Radical Islam and International Security

Radical Islam poses a political challenge in the modern world which is like that of no other radical religious movement. Ideologically, it is perceived by Western policy makers as threatening the liberal-democratic ideology by which most states in the West abide and which most other states rhetorically espouse.

This book serves as a welcome addition to the intellectual and policy debate on the nature of the radical Islam phenomenon and how to respond to it. The collection is divided into three parts, analyzing the phenomenon of radical Islam, the challenges it poses to current international security and the strategic responses available. The first part seeks to understand the Islamic challenge in broad comparative and historical terms, while the second part deals with specific regional case studies, which seek to identify patterns of uniformity and variation in radical Islam across a wide swath of terrain. The third part is policy-oriented, suggesting possible responses to the Islamic challenge. The contributors include distinguished researchers from Europe, North America and the Middle East.

This book will be of much interest to students of Islamism, political violence, international security and Middle Eastern politics.

Hillel Frisch is a senior lecturer in the Departments of Political Science and History of the Middle East at Bar-Ilan University. **Efraim Inbar** is a Professor in Political Studies at Bar-Ilan University and the Director of its Begin-Sadat (BESA) Center for Strategic Studies. He is author of five books and editor of nine collections of articles.

BESA studies in international security
Series Editor: Efraim Inbar

Contents

Illustrations

Figures

Tables

Contributors

Yasemin Akbaba is Assistant Professor at Gettysburg College and is Officer-at-large in Foreign Policy Analysis for the International Studies Association, 2006–2008. She teaches courses on International Relations, War and Ethnic Conflict. Her research focuses on mobilization of ethnic and religious groups as well as international conflict. She is a native of Istanbul, Turkey. She received her Ph.D. from the University of Missouri-Columbia in August 2006.

Daniel Byman is Associate Professor and Director of the Security Studies Program and the Center for Peace and Security Studies at Georgetown University's Edmund A. Walsh School of Foreign Service. He holds a joint appointment with the Georgetown Department of Government, and he is also a Senior Fellow at the Saban Center for Middle East Policy at the Brookings Institution. Dr. Byman has served as a Professional Staff Member with both the National Commission on Terrorist Attacks on the United States ("The 9-11 Commission") and the Joint 9/11 Inquiry Staff of the House and Senate Intelligence Committees. He has also worked as the Research Director of the Center for Middle East Public Policy at the RAND Corporation and as an analyst of the Middle East for the US intelligence community. Dr. Byman has written widely on a range of topics related to terrorism, international security, and the Middle East. His latest books are *The Five Front War: A Better Way to Fight Global Jihad* (Wiley, 2007); *Things Fall Apart: Containing the Spillover from an Iraqi Civil War* (Brookings, 2007; co-authored with Kenneth Pollack); and *Deadly Connections: States that Sponsor Terrorism* (Cambridge University Press, 2005).

Hillel Frisch is a Senior Researcher at the Begin-Sadat (BESA) Center for Strategic Studies specializing in Middle East politics and Senior Lecturer in the Departments of Political Studies and Middle East History at Bar-Ilan University. His publications include "The Role of Religion in the Armies of Egypt, Syria and Jordan," *Orient* (2002) and "Nationalizing a Universal Text: The Qur'an in Arafat's Rhetoric," *Middle Eastern Studies* (2005). He received his Ph.D. in Political Science from the Hebrew University of Jerusalem.

Arye L. Hillman is a Senior Research Associate at the Begin-Sadat (BESA) Center for Strategic Studies and Professor of Economics at Bar-Ilan University where he holds the William Gittes Chair. His research focuses on political economy and public policy. He has also taught at Princeton and UCLA. He is an editor of the *European Journal of Political Economy* published by Elsevier and a former President of the European Public Choice Society. In 1995, he was awarded the Max-Planck Prize in Economics for contributions to political economy. He is the author of *Public Finance and Public Policy: Responsibilities and Limitations of Government* (Cambridge University Press, 2003, 2nd printing 2006, translations in Chinese, Japanese) and *The Political Economy of Protection* (Harwood Academic Publishers, 1989; reprinted in 2001 by Routledge). He received his Ph.D. in Economics from the University of Pennsylvania.

Efraim Inbar is Director of the Begin-Sadat (BESA) Center for Strategic Studies and Professor in Political Studies at Bar-Ilan University. His area of specialization is Middle Eastern strategic issues with a special interest in the politics and strategy of Israeli national security. He has written over 50 articles in professional journals. He has authored four books: *Outcast Countries in the World Community* (University of Denver Press, 1985), *War and Peace in Israeli Politics: Labor Party Positions on National Security* (Lynne Rienner, 1991), *Yitzhak Rabin and Israel's National Security* (Wilson Center and Johns Hopkins University Press, 1999), and *The Israeli–Turkish Entente* (London: King's College Mediterranean Program, 2001), and has edited seven collections of articles. He received his Ph.D. in Political Science from the University of Chicago.

Patrick James is Professor of International Relations at the University of Southern California. He is also a Distinguished Scholar in Foreign Policy Analysis for the International Studies Association (2006–2007), President (2007–2009) of the Association for Canadian Studies in the US, and Vice-President (2008–2009) of the ISA. He is the author of twelve books and over a hundred articles and book chapters. He received his Ph.D. in Government and Politics from the University of Maryland.

Joseph Kostiner is a Senior Research Fellow at the Moshe Dayan Center for Middle Eastern and African Studies and Associate Professor in the Department of Middle Eastern and African History at Tel Aviv University. He specializes in the history and current affairs of the Arabian Peninsula states, social history of the Middle East, and state- and nation-building in the Middle East. He is the author of several books including *From Chieftaincy to Monarchical State: The Making of Saudi Arabia 1916–1936* (1993) and *Yemen: The Tortuous Quest for Unity, 1990–1994* (1996). He is the editor of *Middle East Monarchies* (2000). He received his Ph.D. from the London School of Economics and Political Science.

Michael M. Laskier is Professor of Middle Eastern History and Director of the Menachem Begin Center for Underground & Resistance Movements at

Bar-Ilan University. He is the author of twelve books and 180 articles and chapters on the modern Middle East, the Maghreb, Israel and Western Europe. Among his most recent publications are *North African Jewry in the 20th Century* (New York University Press, 1997), which won the American National Jewish Book Award, *The Jews of the Middle East and North Africa in Modern Times* (Columbia University Press, 2003), *Israel and the Maghreb: From Statehood to Oslo* (University Press of Florida, 2004), and *Israel and the Aliyah from North Africa, 1948–1970* (Ben-Gurion University Press, 2007). He received his Ph.D from the University of California – Los Angeles (UCLA).

Ze'ev Maghen is a Research Associate at the Begin-Sadat (BESA) Center for Strategic Studies and Senior Lecturer in Middle Eastern History and Persian Language at Bar-Ilan University. He specializes in medieval Muslim jurisprudence, modern Islamic fundamentalism and the politics of post-revolutionary Iran. He speaks five regional languages fluently – Arabic, Hebrew, Persian, Russian, and Turkish. He lectures in English and Hebrew at Bar-Ilan University and the Hebrew University. He received his Ph.D. in Middle East History from Columbia University.

Laurent Murawiec is a Senior Fellow at the Hudson Institute. He was a Senior International Policy Analyst with the RAND Corporation (1999–2002), and, prior to moving to the US, a consultant to the French Ministry of Defense. He was co-founder and General Manager of GeoPol Services, S.A. of Geneva, Switzerland (1993–1999), a consulting company that advised multinational corporations and banks on geopolitical and geoeconomic matters. He taught the history of central economic planning at the Ecole des Hautes Etudes en Sciences Sociales (EHESS, Centre d'étude des modes d'industrialisation) in Paris and at the Elliott School of International Affairs at George Washington University, Washington, DC. His latest book is *The Mind of Jihad* (Hudson Institute, 2005). He is currently preparing a second volume.

Jonathan S. Paris is a London-based Middle East and Islamic movement analyst and an Adjunct Fellow at the Hudson Institute. He has completed studies for the US government on radicalization in Europe. From 1995 to 2000, he was a Middle East Fellow at the Council on Foreign Relations. He comments on CNN, BBC, Sky News, Fox News, and NBC News, and has written for *Foreign Affairs*, the *Financial Times*, the *New York Sun*, the *Baltimore Sun*, and *Asharq Alawsat*, an Arab daily newspaper based in London. He co-edited the first book on Indonesia's democratic transition, *The Politics of Post-Suharto Indonesia* (Council on Foreign Relations, 1999), and from 1994 to 1997 lectured at Yale University on Islam and Politics in the Middle East and the Arab–Israeli conflict. A Cleveland native, he is a graduate of Yale and Stanford Law School.

Rushda Siddiqui is an Associate Fellow with the Institute for Defence Studies and Analyses (IDSA) in New Delhi. Her specializations include State and

Religion in West Asia and North Africa, and Religion-based Movements in West Asia and North Africa. She has worked with the Institute of Social Sciences as Research Officer, in the World Bank Project of Resource Centre on Civil Societies in India and for SAPRA India. She received her Ph.D. in West Asian and African Studies from Jawaharlal Nehru University.

Max Singer is a Senior Researcher at the Begin-Sadat (BESA) Center for Strategic Studies at Bar-Ilan University, Senior Fellow Member of the Board of Directors at the Hudson Institute, and Research Director of the Institute for Zionist Strategies. In 1961 he founded the Hudson Institute with Herman Kahn and served as President until 1973. From 1974 to 1976 he was Managing Director of the World Institute in Jerusalem, and in 1977 to 1978 Director of the Institute for Jewish Policy Planning and Research of the Synagogue Council of America. He is the author of *The REAL World Order: Zones of Peace/Zones of Turmoil* (with Aaron Wildavsky) (Chatham House, NJ, revised edn, 1996), which won the 1996 Grawemeyer Award for Ideas Improving World Order, and of *Passage to A Human World: The Dynamics of Creating Global Wealth* (foreword by Irving Kristol) (Transaction Publishers, NJ, 2nd edn, 1989). He has a J.D. from Harvard Law School.

Jonathan Stevenson is Professor of Strategic Studies in the Strategic Research Department of the Naval War College. He specializes in counterterrorism, counterinsurgency and political Islam. He has published widely in such journals as *Foreign Affairs, Foreign Policy, The National Interest* and *Survival*, and is the author of several monographs, including *Counter-terrorism: Containment and Beyond* (Adelphi Paper 367, 2004). He received a J.D. from Boston University School of Law.

Bassam Tibi is Professor of International Relations at the University of Goettingen and a Visiting Faculty Member at Cornell University as the A.D. White Professor-at-large. He has taught and lectured at 30 universities in four continents and is author of six monographs in English, the most recent of which are: *The Challenge of Fundamentalism* (Californian University Press, updated edn, 2002); *Islam between Culture and Politics* (Palgrave, updated and expanded edn, 2005). He was born in Damascus and moved to Germany in 1962. He trained in social science, philosophy and history at the Goethe University of Frankfurt where he received his first Ph.D. in 1971. He received his Dr. Habil (German Ph.D.) from the University of Hamburg.

Introduction

Radical Islam and international security: challenges and responses

Hillel Frisch and Efraim Inbar

Radical Islam poses a political challenge in the modern world like no other radical religious movement. A cursory comparison with other religions shows that though Hindu radicalism generates violence, it is overwhelmingly circumscribed to the Indian subcontinent if not to India itself. Jewish radicalism lacks mass, while Christian fundamentalism, with arguably global reach due mostly to its impact on United States politics and more tenuously on the makings of US foreign policy, is hardly involved in terror and violence or actively pursues extreme political solutions.

In contrast, contemporary radical Islamic movements are geographically dispersed throughout the Far East, Southeast Asia, Europe, Africa and, of course, the Middle East. In fact, there is scarcely a region on the globe where they do not exist. The goals of these movements range from the removal of state-based international systems to the overthrow of regimes to their replacement by theocracies. The violence they engender is rivaled today only by ethno-national movements. Islamism challenges the integrity of state regimes (Egypt, Jordan and India), the very existence of states (Israel and Lebanon), exacerbates relations between states directly (Iran–United States), and indirectly when states support and abet Islamic terror movements (Pakistan–India, Syria–Israel).

Ironically, Islamic radicalism contributes to violence and division within the Islamic world itself, as the ongoing conflict in Iraq demonstrates. In short, radical Islam poses a challenge to the state-based and broadly secular international system that has been in place since the seventeenth century, in addition to the states and societies that make up this system. Ideologically, Islamism has replaced communism and fascism as the greatest threat to liberal-democratic ideals by which most states in the West abide and which most other states rhetorically espouse.

Even a broader categorical and historical comparison, including ideological and religious movements, suggests that the challenge of radical Islam in the twenty-first century might have a similar impact as did radical secular ideologies in the previous 100 years. For the time being, radical Islam does not possess powerful state structures in the same way communism held sway in the Soviet Union, Nazism in Germany and fascism in Italy and Spain. Nevertheless, globalization has advantaged radical Islamic groups in a number of important ways:

large-scale migration of Muslims from poor and dense Islamic hinterlands to Europe and the Americas has led to the emergence of a pool of potential recruits, sympathizers and financial and political supporters; the dissemination of knowledge through modern communication favors the radical underdog in the production of violent means; and modern technology aids Islamists in their means of terrorism, such as the use of airplanes in the events of 9/11.

These new advantages often find their moorings in older, more embedded phenomena such as the direct or indirect support these movements receive from established states (Iran, Pakistan and Saudi Arabia). The danger also exists that "failed" states, a perennial feature of political life, might also be taken over by radical movements, as the recent conflict between secular and religious forces in Somalia demonstrates.

A challenge of this magnitude naturally calls for an effective response. The events of 9/11 painfully pointed out the global reach of radical Islam. Yet since the attack, other terror acts and the potential recurrence of a large-scale event have demonstrated the threat posed to globalization by radical Islamic movements and the states that often sponsor them. Specifically, this "threat" is aimed at the welfare and democratic rights enjoyed by Western nations. In the long term, Western states have much at stake in meeting the challenge. After all, they are the actors possessing the financial and technical know-how, commensurate with the benefits they derive from peaceful and stable globalization.

In countering the radical Islamist threat, allies belonging to and practicing the Islamic faith should not be discounted. In Iraq, massive turn-out at the polls demonstrated that many Muslims disagreed with radical Islamic tenets. In the face of considerable danger, voters showed up not only once to ratify the constitution, but a second time to elect political leadership. Even in places where Islamists have made considerable gains or retain authority, as in the Palestinian Authority, their adherents are hardly a majority and their vote is not necessarily a long-term endorsement of Islamism. The world community of states should ensure that the democratic process, which allowed movements such as the Hamas to come to power, will also ensure the possibility of free and fair competition in the future, including the possibility of voting the movement out of office.

In May 2006, the Begin–Sadat (BESA) Center for Strategic Studies at Bar-Ilan University convened a number of international experts for a conference exploring the radical Islamic challenge and the ways to respond to this phenomenon. This book, a compendium of articles, emerged from this conference. The book is divided into three parts: general themes, case studies and policy-oriented papers. In the first part, the Islamic challenge is understood in broad comparative and historical terms. Part II seeks to identify contrasting patterns of uniformity and variation in radical Islam across a wide swath of terrain. Part III suggests possible responses to the Islamist challenge.

Opening the book is a chapter by Bassam Tibi, who argues that radical Islam has little to do with traditional Islamic precepts, and since the Six Day War there has been a religionization of politics along with a politicization of Islam. An emerging irregular war waged in the name of Islam in the context of a religio-culturalization is the major feature of the Islamist challenge. The conflict over the Holy Land of Israel/Palestine is its major arena, and the global attempt to replace a liberal order of states by establishing a theocratic order dominated by Islamism is the movement's major thrust.

Championing a state based on Shari'a law and perceiving the world as an arena for an almost perpetual *jihad*, what he terms the twin processes of Shari'azation and *jihadization* are the ideological tools to achieve the latter goal. Tibi rebukes European cultural and political elites for not recognizing the magnitude of the danger posed by the Islamists and their conviction and sincerity which will hardly be swayed by strategies of "engagement." Similarly, he rejects Huntington's "clash of civilizations," not because a clash does not exist but because the Islamism these extremists espouse is an invention of tradition, not Islam itself. Rather than this clash of civilizations, he believes there is a clash between Islamists and proponents of free and democratic societies. To portray the conflict as a clash of civilizations rather than a clash of ideologies is to play into the hands of the Islamists.

From a more historical perspective, Ze'ev Maghen nevertheless concurs with Tibi's prognosis (Chapter 2) that views Islam in evolutionary rather than essential terms. Maghen asks why, in the minds of most Westerners and some Easterners, is Islam associated today with fury, fierceness, fanaticism and intransigence? "Perceived to be a harsh and uncompromising faith, as deaf to the cries of the innocents slaughtered in its name as it is to the pleas for reform emanating from within its own walls," for most of its 1400-year history and across "the Abode of Islam," the Shari'a was rarely enforced, and Muhammad was almost a paragon of flexibility to the point of championing canonical laxity.

His answer paradoxically lies in the tremendous influence of Western thought on the Islamic world rather than in its rejection, as argued by Bernard Lewis and others. He boldly suggests that the Western tradition of scientific rationalism, hailing from Greek times and having been revived considerably since the Renaissance, described the world in logical and almost mathematical terms. By the end of the nineteenth century, powerful attempts were being made to apply scientific principles to all walks of life. Humanity and its institutions are ultimately and ideally a machine – and machines require precision.

Maghen's reading of recently written fundamentalist tracts and treatises provides evidence that this new Western way of looking at things had begun to penetrate the consciousness of the educated classes in Middle Eastern countries by the end of the first half of the twentieth century. The Islamists were no exception. This is when a fascinating and monstrous hybrid began to grow. Suddenly, the blurry lines and rounded edges characterizing Islamic law and life were unacceptable. "Islam, they frowned, is no laughing matter!" One wonders if that means that the Islamists are a half-century behind Western intellectual development. Ominously, one knows in retrospect the political impact of the "scientific" ideologies of Nazism and communism and what it entailed until these ideologies and the powers behind them were defeated: a massive world war against the former and a cold war against the latter. Perhaps this is why Maghen concludes with a fervent wish to see "the religious corner-cutting, legal laxity and a 'laid-back' outlook" formerly characterizing Islam renewed.

Successful integration of states and regions inhabited by Muslims into the world economy might plausibly dissipate Islamist fervor. In Chapter 3, economist Arye Hillman warns, however, that the world-view of the Islamists is inimical to economic development and, inasmuch as they have political influence, reduces the chances of such integration. A focus on economic consequences of *radical* Islam introduces two explanatory concepts: supreme values and rent-seeking behavior. A supreme-value system, by ranking objectives hierarchically, delegitimizes trade-offs and distractions that compromise the achievement of as-yet unattained priority goals. It subordinates economic achievement to religiously ordained geo-political goals.

A rent-seeking perspective emphasizes that contestable rents impede economic development by distracting personal talent and initiative away from productive endeavor towards, in our case, increasing the domain of Islam where wealth is achieved by sequestering land rather than developing its productivity. Hillman shows that the greater the influence of the Islamist value-system and ideology, the poorer the economic performance of that society is compared both to states with similar physical endowment yet different political cultures and, to a lesser degree, compared to states with an Islamic majority where Islamist thought has less influence on the state and society.

Joseph Kostiner's survey of *jihadi* trends and the role of the Saudi state both in propagating and fighting these trends since the Iraq–Kuwait War is the first of several chapters comprising Part II. Kostiner credits the Saudi Arabian elite for embarking on a policy of reconciliation between the different religious groups. In such a policy, the voices of religious radicals would be diluted to a more moderate form of preaching as to blunt the edge of the radicals' works and depict terrorism as a marginal issue. The rise of more moderate, yet active and vocal clerics in the public sphere demonstrates partial success. Ironically, this invariably meant cajoling *sahwa* clerics to retract on their earlier support of the "*jihadists*," often with the encouragement of the government itself. A controversy between these clerics soon emerged.

The government hardly relied on discourse alone. Since May 2003, about 1000 suspects have been detained, and about 2000 clergymen have been questioned. Security forces cracked down on several terrorist cells, discovering and destroying tons of explosives and arms. Several "charity foundations" that had been channeling money for the funding of terrorism, notably the "al-Haramayn" fund, were shut down. Shoot-outs with terrorists occurred daily. The series of blows peaked in June 2004, when some of the principal terrorists were killed, leading to a lull in terrorist activity. However, the infrastructure of many young Saudi cells still exists and could be reset into operational mode, especially since Wahhabism continues to be the official state doctrine. The readiness of bin Laden to start another campaign is also beyond doubt. The possibility of a new extremist or terrorist wave in Saudi Arabia is therefore most tangible.

Two case studies explore the role of radical Islam in Europe. In Chapter 5 Michael Laskier looks specifically at the involvement of Islamists from the Maghreb (North Africa). He presents four basic theses. First, growing numbers of young Maghrebi Muslim immigrants as well as second and third generation Maghrebi Europeans are a potential threat to the continent's internal security, in addition to becoming increasingly burdensome to Europe's social welfare system. Second, he discards claims that Islamists opposing European values and rejecting their Western surroundings are a negligible force. Third, as far-fetched as the dream of transforming the EU into an Islamic bastion, annexing it to the Maghreb, and creating a greater Islamist state, there are a variety of Islamist groups who take these goals seriously. Fourth, Maghrebi Islamist organizations have emerged in several key member-states of the EU due to immigration, the presence of foreign students, prisoners in European jails, and second/third generation European Muslims.

Combating ideas with ideas is the solution Jonathan Paris proposes in Chapter 6, "Explaining the causes of radical Islam in Europe." The best defense against political Islam may be nationalism, which, like religion, draws on primordial bonds dating back generations, not only in Europe but in the Muslim world itself. "If Kuwaitis think like Kuwaitis, not like Muslims, they can be weaned away from global extremist influences like al Qaeda." Paris warns, however, that though this strategy may work in the United States where Jacksonian nationalism remains strong, the erosion of nationalism in Europe makes it difficult to persuade French or Dutch Muslims to enthusiastically identify themselves as French or Dutch citizens. Moreover, the second and third generations of Muslims in Europe have largely rejected the traditional ethnic roots of their parents, but have failed to become wholly accepted by the majorities in European states despite their linguistic and cultural education in their host countries. They become easy prey to those who promise a future with power and respect derived from a politicized version of Muslim identity – hence the allure of the born-again Muslims.

Patrick James and Yasemin Akbaba (Chapter 7) employ the tools of international relations theory to study radical Islam in Turkey, particularly as it was influenced by the Islamic Republic of Iran. Iran and Turkey form an interesting dyad due to their contrasting ideologies. While Turkey disregards the role of religion in its state identity, Iran designates Islam as its reason for existence. In their analysis, Iran is by far the more aggressive state and uses radical Muslim organizations as tools both in leveraging against Turkey and in bolstering domestic legitimacy. Akbaba and James inadvertently demonstrate how in the war on Islamic terror it is crucial to deal with the state powers behind the proxies.

The state–proxy nexus takes on much greater importance in Rushda Siddiqui's analysis of the Islamic dimension of Pakistan's foreign policy, where support for proxy insurgents is a means to balance against a vastly more powerful neighbor. According to Siddiqui, Pakistan has been one of the first states in contemporary history to employ non-state proxies to safeguard its interests in the region and in the international arena. Initially, Pakistan benefited from its non-state actors and the mechanisms they employed to support terrorist activities in Kashmir. In the long run, however, the use of non-state actors backfired, increasing the state's vulnerability to a backlash not only by the states affected by Pakistan's terrorist proxies, but also by the non-state actors within Pakistan. Today, the country is considered a "state sponsor of terrorism" or a "passive sponsor of terrorism."

Responding to the Islamist challenge is the focus of the chapters in Part III of the book. In Chapter 4, Max Singer presents an especially bold diagnosis and strategy to meet the challenge of preventing a greater *jihad* than the West faces at present. While many in the Muslim world support *jihad*, far less are actively involved in supporting "*jihad*-now." He suggests that US policy should focus on deterring passive supporters of *jihad*-now from becoming active supporters. The way to do this is through an intensive long-term campaign against the minority who are currently engaged in it. "Our immediate danger comes not from support for *jihad* but from *jihad*-now. The choice between these two depends on decisions on which we can have a decisive influence by demonstrating how much harm will come to Muslims from *jihad*-now," he writes.

Singer's combative strategy is more than echoed in Laurent Murawiec's chapter entitled "Deterring those who are already dead?" In a sharp rebuttal to Tibi, Murawiec believes that *jihad* is integral to Islam and derives from its most fundamental tenets that world society cannot eliminate these beliefs, but can only make the strain dormant instead of virulent. The strategy crystallizes from the study of history: when Islamic conquerors met their match, they stopped, when they met crushing defeat, they retreated, and found the *'ulama'* and the *faqih* to justify passive theological alternatives like *jihad al-nafs* (spiritual self-exertion). The author counsels the West to render the same to present-day *jihadists*.

Can one of the tools in meeting the challenge of radical Islam be as benign as democratic regime change? Daniel Byman (Chapter 11) believes as much, provided that democracies, principally the United States, are selective in choosing their targets, and are creative and adaptive in fine-tuning the strategy. Essentially, regime change towards democracy highlights a difficult dilemma: the creation of a less suppressive environment for the radical Islamists to operate. The answer is neither to embrace democracy uncritically nor to reject it completely. Rather, policy makers should recognize when the promotion of democracy should be pursued and when it should be rejected. Byman counsels focusing on consolidating democracy in Muslim countries that are already in transition – a daunting task in itself. Where democracy is non-existent and democratic groups are weak, Western attention would be better spent building institutions, such as the courts and the police. These institutions will strengthen government counter-terrorism efforts and, if democratization occurs, make strife and government weakness less likely.

If Byman is willing to recognize benign strategies, Jonathan Stevenson (Chapter 12) calls to warmly embrace them. What is virtue to Singer and

Murawiec amounts to the wrong strategy as far as Stevenson is concerned. Iraq, he argues, is the litmus test of overly aggressive strategies. The United States now faces a dilemma. It can either expeditiously withdraw from Iraq or stay there indefinitely to complete the task of state-building. Either way, the *jihadists* are handed a propaganda victory: withdrawal reads as a superpower's humiliation, ongoing occupation as its imperialism. The only hope seems to be for the US to stay long enough to prove itself a benevolent midwife rather than a malign hegemon.

In Europe, an exclusively military strategy is also wide of the mark. In these societies, the rule of law prevails and social discontent feeds the radicals with recruits. The global *jihad* will collectively regard itself as better off as a maximally decentralized and virtual network fully infiltrated into locales in which the military instrument is subject to severe political and operational limitations. He counsels a removal of emphasis on direct military action in general, such that "hard" counter-terrorism becomes primarily a function of civilian intelligence and law-enforcement cooperation. The premium should be an internationally coordinated blend of regional economic initiatives and proactive conflict management in key areas (especially the Middle East, but also Kashmir and Chechnya), and to quietly urge and support national efforts – customized according to particular circumstances – in order to better integrate alienated segments of society which are otherwise vulnerable to radicalization.

Hopefully this volume will be a welcome addition to the intellectual and policy debate on the nature of the radical Islam phenomenon and on how to deal with the challenges it poses to Western civilization. Unfortunately, this strategic problem will not easily go away. Meeting the challenge obviously requires much more than writing articles and books, although intellectual clarity is unquestionably a prerequisite for effective strategic action. Indeed, the goal of this collection is modest: to clarify the radical Islam phenomenon and to discuss ways to combat the challenge.

Special thanks are due to the BESA administrative team who worked hard to make the conference a success and to produce this volume. We also wish to express our appreciation to Rebecca Goldberg for her invaluable assistance in the editing of the book. Ian Bomberg and Sara Krulewich worked hard to add the final touches. Finally, our deep gratitude goes to the contributors to this volume who put up with successive demands for revisions and worked hard to meet the requirements of the editors, their staff and the deadline. We have learned enormously from them and we hope that this will also be the reaction of our readers.

Part I

The challenge of radical Islam

General themes

1 Religious extremism or religionization of politics?

The ideological foundations of political Islam

Bassam Tibi

Political Islam is a transnational movement that cannot be well understood through the terms "extreme, extremist, extremism." These terms with their negative connotations refer to a delinquent mindset and to behavior diverging from society's mainstream. Political Islam is today the mainstream opposition in the world of Islam, particularly in the Middle East. Implicitly, the rejected terms imply a value-judgment because of their connotations and they do not reflect the existing political realities.

Having stated the case, this chapter presents a different approach. Durkheim's sociology of religion and the methodology of the Frankfurt School established by Theodor Adorno and Max Horkheimer are the basis of the subsequent inquiry into the current state of Islam in Middle Eastern politics. This idea is based in the social-scientific view that religion matters as a *fait social* rather than as a belief system. Based on this methodological wisdom, it is not an expression of pedantry to insist on a proper use of the language and to question the application of the term "extremism" (in Arabic: *Tatarruf*) to political Islam. Questioning the use of "extremism" is important in knowing that political Islam is not a fringe phenomenon of delinquency, but rather an ideology and related practice of political movements that represent the major opposition in most countries of the world of Islam, particularly in the Middle East (e.g. Muslim Brotherhood in Egypt). Some of these movements of political Islam (e.g. Hizballah in Lebanon, SCIRI and al-Mahdi Army in Iraq) already participate in power and governance.

This chapter begins by suggesting the use of value-free, analytical terms and tools for conceptualizing the *fait social* of the use of religion as a legitimatory device in Middle Eastern politics, in particular since the Arab defeat in the Six Day War. The suggestion to see in this process a religionization of politics[1] is supported among many other things by the 2006 Lebanon War provoked by the Shi'a Hizballah and viewed by the Sunni Muslim Brotherhood as their "victory by extension."[2] The perception of its alleged victory was presented as a "divine victory." This is not only an indication of a religionization of politics along the politicization of Islam, but also an emerging irregular war,[3] waged in the name of Islam and in the context of a religio-culturalization of conflict.

It is assumed that the Middle East conflict over the "Holy Land" is a political conflict that can be resolved rationally through negotiations between the conflicting parties and assisted by third-party mediation. However, this assumption does not apply to a situation in which a political conflict is religionized in a way that makes the issues non-negotiable. Given the fact that religion claims to indicate the absolute, a religionization means that there can be no room left for a rational and compromising resolution. The formula *Filastin Islamiyya* versus Israel indicates an Islamization of the conflict with non-negotiable claims.[4]

In order to understand the religionization of politics, the study of the ideological foundations of Islamism, acting as transnational political religion in global networks, becomes pertinent. This kind of new analysis promises to provide an enlightening contribution; and this is the goal of this inquiry.

The scope of the inquiry: Islam and Islamism

Islam is a faith. In this capacity it by no means supports any kind of action that can be identified as extremism. There can be an understanding of religion that leads to fanaticism, but this is different from Islamism. Neither theological questions nor psychological fanaticism are the basic concern of this chapter. The issue is the embedding of faith in social realities in an ongoing process of a religionization of politics and a politicization of religion. In this context, religion is viewed as a ground for political order. In the current form of political Islam, this process leads to a Shari'atization and *jihadization* of faith pronounced as a return to tradition.[5] The outcome is the ideology of Islamism, which is different than the religion of Islam itself. This distinction is the point of departure for the study of Islamism, which is the ideological foundation of political Islam, an aspect of the overall phenomenon of religious fundamentalism.

While outlining the distinction between Islam as a faith and Islamism as a political ideology, one has to refute the claims of Islamists that their religion-based worldview qualifies them as the "True Believers."[6] It follows that countering their *jihadist* terrorism is not "a war on Islam" as they propagate in a war of ideas. In a summary fashion it can be stated that Islamism is not a delinquency, but stands as a political phenomenon within Islam as a social reality. At issue is a transnational movement that uses existing institutions to promote the practice of irregular war while working to remake the world.

Different peoples are entitled to their own religions, but not to their own facts. Facts must be contextually understood in their place in the ideology of Islamism and into its branch of *jihadism*. In the current analysis, politicization of religion will be discussed, and it will be shown how this process contributes to an intensification of the conflict. This conflict occurs in a context of a war of ideas and worldviews where issues are complicated by religious ideologies. The war of ideas enables Islamists to ideologically defame their foes, including fellow-Muslims, in order to legitimate a fight against them. The new notion of a "war of ideas" refers to a competition between political concepts of order and life, and it also includes the instrumental defamation of critics with notions like "Islam-bashing."

In recognizing this dimension of conflict, which hampers the attainment of a peaceful conflict resolution, I focus on the ideology of Islamism. At issue is to first understand the new thinking and to find ways of dealing with it. As Islamism includes a branch of terrorism underpinned by the idea of *jihadism*, conceptualized here as irregular war, the analysis must also analyze the constructed relationship between "Religion and Terror."[7] This interpretation makes use of religious themes which work to justify the practice of terror in the name of Islam. In this context, the formula of "politicization of religion and religionization of politics" has been employed to identify the ideological foundations of Islamism. Applied to the politicization of Islam, political Islam can be expressed in two directions: as institutionally peaceful and as a *jihadist* terrorist branch. *Jihadism* is a recent addition; it is different than traditional Islamic *jihad*. This practice is equally directed against secular world peace and the underlying secular system of states in an invention of tradition.[8]

In a project at Cornell University, the study of the politics of a "transnational religion"[9] has been an essential part of international studies in the process of an expanding Europe. The issue of political Islam heralds a prominent case of transnational religion. It is related to the foundation of the Society of Muslim Brothers[10] in Cairo in 1928. This movement, which is active in Western Europe, is not only the first movement based on Islamic fundamentalism, but has recently developed a huge network. This example of a transnational religion displays an international movement that also covers the Islamic diaspora in Europe. Hamas, also active in Europe, is an offshoot of the Muslim Brotherhood. The founder of this movement, Hasan al-Banna, published his "Essay on *Jihad* (*Risalat al-Djihad*)[11] in the early twentieth century, which is used today as a basic reading for the indoctrination of the *jihadist* ideology.

More significant and more powerful than the writings of al-Banna are the many catechisms/pamphlets authored by Sayyid Qutb. Qutb was the foremost thinker of political Islam and continues to be the most influential ideological precursor of contemporary Islamism.[12] The central tenet in Qutb's thinking is the idea of "*jihad* as a permanent Islamic world revolution"[13] in the pursuit of establishing what he termed as "God's rule" (*Hakimiyyat Allah*) on global grounds. Along these lines, Islamists envision a new order for the world. It is based on their understanding of a reinvented Shariʻa and is aimed at replacing the Western secular Westphalian system with an Islamic order.[14] These claims, expressed in the ideology of Islamism, make clear that more than religious extremism is involved. The sensational coverage of suicide terrorism[15] should not detract our attention from the real issue; the new *jihad* is warfare for a new world order. This new world begins with Islam and is based on the religionization of politics.

The ideology of Islamism and its *jihadist* virus are currently spreading with the assistance of *madrassas* and faith-based schools throughout the Islamic and Western worlds. Respective Islamist organizations pursue a policy of recruitment by first teaching *jihadism*, then creating an appeal, and finally recruiting for action. Knowing this approach, a two-track strategy is needed to deal with Islam and Islamism. This strategy is first based on winning the hearts and minds of young Muslims through proper education and enlightenment in the ongoing war of ideas, and second, on countering the *jihadist* warfare that should be incorporated into a new security approach in the war on terror. To be successful, this strategy needs to be based on a joint Western–Islamic effort, to avoid the war being perceived as a "war on Islam."

Islamism is gradually favoring a transnational religion based on a "reimagining of the *umma*."[16] The ideological foundations of Islamism, post-Cold War, justify replacing the international order of secular states with a global Islamicate of a *Dar al-Islam*. In its present shape, the phenomenon of Islamism is rooted in the international political state of the post-Cold War. There are many new cultural factors, including the aforementioned "return of the sacred,"[17] which exist in political form. Another factor is the ascendancy of non-state actors in world politics, expressed in the emergence of global terrorist movements. Contemporary Islamism is the internationalism of religion carried out by non-state actors. At present, the pertinence of the current rise of politicized religion to international affairs is becoming evident.[18]

These new policies have international ramifications beyond the state, as they are designed and carried out by non-state actors committed to political Islam. Nevertheless, Islamism is a concept of order in the global phenomenon of religious fundamentalism, aimed at remaking the world based on *Hakimiyyat Allah*.[19] The classic Islamicate,[20] a term coined by Hodgson, was an order that should not be equated with the current vision of a global *Pax Islamica*. This is one of the distinctions between Islam and Islamism. In addition, it is essential not to overlook the common misconception between the orthodox Salafism and Islamism. While both appear to seek international hegemonic power, Islamists no longer discuss a restoration of the caliphate, which orthodox Islam supports.

One cannot discuss Islam and Islamism without addressing the idea of Islamophobia. Islamists themselves are exploiting the suspicion of Islamophobia by stating that Western nations "demonize Islam" by associating it with violence. This connection supports the rise of anti-Islamist sentiments after September 11th. Foremost, September 11th made clear that Islamists were in action; however, it also revived the Islamic negative stereotype of Islam as a religion of terrorism. In responding to this flaw, the well-known and fashionable accusation, Orientalism, has been reintroduced. Followers of this belief view terrorists simply as criminals, or as a "crazed gang," according to Edward Said. It is contended that they had nothing to do with Islam; rather, they were created as an image by "Islamophobic Orientalists." There exists another extreme, namely attributing all evils to a "militant Islam," equating militancy with Islam itself. The current analysis aims at cautiously avoiding both extremes, while working to introduce the idea into security studies that "culture matters," through the analysis of the ideology of political Islam.

Culturally, political Islam is inspired by an Islamic nostalgia aimed at reinventing Islam's past glory into a new Islamic shape. The political implication of this cultural nostalgia is that an Islamic world order needs to re-emerge. The self-assertive "Revolt against the West"[21] taking place as an "Islamic Awakening" (*Sahwa Islamiyya*) underlies this nostalgia. Through a war of collective memories it indicates a return of a history of civilizations rather than the "End of History" as suggested by Francis Fukuyama.[22]

As a preliminary conclusion one can state that the addressed new revolt is not restricted to an upheaval against the hegemony of the West. The target is much broader; it is the secular Western order and its values. In addressing this target, new areas must be considered. Hedley Bull appropriately analyzes the pending issue by unraveling the fallacy of the "global village" in stating that:

> it is also clear that the shrinking of the globe, while it has brought societies to a degree of mutual awareness and interaction they have not had before, does not in itself create a unity of outlook and has not in fact done so.... Humanity is becoming simultaneously more unified and more fragmented.[23]

Based on this observation, this chapter first develops the general concept of a world structurally globalized and culturally fragmented.[24] Second, the work applies it to contemporary radical Islam that combines modernity with a medieval worldview.[25] This ideology emerges from a gap between the unfulfilled claim of a universalization of Western values and the degree of structural globalization reached. In short, the claim does not match the reality. For this reason, this work distinguishes between the globalization of structures and the universalization of values. Based on this distinction, it is inferred that the globalization of structures parallels a cultural fragmentation. This fragmentation neglects the international norms and values that claim universal validity; instead, political Islam promotes Shari'a and its alternative order of a "*nizam Islami.*" To be sure, this is *not* the restoration of the traditional caliphate.

In this context, the world encounters new opposition: non-state actors fighting against Western values while more or less successfully launching a process of de-Westernization.[26] The related war of ideas touches on secular knowledge, values and worldviews, moving subsequently to question the existing political order itself. These are the ideological foundations of Islamist politics. This is not a problem of "rough states,"[27] as a state-centered view of realism stubbornly suggests.

In short, political Islam is neither a mere expression of a religious extremism or fanaticism, nor is it related to failed states. Rather, it reflects a complex issue that compels scholars to look beyond traditional wisdoms in order to understand how culture matters in the twenty-first century. Religion is a cultural system embedded in both politics and the new irregular warfare by non-state actors.

The ideology of *jihadist* Islamism and its pillars

The political movements representing Islamism are carried out by non-state actors in local, regional, and international politics who work to reinvent tradition. Their subsequent realities create an indication of the return of Islamic civilization to world politics and its claim to international domination. Even though Islamic civilization is often described as a "World of Islam," its states are still considered to be part of the international system. Islamic states exist independently, solely as a grouping of states with a distinct civilization based on religion. These states are assembled in the only international organization identified by religion: the Organization of Islamic Conference (OIC). Political Islam is not the ideology of the OIC; rather it is the orientation of the Islamist movements not only politically opposed to the current international order, but also to the existing regimes in Islamic countries. Many who study traditional Islam or who are part of the Middle Eastern studies establishment act outside of social sciences and international relations and have an inappropriate, not to say an unprofessional understanding of world politics. Neither Orientalist philologians nor cultural anthropologists in Middle Eastern studies are professionally in a position to deal with the addressed current issues beyond their confines. In contrast, an International Relations (IR)-oriented expert is able to place Islamism in security studies. Therefore, international relations are more promising for the understanding of political Islam and of its ambitions for a remaking of world order.

The unequivocal call to replace the existing order of the nation-state with a *Hakimiyyat Allah* is based on the ideology of an Islamic state and of a new world order along the lines of the Shari'a. In summary, the goal of the Islamists is not the restoration of the Caliphate as some self-proclaimed experts contend; rather, the establishment of an "Islamic Order" (*nizam Islami*)[28] is the top priority of political Islam. In the twenty-first century this has become a competition between *Pax Islamica* and *Pax Americana*. This is the basis of Islamic fundamentalism represented by both the peaceful institution of Islamism and by terrorist *jihadism*. Despite the difference in the employed means, the final goal of Islamic order is shared by both.

The major target of Islamist movements is currently the toppling of existing regimes. However, it is wrong to exclusively identify the concerns of Islamism as solely within the world of Islam. Michael Doran published an essay in *Foreign Affairs*[29] in 2002, directly after 9/11, and found wide dissemination. Doran claims that in September 2001, al Qaeda wanted primarily to target its enemies in the world of Islam via the United States. Despite Doran's well-reasoned essay, he overlooks or even confuses the two levels of order in the ideology and strategy of Islamism. First, he discusses the replacement of secular regimes in the world of Islam by the system of *Hakimiyyat Allah*. Second, he fails to understand the vision of a global *Pax Islamica* to be established via an Islamic "world revolution" (*thawra 'alamiyya*). Thus, on September 11th, the levels were both confused and intermingled. It is only in this sense that one may speak of "somebody else's war" when addressing the assault of September 11th. However the general implication of this notion is utterly wrong. In fact, *Jihadist* Islamism is both domestic ("the world of Islam") and international (world politics). Both levels are interconnected through the Islamic diaspora in Western Europe. It follows in the context of transnational religion that internationalism is intrinsic to Islamism. The global networks of transnational religion encompass the Islamic diaspora in the West. This fact explains the need to relate the study of security to the analysis of the global migration crisis.[30]

It is an established fact that Islamists, despite their deep contempt for Western democracy, make full use of democratic systems and civil rights to establish a logistical base for their movements in Western Europe. These tactics allow them to win most cases in European courts. In this context, the study of the anti-Western ideology of Islamic fundamentalism matters greatly to Europe itself. For a proper understanding of this issue it is necessary to analyze the legal dimension of establishing political Islam in Europe. Increasing Islamic migration complicates the issue. Among the established facts is the link between radical Islamic movements in Western Europe and the al Qaeda camps that once existed in Afghanistan under the rule of the Taliban. Young diaspora Muslims were not only trained there as terrorists, but were also indoctrinated in the ideology of Islamism and infected by its virus of *jihadism*.

The major section of this chapter refers to the distinction between Islam and Islamism in the context of the politicization of religion and religionization of politics. This is the background for a proper understanding of *jihadist* Islamism. This analysis is much more than "religious extremism" attributed to a "radical Islam" according to traditional wisdom. The American Academy of Arts and Sciences accurately addresses this topic through a comparative study of religious fundamentalisms. Their study resulted in the publication of five volumes.[31] These findings are highly important for demonstrating the links that currently exist between religion, society, state, and international politics.

To begin, politicized religion emerges from a political crisis within states as well as in the regional and international environment to which they belong. This crisis materialized as the end of the Cold War gave a new defense to the return of the sacred and is the overall context of the "cultural turn" of the twenty-first century. In addition to the political crisis of legitimacy, one can state a crisis of meaning growing from the crisis of cultural modernity. The result is further globalization, but not a successful universalization of shared values. In reality, there is an effort to de-Westernize non-Western cultures, particularly in countries with Islamic majorities. Even the brilliant political philosopher Jürgen Habermas fails to understand the ideological challenge to universal values in non-Western civilizations. Few recognize that the current conflict at work indicates the competition of the divine order against the secular. These opposing worldviews clash as one cultivates the ideology of neo-absolutism while the other subscribes to cultural relativism. What Habermas addresses as "post-secular society" is in fact a politicization of religion focused on Islam.[32] This neo-absolutism challenges the tenets of a paradoxically open society, making full use of cultural relativism to establish itself.

Similar to the errors of Habermas, most Europeans fail to grasp the ideology of contemporary neo-absolutist political Islam, which claims to eclipse the West and replace its Westphalian secular order with a divine Islamic one. The German-Jewish political scientist Michael Wolffsohn accused most Germans of being "religion illiterates"[33] (*Religionsanalphabeten*), because they misunderstand the reference to religion in politics (e.g. Hamas). This society replaced the proper understanding with moralizing arguments based on the alleged injustice of globalization or wrong lessons from the shameful German viewpoint. These moralists fail to understand politicized religion and the related worldview in the Islamist concept of order. The concept of "unity of religion and state" (*din-wa-dawla*) challenges the validity of the secular nation-state in the world of Islam. It further supports the use of the concept of *dar-al Islam* over the entire globe. The religious legitimization of terror is to be placed in this context,[34] even though it is not intrinsic to it. *Jihadism* is only a means, not an end in itself.

Using philosophical approaches to international relations presented in the work of Raymond Aron and Hedley Bull, this chapter relates the study of religion to their study of values in international affairs. In this context, Islamism is interpreted as an expression of Islamic revival being politically, culturally and religiously equal. In short, the ideology of Islamism is not a call for justice, but is rather a civilizational project that challenges the existing world order.[35] The Islamist claim to an alternative new order is perceived to replace the alleged "Judeo-Christian conspiracy" directed against Islam.[36] Therefore, the call for a "Revolt against the West" aims to counter that conspiracy.

To understand the issue properly, two aspects should be considered. The first is an international relations-oriented study of politicization of religion that underpins the emergence of religious fundamentalism. The prevailing media clichés describe the phenomenon through the terms "fanaticism, terrorism and extremism." These terms must be replaced by non-extreme vocabulary, but this is not the business of the IR discipline. However, it is dishonest to describe the *jihadist* threat of Islamism as a creation by the media, not as a reality. The accusation of Islamophobia has become a cover for *jihadism*. Although the addressed threat emerges from the politicization of Islam, it is not Islam as a faith that is under issue. Critical efforts at "covering Islam" have been denounced as a tool for the Western media to criticize Islam. This is not helpful either for defending Islam or for countering *jihadism*. This chapter does not defend the Western media; instead, it simply challenges the common view that the defamation of Western civilization – wrongly presented as a criticism – is needed for defending Islam.

Second, it is necessary to understand that the process of the religionization of politics and the politicization of religion reaches a pinnacle when it embraces Islamic universalism. The worldview is transformed to an internationalism that legitimates fighting for an Islamic world order. True, Islam is unique because of its universalism. In comparison, the politicization of religion in Hinduism only leads to a concept of order restricted to the envisaged Hindu nation in South Asia. It therefore remains exclusively regional and refrains from exclusive claims. In contrast, Islam is a universalist religion and its politicization touches on the international order. As the intellectual precursor of political Islam, Sayyid Qutb once proposed that international peace can only be based on establishing *Hakimiyyat Allah* on global grounds. The implication of this view is that there can be no world peace without the global domination of "Islam" (*Siyadat al-*

Islam). This is the articulation of an Islamist internationalism made by Qutb with a bid for a related new world order. This is the ideological background of the geopolitics of Islam and the West.[37]

Can we deal with the religionization of politics with an approach to cultural diversity and the heterogeneity of civilizations? The validity of political Islam and its related vision of a political order is suspect. At issue is a cultural difference that claims recognition as a cultural right. However, the "cultural difference" should not be tolerated, as it creates divisions in society. The dangers did not become apparent in the 1950s, when Qutb challenged the existing world order. He maintained that the deep civilizational crisis facing the West could only be resolved by creating Islamic dominance. In his writings, in particular *Signposts along the Road* and *World Peace and Islam*,[38] he proposed that solely Islam can save humanity by overcoming this civilizational crisis. It is only the action of al Qaeda *jihad* fighters and their offspring, combined with a demise of bipolarity, that made the new challenge clear and visible. At issue is not a "crazed gang," but a new totalitarianism represented by a powerful political movement based on transnational religion.

Jihadist Islamism is a revolt against the Westphalian order of world politics[39] in the hope of replacing it with an Islamic order. Without knowing the work of Qutb, Hedley Bull was aware of the fact when he identified the civilizational "Revolt against the West" as best "exemplified in Islamic fundamentalism."[40] In the twenty-first century, Qutbian ideas have become more topical and play a role in mobilizing the world of Islam. The reference to these ideas, articulated by the Islamists, reinforces Islam's new role as well as its public appeal. Political Islam can be traced back to 1928 when the Society of Muslim Brothers was established. This evidence is employed to show how Islamism pre-dates both the demise of the Cold War as well as the "Islamic Revolution" of Iran. Its appeal as a mobilizing form reached its zenith only after the fall of the USSR. The demise of the bipolar world allowed the heterogeneity of civilizations to become apparent. An integral part of the differences between these civilizations occurs as a result of politicized religions. In Islam, this has been translated to mean the establishment of the "the Islamic State" (*al-dawla al-Islamiyya*). The Islamist neo-*jihad* in the twenty-first century is an effort, fought through irregular warfare, to achieve political Islam's new order both at home and internationally.

One may ask if we are heading in a direction "Beyond Westphalia?" There are clearly problems inherent to the Westphalian order, and must therefore be questioned in a changed world. However, neither the violent *jihadist* means of Islamism nor the ideology of "divine rule" (*Hakimiyyat Allah*) appear to offer an appropriate alternative for a safe and secure international order. For a religiously diverse humanity, no alternatives based on the political concepts of order grounded on one religion can be accepted. There is no alternative to an order which acknowledges pluralism on all grounds.

In addition to the argument of religious and cultural pluralism, one needs to acknowledge that the "Islamic system" (*nizam Islami*) is a totalitarian political concept without the full support of the entire Islamic society. In particular, those committed to freedom and democracy reject this system. Again, it is essential to recognize the difference between the traditional Caliphate and this "new totalitarianism."[41] This Qutb concept of a *Hakimiyyat Allah* is not the rhetoric of a romantic order, nor a simple nostalgia for past Islamic glory. It is an indication of a new system of government opposed to democracy, and supporting the call for *jihad* as an Islamic world revolution. This call is not only restricted to political opposition to the existing regimes in the world of Islam by Islamists. In addition, Islamism pursues world political visions not limited to a legitimacy crisis. This study comes to the conclusion that the Islamist is a political man of action, who views himself as the "true believer." Jansen addresses this fact appropriately as "the dual nature of Islamic fundamentalism."[42] The terror practiced is believed to be conducted "in the mind of God."[43] It is not instrumental; instead it is based on an intrinsic belief regardless of its consonance with or contradiction of "true" Islamic beliefs fixed in scripture.

In post-bipolar politics it is imperative to deal with the significance of religion, ethnicity and culture as sources of social and economic issues. Earlier, these issue areas were ignored or perceived as offshoots or fall-outs from the East–West rivalry. Since the demise of bipolarity, suppressed conflicts related to political Islam are now on the rise. Islamist movements are among the new forces relating to politicized religion and the scholar is challenged to engage in cultural studies without falling into the trap of culturalism.[44] In explicitly arguing against Gilles Kepel, this study states that Islamism is neither declining; nor is it a passing phenomenon. Kepel, and similar-minded self-proclaimed experts, are clearly mistaken and they are contradicted by the facts.[45] Currently, most regional conflicts throughout the world are related to a religionization of politics and to a politicization of religion. This process is, in some cases, combined with ethnicity. In recent history, the Balkans, Chechnya and Kashmir provide examples of this combination of ethno-fundamentalism.

In conclusion, the common understanding of *jihadism* is flawed. To understand the ideological foundations of political Islam it is crucial to incorporate into the analysis a variety of issues: religious, ethnic, cultural and civilizational. Hereby, one needs to include the realities of de-Westernization[46] without derailing the analysis into the misleading rhetoric of a clash of civilizations. To be sure, this clash can be averted,[47] for example, by a reform of Islamic Shari‘a[48] and also by a rethinking of other outdated Islamic doctrines.

Jihadist Islamism and its challenge to security: the new irregular war

In relating the study of *Jihadist* Islamism to security, one is in a position to deal with the new challenges of irregular warfare. It is necessary to go beyond traditional wisdoms (for example, state-focused efforts) to counter the new threat posed by irregular warfare. In his work, Barry Buzan[49] was among those who made pioneering efforts in looking at security beyond the conventional military wisdoms. In addition, September 11th reminded states that security studies need to change in order to deal properly with the violence of terrorism. Cultural, religious and ideological strategies must be employed which differ from the traditional constraints of countering organized military forces. These strategies have the greater potential of countering terrorism.

Jihadism is the ideology of irregular warfare by non-state actors for fighting Western civilization. This form of war is a threat to international security. In the course of a politicization of the world religion of Islam, the call for a *jihadist* revolution is used for mobilizing the followers. *Jihadists* imagine that together all Muslims constitute a transnational community, the Islamic *umma*. In the ideology of al Qaeda, this reimagining of the *umma* by political Islam serves as grounds for political mobilization. This is a core issue in the *jihadist* ideology of political Islam.

It is important to note that the new facets of Islamism, a reimagined *umma* and *jihadism* in the shape of terrorism, are not evident in classical Islamic doctrine.[50] Again, the differentiation between Islam and Islamism must be understood. Islam is a faith which builds the framework for a respective civilization[51] with great cultural and religious diversity, as well as the differentiation between Sunni and Shiʿa Muslims.[52] Within this positive society the element of *jihadist* Islamism arises, a Sunni Arab ideology. It reimagines for the *umma* to mobilize Islam[53] in the pursuit of establishing a new world order. This worldview contributes to an essentialization of Islam. In a similar vein, I question Huntington's "clash of civilizations" that contends for the existence of an overall Islam acting collectively as a monolith, which is also a kind of an essentialization.

Despite great diversity within Islam, it can be stated that all Sunni Islamist groups adhere to similar concepts of political order based on politicized religion and Shariʿa. In a variety of ways these groups are committed to an interpretation of *jihad* as a formal irregular war. This interpretation is different from basic Islamic teachings. However, *jihadism* is a general phenomenon which must consequently be studied through a new security approach based on empirical truths. Scholars who refuse to include Islamism in security studies are fearful of the accusation of Islamophobia. This sentiment adds to the confusion between Islam and Islamism.

While disassociating the current analysis from Huntington's clash-rhetoric, the interpretation of *jihadist* Islamism as a "revolt against the West" acknowledges a civilizational conflict. Unlike a "clash," a conflict can be resolved peacefully. In this case the conflict is based on international grounds determined by the continual religionization of politics. The wars of collective memories contribute to constructing a worldview in which the "Crusades" against Islam are continually being fought. In the return of history a perceptual "War of Civilizations" occurs in which different worldviews, each honoring different sets of norms and values, ignite tensions and result in conflict. This is not simply a cultural concern. After all, the idea of order is always based on civilizational values. Therefore, this analysis contends to see a war of ideas underlying the conflict. It is expressed in tensions resulting from constructed world views and of collective memories. As "the war of ideas" becomes an established term, an important analysis on political Islam by the Turkish–American analyst Zeyno Baran, published in 2005, bears the title "Fighting the War of Ideas." This is an essential part of the new security.

The transformation of political Islam into *jihadism*, involved in conflicting civilizations, contributes to militarizing the claims to be accomplished in irregular warfare. *Jihadism*, particularly through its acts of terrorism, is based on political Islam, which is not indicative of all religious extremism. At issue is rather a new warfare. The irregular war of *jihadism* – unlike classical *jihad* – is a war without rules and without a limit of targets. This new type of *jihad* indicates a radical change in international affairs. Politically, it is related to a politicization of Islamic universalism that strives for a new Islamic world order. The contestation of existing concepts about world order is the substance of a war of ideas that leads to a conflict between the competing forces of world order. This conflict determines the mindset of *jihadist* terrorists in their irregular warfare. The ideology of Islamism promotes this conflict.

Among the few scholars who grasp the overall context of the described conflict is John Kelsay, who states, "In encounters between the West and Islam, the struggle is over who will provide the primary definition to the world order." Kelsay continues:

> Will it be the West, with its notions of territorial boundaries, market economies, private religiosity, and the priority of individual rights? Or will it be Islam, with its emphasis on the universal mission of a transtribal community called to build a social order founded on pure monotheism natural to humanity?[54]

Unfortunately, established Western students of Islam suppress these necessary questions. In contrast, Islamic fundamentalists ask these questions and have clear answers, as seen through Qutb's writings. In his *Signs along the Road* he states that only Islam is designed to lead humanity to overcome the contended crisis by establishing a just Islamic world order in the future.

The competition between Western and Islamist concepts of world order, particularly opposing understandings of war, peace, law and justice, is the focus of this chapter. The perceptual "war of civilizations" also as a war of ideas is rooted in these conflicting viewpoints.[55] By studying this conflict it is assumed that it can be averted. This "war" presents new areas of both security studies and conflict resolution under the environment of a "New Cold War." In this opposition, *jihadism* escalates the conflict beyond basic differing worldviews to militarization. The conflict eventually reaches an irregular war with the introduction of terrorism. Thus, the politicization of religion is not simply a state of mind or a dispute over cultural differences which can be treated with "tolerance." This strategy does not work when groups practice terrorism in the hope of achieving ideological goals pursued by political-military movements.

Long before the world was confronted with the implications of September 11th and the ensuing assaults, there were the earlier cases of Kosovo, Macedonia, Chechnya, Kashmir and the al-Aqsa Intifada. In all these cases, *jihadism* prevailed as the new kind of war without rules, i.e. irregular warfare. For instance, the fight between Israel and Hamas is based on a religionized conflict rooted in clashing civilizational worldviews. Even the late secular Palestinian leader, Yasser Arafat, declared this mindset. On 26 January 2002, he called for Islamic *jihad* as a response to the Israeli tanks encircling his residence. During these events, Arafat was seen on BBC-World shouting repeatedly, "My answer is *jihad*...." Although it is appealing to fight this irregular war through conventional means, it is equally as difficult.

The preceding analysis offers some general conclusions about the combined religionization and militarization of the conflict through *jihad*. These conclusions are as follows.

The problem of political order

Islamic fundamentalism as expressed in Sunni Islam is a powerful example of the politicization of religion. It not only illuminates existing cultural differences; it also promotes greater opposition to fight traditional rules and values of the current international community. The conflict is focused on the issue of international order. In terms of security *jihadists* are most appealing and subsequently successful when they mobilize on religious grounds. In addition to the need for military security, other measures are measured to counter irregular warfare and *jihadi* quests for a new world order. One cannot fight fundamentalists with armies; nor is it possible to overcome ideologies with militaries. This fight can only be won by undermining the ideology's appeal for an Islamic order and by delegitimizing it. A new security approach is needed to counter these challenges. This strategy can neither be fixed by the state nor on the predominance of conventional military thinking. The ideological appeal of *jihadism* will not be eradicated solely by destroying its terrorism arm. The war of ideas continues unabated.

Holy terror as a war of ideas

There are Sunni fundamentalists, such as the Turkish AKP-Islamists, who fight for their goals through peaceful political means in established institutions. Others fight within the framework of terrorism and violence to achieve their ideological goals. *Jihadism* often follows the latter path as a variety of "terror in the mind of God." *Jihadism* is a branch of fundamentalism that combines the views of Islamic world order with terrorism, turning the fight into a "holy war." Although there are clear differences, Islamists who choose to fight an irregular war are similar to Islamists who fight through traditional institutional means, as both are committed to the idea of an Islamic Shari'a state.

"Islamism" as the "Islamic variety of religious fundamentalism"

In this section, the terms *political Islam*, *Islamism*, and *Islamic fundamentalism* are used interchangeably. This use is debated, as some scholars dispute the application of fundamentalism to Islam in order to combat spreading prejudice against Islam. Fundamentalism is an analytical term and the rejection of it is misleading. Moreover, while the term has been given negative connotations, it is a helpful scholarly and analytical concept used in studying the politicization of religion. Scholars who use the term "Islamism" as an alternative to fundament-alism are unknowingly contributing to the stereotyping of Islam by implicitly restricting the general phenomenon of the politicization of religion to it. In con-trast, this work argues that "Islamism" is an element of the phenomenon of polit-ical religion known as a variety of religious fundamentalism. This phenomenon is not limited to Islam; it is also present in other religions. However, *jihadism* as the military dimension of this phenomenon is specific to Islamism as an interpre-tation of Islam. This compels the inquiry of Islamism to be included in the field of security studies. The new conclusions may be described as "new frontiers of security"[56] which extend beyond the traditional concepts of security dominated by military thinking. This new thinking broadens the scope and deepens the insights of the analysis. It enables the scholar to deal with the problem of reli-gion and extremism, particularly through the new pattern of irregular warfare. It must be remembered that *jihadism* is not only an ideology of religious extrem-ism, but also a new concept of warfare and the quest for a new world order represented by movements based in transnational religion with global networks.

The military dimension of Islamism

Since the end of the Cold War, the potential for conventional Clausewitzian wars appeared to decrease. Wars between states with organized and institution-alized armies have largely disappeared, being replaced by wars waged by non-state actors. This pattern is likely to prevail in the foreseeable future and therefore new analyses must be produced. Security experts have been arguing that this change be considered and have underscored the need for a new security approach. Earlier scholars like Barry Buzan, and later Martin van Creveld and Kalevi Holsti, have ventured into ground-breaking studies of security and war. These studies extend beyond the dependence on institutionalized armies. Others, like Anthony Cordesman, are reluctant to acknowledge the change. The chang-ing styles of war along with non-military factors must become the central sub-jects of future security studies. The militarization of the religious Islamist ideology, which combines Islamism with *jihadism*, compels new security approaches to be examined. *Jihadism* is the militarization of the war of ideas for a new international order. The new important war has proved to be very power-ful. In this war, the new missiles are human bodies with the ability to accurately strike the target, causing extensive damage.

Between 1948 and 1982, five interstate wars took place in the Middle East.

This is in contrast to current circumstances where an Arab–Israeli or Indian–Pakistani interstate war is unlikely. Instead, we are confronted with irregular warfare enacted by violent *jihadists*, in particular suicide bombers. Prior to these recent developments, earlier events in Algeria, Egypt, Israel, Afghanistan, as well as in Xinjiang, Kashmir, Kosovo and Macedonia, highlighted the need to confront the new *jihadist* warfare. September 11th served as a watershed event for the West. It is certain that the West will not be able to counter *jihadism* and its related challenges to international security using the old framework of the state-centered approach. In earlier conflicts, the North Atlantic Treaty Organization (NATO) was able to outpower its foes, such as the Serbian army with its regular and armed forces in 1999 and Iraqi forces in 2003. In contrast, neither the religious-ethnic UÇK acts of revenge against the Christian Serbs, Macedonians, and others, nor the irregular war against coalition troops in Iraq and in Afghanistan could be curtailed by conventional means. Moreover, the Israeli Defense Force (IDF) has been unable to cope with the Palestinian Intifada. The inability to fight an irregular war also applies to the recent Hizballah war against Israel. On the cover of the 19–25 August 2006 issue of *The Economist* was a picture of the Hizballah leader under the headline, "Nasrallah Wins the War." This perception was shared throughout the Middle East. This war was a prime example of combining an irregular war with a media war and war of ideas.[57]

Islam and Islamism in Europe: anti-Semitic Islamism and the reintroduction of anti-Semitism to Europe via global migration

According to German Intelligence, Hezbollah has 900 members among the Islamic diaspora in Germany. This diaspora has the potential to be hijacked by organized Islamists who claim to be the ultimate representatives of the "true voice of Islam." While the majority of Muslim immigrants behave as law-abiding citizens, a minority of Islamists seek to transform Europe into a new "hinterland" for global *jihad*. These *jihadists* abuse basic democratic rights (e.g. asylum) while at the same time successfully demonizing their critics as the "voice of Islamophobia." These acts camouflage their pursuit of establishing Islamist logistics in Europe. Important components of Islamist *jihadism* exist throughout Europe; Germany being a prominent case in point. The new German tolerance vis-à-vis Islamism is – as Michael Wolffsohn rightly argues – among the wrong lessons which contemporary German scholars have drawn from their shameful past.[58] Another German Jew, Henryk Broder, strongly coined the formulas of *Hurra, wir kapitulieren* to describe appeasing Islamism, in his essay in *Der Spiegel* of 2006. Expanded into a book under the same title it became a bestseller, but it did not succeed in altering the distorted public opinion in Germany. A disturbing example was the recent Lebanon War in July 2006, where it was most irritating to see European opinion leaders implicitly comparing Jews to Nazis and Hamas and Hezbollah's Islamists to their victims. This reversal serves as a self-congratulatory accusation of the other to acquit oneself of German crimes against Jews.

The study of Islam and Islamism in Europe is poor if not absent. In contrast, this research topic is covered in many seminal international projects run in the US that deal with migration, security and cultural studies equally based in Middle Eastern, Islamic and European studies. At the University of California at Berkeley, a research project was launched entitled "Islam and the Changing Identity of Europe." The project, conducted by two major Berkeley centers for European and Middle Eastern studies, led to the book *Muslim Europe or Euro-Islam?*[59] The work examines the feasibility of a European Islam. If Euro-Islam fails, then the Islamist dream of "Muslim Europe" is attainable through a gradual Islamization of the European political sphere. This scholarly analysis was continued in a Cornell project where I dealt with the threat and challenge of Islam to Europe's civilizational identity.

It is crucial to understand that although terrorist operations on September 11th were carried out in New York and Washington, they were prepared and rooted in the German Islamic diaspora. This highlights the fact that the networking of Islamism and the related supporting systems of *jihadism* (financing, recruitment, propaganda, indoctrination) are based and located in the Islamic diaspora in Western Europe. Therefore, I share Fukuyama's view that Europe has become a battlefront of Islamism.

To avoid misunderstandings, it is important to note that at issue is a small but highly active minority among the Islamic diaspora, not the entire diaspora itself. In the case of Germany there are approximately 100,000 Islamists among the diaspora community of 3.7 million. This figure varies from one country to another. The Islamists comprise 10 percent of the diaspora in the Netherlands. In general, the figures range between 3 to 5 percent and only rarely reach 10 percent. Nevertheless, the issue is not the number of organized Islamists; rather, their relative power and number of sympathizers is important. The small community of Islamists is institutionally well organized which allows them to be highly influential. Due to their abundant resources, they control the major mosques of the European diaspora and are able to launch highly costly lawsuits against their rivals. The propaganda war placed in the repeatedly mentioned war of ideas is the most powerful means for the transmission of their message: the victimization of Muslims. The accusation of Islamophobia is not only employed against non-Muslim critics; it also targets Muslim foes suspected of being "Westernized."

Although the study of Islam in Europe covers a variety of issues, the focus is the spread of anti-Semitism among Muslim diasporic communities. Professor Wolfgang Benz, director of an international Research Center on anti-Semitism, observed an increase in anti-Semitism among young Muslims of the diaspora. Unfortunately, some EU functionaries silenced this study due to fear of an alleged Islamophobia.[60] This propaganda weapon works most effectively, even against Jews living in Europe.

It is necessary first to address the general question of the "Europeanization of

Islam or Islamization of Europe." A European Islam, in contrast to Islamism, would not allow anti-Semitism to occur in the name of Islam. This view can be traced to the historian Bernard Lewis, who supports the belief that anti-Semitism, or Judeophobia, is alien to Islam and its history. However, this has changed in contemporary history, as anti-Semitism was exported from Europe to the Muslim Middle East (including Iran). While anti-Semitism was originally exported from Europe, it has taken a firm hold in the Arab world. Today's anti-Semitism is now being transmitted back to Europe via Islamic migration. Islamist anti-Semitism continues to be popular[61] both in the world of Islam and in its European diaspora. Europeans favor hiding this phenomenon and deterring the accusation of anti-Semitism, preferring to highlight the Islamist accusation of Islamophobia.

The language of political Islam is popular for declaring *jihad* on the West, believed to be waged in the name of "belief" (*iman*) against "international belief" (*al-kufr al-'alami*). This idea is also taught in religious schools in the Islamic diaspora throughout Europe. The novelty, however, is that this *jihad* incorporates, next to the Crusaders, the Jews. We also find this sentiment in the Islamic diaspora in Europe. The Islamists came to Europe to join an increasing number of migrant asylum seekers. In this way, political Islam has been exported to the West. Its ideology, including its anti-Semitism, is becoming apparent in domestic European affairs.

Being myself a liberal Muslim, I have been warning for years that totalitarian-minded Islamists have been abusing both democratic freedoms and the European Islam diaspora for establishing a logistical basis for their activities in the West. The best impartial way for stating the response is to quote *Newsweek* writing after September 11th about the issue: "Bassam Tibi ... has warned for years that Westerners need to differentiate between good Muslims and the bad ... no one wanted to hear that, verging as it does on the politically incorrect."[62] In Europe, it is politically incorrect to state the fact of a new anti-Semitism spreading in the Islamic diaspora.

The incorrect understanding of an "open society"[63] has allowed fundamental-ist activities in Europe and the West to be tolerated or even ignored. European politicians, despite alerts by the security apparatus, are more concerned about political correctness while turning a deaf ear to the warnings. These findings show that anti-Semitism in Europe seems to be the lesser evil than the alleged Islamophobia. This chapter supports the lessening of prejudices against non-Western cultures and combating racism against both Jews and Muslims. However, Islamophobia is a constructed weapon used instrumentally by the Islamists. Thus it should not be considered to be a greater prejudice than anti-Semitism. In reality, anti-Semitism is the "new totalitarianism." Hannah Arendt, the source of the theory of totalitarianism, identifies anti-Semitism as one of its basic elements. On these grounds I identify Islamism as the third most recent variety of totalitarianism in a study devoted to this subject matter.[64]

The success of Islamist networking in Europe's civil society and the spread of the related ideology in the diaspora made the Islamist movement powerful in

Europe. Islamists have succeeded in incorrectly connecting a critique of *jihadist* Islamism with an ugly Islamophobia in a war of ideas. This is most evident in Germany as the country assists in protecting Islamic fundamentalism while overlooking the interrelation between migration and security. European opinion leaders are less concerned with anti-Semitism in society, focusing instead on their own preoccupation of having multicultural views. Those who disagree with them, including myself, were silenced by "democratic" means, while the abuse of the Islamic diaspora in Europe continues unabated.[65]

Islamists, who act as enemies to open society, may be found within contemporary Europe. These neo-absolutist Islamists protect themselves through instrumentalizing the culture of political correctness, advocated primarily by the left. Even liberal Muslims engaged in Islamic reform have been victimized in the name of combating a "Feindbild Islam" (the German formula for Islamophobia). Europeans leftists support this victimization by allegedly practicing tolerance towards differing religions, i.e. Islam. Consequently, it is not surprising that Islamists have been given priority in Scandinavia and Germany for establishing their logistical bases and propaganda networks. In Sweden, "Radio Islam" is one of the influential means for the spread of anti-Semitism in Europe, according to Professor Benz. Germany – due to its shameful past – is one of the European countries with the highest standards of political correctness when it comes to non-Western cultures. An example may be seen through the liberal German journalist Udo Ulfkotte, who disclosed similar findings in his book *Krieg in unseren Städten.* Although his findings are legitimate, he has been silenced by dozens of lawsuits and arbitrary court decisions. The legal expenses of the Islamist claimants were, in most cases, paid by the German state, as most of them live on welfare payments by claiming to be "poor." An article in the *New York Times* and republished in the *International Herald Tribune* describes Germany as a "safe haven" for Islamist activities.[66] In addition, the cover of *Newsweek* asked, "Why terrorists like Europe?" In Germany this was answered with the formula "Tolerating the Intolerable."[67] Three of the four neo-*jihad* terror-pilots from 9/11 came from Germany. The terrorists used the country to accumulate finances and create an infrastructure for the operation. Their apartment in Hamburg was given the name "House of Supporters" (*Dar al-Ansar*).

In my book *The New Totalitarianism* (2004), I argue that the European awareness of the security threat is as weak as their willingness to combat Islamist anti-Semitism in Europe. A French author described the problem as "Democracy against itself."[68] This statement highlights a critical dilemma of Western democracy. What is the proper balance between ensuring security and protecting civil rights, while preserving democratic rules and values? Is tolerating the enemy of "open society" a part of democracy?

Islamist totalitarianism and its ideology as tolerated in the West can be countered by the democratic mean of successfully integrating into the framework of a Euro-Islam.[69] The proposed concept of *Leitkultur* (guiding culture of a civil society and pluralism) for the integration of immigrants has failed to find acceptance in the Jewish community in Germany despite its positive arguments.

Leitkultur obliges not only Muslim immigrants to embrace democracy and also to reject anti-Semitism, but also Europeans not to treat these newcomers as they did the Jews. As far as Muslims are concerned, European Islam should be the *Leitkultur* of the Muslim diaspora in Europe. Only a Euro-Islam can help reach the goal of making the Muslim diaspora in Europe immune to the susceptibility of the Islamist ideology and its anti-Semitism. Euro-Islam is an alternative to multicultural communitarianism[70] which implies "anything goes," and which also applies to the anti-Semitism of the diasporic Islam.

Conclusions

Among the major findings of this study is the knowledge that the term "religious extremism" is not the proper term for dealing with the pending challenges arising from the religionization of politics and politicization of religion. There are many political organizations and also some religious institutions which follow the ideology of Islamism. This fundamentalist challenge can be countered through a proper security approach in addition to a democratic strategy. The ideology of Islamism preaches a "clash of civilizations." The assistance and cooperation of Muslims in the pursuit of countering Islamism is imperative. In the case of the Islamic diaspora in Western Europe a line has to be drawn between Islam and Islamism for properly countering the challenge. This is not only to protect Muslims living in Europe from general suspicions, but also to undermine the actions of the Islamists drawing the fault-line between "we" (Muslims) and "they" (Crusaders and Jews). If this cannot be countered in the ongoing war of ideas, Europe will face civil strife and turmoil in the foreseeable future. The uprising in the *banlieues* of Paris was only a warning that seems not to have been taken seriously.

In Germany, the discrimination and denial of young Muslims to join the core community make them susceptible to the appeal of political Islam. Despite my background as both a Muslim descended from the "nobility" (*ashraf*) of Damascus and as a middle-class university professor, I have been regularly and repeatedly treated in German society as a "guest worker," i.e. a second-class citizen. This has led to discriminatory acts against me during my entire university career. An education in rationalism saved me from becoming a Muslim fundamentalist. From my Jewish academic teachers in Frankfurt, Max Horkheimer and Theodor Adorno, I learned to identify with the plight of German Jews and to cope with the exclusion of an ethnic-exclusive society in a rational manner.

The thriving of radical Islam in the European diaspora is related to the exclusion of Muslim citizens, and not only to the lower classes. Having lived in Germany for more than four decades, I acknowledge that my education in rational philosophy and the knowledge about a proper Islam have helped me to distinguish between Islam and Islamism. This has protected me from the appeal of a *jihadist* defensive culture, despite the enduring experience of discrimination in Europe. In an interview with the German magazine *Focus* following the *jihadist* assaults of London on 7 July 2005, I bluntly stated, "Had I not been educated in

European philosophy by my Jewish academic teachers, Horkheimer and Adorno, I would have become in view of the discrimination subjected to a *jihadist* fighting against Europe."[71]

The repeated references to the diaspora serve to explain an important social fact. The poorly educated Muslim immigrants who lack the education to protect them against their "othering" by European societies become an easy catch for *jihad*-Islamists. The problem becomes worse with the spread of anti-Semitism, putting the blame on Jews. I share Francis Fukuyama's view that Europe, due to the appeal of a safe haven for *jihadism,* is becoming the battlefront for Islamic fundamentalists. People like the Egyptian Mohammed Atta of Hamburg and even the German-born Moroccan Said Bahaji joined the fundamentalist network for religio-ideological reasons. A Muslim with a combined European civilizational identity would presumably not act as a *jihadist*, but rather as a guardian of Western values. The Europeans must first stop the "othering" of young Muslim immigrants (even those born in Europe), i.e. treating them as aliens and an underclass while denying them full membership in the polity. The best way for Europeans to accomplish this while also undermining Islamism is to adopt a policy of real integration, not superficial acts. My life experiences give German society a poor record for such a political will of inclusion. Europeans should simultaneously engage in an effort of integration to combat Islamism. Giving in to the combatants of Islam in the name of civil rights is counterproductive. Therefore I argue for the Europeanization of Muslim immigrants – to make them "citizens of heart" – as a solution.[72]

Among the conclusions is also the statement that the ideology of Islamism – in contrast to an enlightened Islam – is thriving in the world triangle of Islam, Europe and the Islamic diaspora. In Europe there is a rhetoric for an integration of Muslim migrants but no political solutions. I reiterate that this policy would be the most effective long-term security approach against *jihadism*. In the world of Islam itself, Islamists create the major opposition. They cannot be solely undermined by security policies of the existing oppressive regimes in the Arab world and other parts of the world of Islam. A simple procedural democratization would only bring these Islamists peacefully to power. This is the dilemma the Arab world has to cope with in the years to come.

An understanding of the addressed roots of the ideological use of Islam in the politicization of religion and the religionization of politics is essential. This use of Islam serves to legitimize the use of irregular warfare waged by Islamist *jihadists* as a new weapon. A lack of this understanding contributes to ignoring the source of tensions and conflicts in post-bipolar politics. To deter the threat of Islamism in the addressed triangle, the world of Islam, the West and the Islamic diaspora in Europe, we need to engage in a war of ideas and not only of politics restricted to military means. There should be no promotion of existing faultlines; instead, Islam and democracy should be harmonized with one another.[73]

In short, Islamism is an Islamic variety of religious fundamentalism. Its emergence relates to a structural phenomenon in world politics and is not simply terrorism. However, *Jihadism* transfers this general phenomenon of the politicization of religion into terrorism as the new warfare. This chapter is an effort to analyze and shed light on the challenge posed by the ideology of Islamism and by its *jihadist* branch. Political Islam is also a home-made problem that challenges Muslims themselves. They are an essential part of the issue.

The solution for Europe lies in Europeanizing Islam to counter the efforts of an Islamization of Europe. In the world of Islam, the task is more complex. The option is either to succumb to the new totalitarianism or to accept reforms for an Islamic embracing of secular democracy in espousing an open liberal Islam. This would open the way for Muslims to join the rest of the world within the framework of democratic peace. The Islamist *shari'a-jihad*[74] inspired dream is not consonant with a world inspired by democracy and pluralism. Muslims need to come to terms with the rest of the world and to give up the illusion of a global Islamization. The *jihadist*-terrorist internationalism of political Islam is not a contribution to world peace, but rather to a new world disorder.

I cannot conclude this chapter without refuting the idea of "multiple modernities." Islamism is not another modernity; it alienates Muslims from the rest of humanity in a modern world. Therefore, Muslim politicians are best advised to pay the price of reforms and to join the war on terror, and to unequivocally dissociate themselves from global *jihad*. The European approach of a democratization of the EU's neighborhood[75] is the best way to counter ideological terrorism. This is true only if it is accepted that democracy is above all a political culture, and not a simple procedure of voting. The electoral victory of the Hamas theocrats over the Fatah autocrats is not an indication of democratization. In their dealings with Islam and Islamism, Europeans need real political will and not to restrict themselves to rhetorical pronouncements of goodwill. The challenge generated by Hamas is a real test for the European Union, as is the electoral victory of the Shi'a Islamist parties in Iraq and the growth of Hezbollah in Lebanon. The outcome in Iraq is a challenge to all assumptions of US policies in the Middle East. These policies are not the right response to *jihadist* Islamism.[76]

In going beyond these topicalities, the foremost conclusion among the findings of this study is the pertinence of culture for understanding post-bipolar politics imbued by the cultural turn. In short, "culture matters."[77] In looking at religion as a "cultural system," it follows that the religionization of politics is much more than a delinquent religious extremism. Instead, it is a culturalization of conflict, which complicates both the issue and the needed conflict resolution, making it a virtually impossible task. Political issues are negotiable and can be put on the table, but not politicized faith.

Notes

1 This is an adoption of the terminology employed in "The World Cultures Project," the findings of which were published in a volume by H. Anheier and Y. R. Isar (eds), Cultures and Globalization series: *Cultures and Tensions,* London: Sage, 2007. The volume includes my chapter "Islam: Between Religious-cultural Practice and Identity Politics." The study deals with tensions leading to conflict in situations intensified by the use of religion in politics as a cultural system within the framework of identity

politics. On the notion of the "return of the sacred" as a process of desecularization, see notes 14 and 17 below.

2 M. Slackman, "In Mideast. A Wave of Political Islam," *International Herald Tribune*, 19–20 August 2006, front page; also by Slackman, "Islamic Radicals Spread Instability across Middle East," *International Herald Tribune*, 9 September 2006, p. 7, also published in *New York Times*.

3 In my work I have coined the term "irregular war" for conceptualizing the *jihadization* of Islam to jihadism. See B. Tibi, *The Challenge of Fundamentalism. Political Islam and the New World Disorder*, Berkeley: University of California Press, 1998, updated edn 2002, pp. 86–88; for a more elaborated view of the strategic consequences, see also Tibi, "Islam and Islamism: A Dialogue with Islam and a Security Approach vis-à-vis Islamism," in T. A. Jacoby and B. Sasley (eds), *Redefining Security in the Middle East*, Manchester and New York: Manchester University Press and Palgrave, 2002, pp. 62–82; and more recently my article "The Totalitarianism of Jihadist Islamism," in *Totalitarian Movements and Political Religion*, 2007, vol. 8, no. 1, pp. 35–54.

4 For a case study see B. Milton-Edwards, *Islamic Politics in Palestine*, London: Tauris, 1996.

5 This interpretation of an invention of tradition is borrowed from E. Hobsbawm, (ed.), *The Invention of Tradition*, Cambridge: Cambridge University Press, reprinted 1996, "Introduction," pp. 1–14. It is employed in a new approach for the study of contemporary Islam by B. Tibi, *Islam between Culture and Politics*, New York: Palgrave, 2nd enlarged edn, 2005. On the contemporary use of Shari'a as an invention of tradition see ch. 7, and similarly on the *jihadization* of Islam see Part V, added to the new edition, pp. 231–272. On the distinction between Islam and Islamism see Tibi, "Islam and Islamism," op. cit.

6 On this concept see E. Hoffer, *The True Believer. Thoughts on the Nature of Mass Movements*, New York: Perennial Library, 2002, reprint of the original 1951 publication; and on violence of these "true believers" combined with a war of ideas see B. Tibi, "Countering Terrorism als Krieg der Weltanschauungen," in M. van Creveld and K. von Knop (eds), *Countering Modern Terrorism. History, Current Issues and Future Threats,* Bielefeld: Bertelsmann, 2005, pp. 131–172.

7 Unlike in B. Lincoln, *Holy Terrors. Thinking about Religion after September 11*, Chicago, IL: The University of Chicago Press, 2003; M. Juergensmeyer, *Terror in the Mind of God*, Berkeley: The University of California Press, 2000; and most recently Mary Habeck, *Knowing the Enemy. Jihadist Ideology and the War on Terror*, New Haven, CT: Yale University Press, 2006, who restrict their analysis to studying the connection between religion and violence, I view terror in an international relations perspective as the new warfare of non-state actors.

8 See note 5 above. *Jihadism* is an example for such an invention; it transforms classical *jihad* into *jihadist* terrorism. For more details see B. Tibi, "From Islamist Jihadism to Democratic Peace? Islam at the Crossroads in Post-bipolar International Politics," *Ankara Paper 16*, London: Taylor & Francis, 2005; and my most recent TMPR article referenced in note 3 above. In a war of ideas *jihadism* engages against the vision of world peace as a democratic peace explained by B. Russet, *Grasping Democratic Peace*, Princeton, NJ: Princeton University Press, 1993. The origin of the concept is I. Kant, *Zum ewigen Frieden*, reprinted in Z. Batscha and R. Saage (eds), *Friedensutopien*, Frankfurt: Suhrkamp, 1979, pp. 37–82. In Islam the Islamic concept of peace is a different one. On this issue see B. Tibi, "War and Peace in Islam," in T. Nardin (ed.), *The Ethics of War and Peace,* Princeton, NJ: Princeton University Press, 1996, reprinted 1998, pp. 128–145. This study is also included in Sahail Hashmi (ed.), *Islamic Political Ethics*, Princeton, NJ: Princeton University Press, 2002, pp. 175–193.

9 The findings of this project are published in the volume by P. Katzenstein and T. Byrnes (eds), *Religion in an Expanding Europe*, Cambridge: Cambridge Univer-

sity Press, 2006. My contribution to this project is the chapter, "Europeanizing Islam or the Islamization of Europe," pp. 204–224.
10 See the classic by R. Mitchell, *The Society of the Muslim Brothers*, London: Oxford University Press, 1969.
11 This authoritative essay by H. al-Banna, *"Risalat al-jihad* (Essay on *Jihad*)," is included in the collected writings of al-Banna, *Majmu'at Rasail al-Banna*, Cairo: Dar al-Da'wa, 1990, pp. 271–292.
12 On the political thought of Sayyid Qutb as the precursor of Islamism and his impact see R. E. Euben, *The Enemy in the Mirror. Islamic Fundamentalism and the Limits of Modern Nationalism*, Princeton, NJ: Princeton University Press, 1999, ch. 3.
13 Sayyid Qutb, *al-Salam al-Alami wa al-Islam* [World Peace and Islam], Cairo: al-Shuruq, 1992, p. 172. In this book classical *jihad* is reinterpreted as an "Islamic World Revolution for achieving Islamic World Peace." This is a formula coined by Sayyid Qutb. His work leans obviously on Leninism.
14 D. Philipott, "The Challenge of September 11 to Secularism in International Relations," *World Politics*, 2002, vol. 55, no. 1, pp. 66–95. Much earlier, Mark Juergensmeyer referred to this in a question put as the title: *The New Cold War?: Religious Nationalism Confronts the Secular State*, Berkeley: University of California Press, 1993. On this subject see also B. Tibi, "Secularization and Desecularization in Modern Islam," *Religion, Staat, Gesellschaft*, 2000, vol. 1, no. 1, pp. 95–117.
15 R. Pape, *Dying to Win. The Strategic Logic of Suicide Terrorism*, New York: Random House, 2005, fails to understand the fact and notion of religionized violence and misinterprets the worldview and action of suicide bombers.
16 On the Islamist *umma* internationalism, see P. Mandevile, *Transnational Muslim Politics. Reimagining the Umma*, London: Routledge, 2004, in particular ch. 6, pp. 178–191. See also B. Tibi, *Political Islam, World Politics and Europe*, London, Routledge, 2007. On the internationalization of al Qaeda as a case in point for reimagining the *umma* and the related internationalism, see P. L. Bergen, *Holy War Inc. Inside the Secret World of Osama Bin Laden*, New York: Free Press, 2001, in particular ch. 10.
17 On this debate and for a critique on Habermas see B. Tibi, "Habermas and the Return of the Sacred. Is it a Religious Renaissance? Political Religion as a New Totalitarianism," in *Religion, Staat, Gesellschaft*, 2002, vol. 3, no. 2, pp. 265–296, and also the references in note 1 above.
18 On this politicization and on its pertinence for world affairs see the contributions to the special issue of *Millennium, Journal of International Affairs*, 2000, vol. 29, no. 3, a special issue on "Religion and International Relations," which also includes B. Tibi, "Post-bipolar Order in Crisis: The Challenge of Politicized Islam," pp. 843–859. See also J. Haynes, *Religion in Global Politics*, London: Longman, 1998, in particular ch. 7 on the Middle East.
19 On the concept of "order" see the classical study by H. Bull, *The Anarchical Society. A Study of Order in World Politics*, New York: Columbia University Press, 1977, in particular part 1. For an appreciation of Bull, see the essay by Stanley Hoffmann, "Bull and the Contribution to International Relations," in *World Disorders. Troubled Peace in the Post-Cold War Era*, New York: Rowman & Littlefield, 1998, pp. 13–34. The contemporary phenomenon of remaking the order of the world along religious tenets is related to fundamentalism. The most authoritative work on religious fundamentalism ever was accomplished in a project at the American Academy of Arts and Sciences chaired by Martin Marty and Scott Appleby, who are also the editors of *The Fundamentalism Project*, Chicago: Chicago University Press, 1991–1995. My book, *The Challenge of Fundamentalism, Political Islam and the New World Disorder*, op. cit., grew from this project. It was a great honor to be part of this project and to be involved in the research that fundamentalism is not an expression of a traditionalism and that Islamists draw on modern technology, even adopt –

instrumentally – its accomplishments; for an inquiry on this issue completed for this project, see B. Tibi, "The Worldview of Sunni-Arab Fundamentalists: Attitudes Towards Modern Science and Technology," in *Fundamentalisms and Society, Vol. 2,* Chicago, IL: Chicago University Press, 1993, pp. 73–102. For a recent work on the use of modern technology by Islamists for terrorist ends see G. Bunt, *Islam in the Digital Age. E-Jihad, Online-Fatwas and Cyber Islamic Environments*, London: Pluto Press, 2003. On "remaking the world," see the respective chapters in the part "Remaking the World through Militancy," in *The Fundamentalism Project*, vol. 3, op. cit. And finally, in this concept of divine order see the analysis of the referenced authentic Islamist sources included in B. Tibi, *Fundamentalisms in Islam (Eine Gefahr für den Weltfrieden)*, Darmstadt: Primus Verlag, 2000, 3rd edn 2002, chs 2, 4 and 5. The origin of this concept is by Sayyid Qutb, *Ma'alim fi al-Tariq* ("Signposts along the Road"), 13th legal edn, Cairo: Dar al-Shuruq, 1989.

20 See M. Hodgson, *The Venture of Islam. Conscience and History in a World Civil-ization*, 3 Volumes, Chicago, IL: Chicago University Press, 1977. Hodgson describes *Dar al-Islam* when it was the hegemonic order of the world from the seventh through the seventeenth century.

21 H. Bull, "The Revolt against the West," in Hedley Bull and A. Watson (eds), *The Expansion of International Society*, Oxford: Clarendon Press, 1984, pp. 217–218; see also the references in notes 14 and 19 above.

22 Decades ahead of Huntington, the notion of civilization was applied to world politics by S. Qutb. In his work, Qutb argues for a return of history as a return of Islamic civilization to dominance. In the US, debate on the issue of Sayyid Qutb's book *al-Islam wa Mushkilat al-Hadara* [Islam and the Problems of Civilization], Cairo: Dar al-Shuruq, reprinted 1988, is not known. This approach is continued by the Egyptian Islamist Mohammed Imara in *al-Sahwa al-Islamiyya wa al-Tahaddi al-Hadari*, Cairo: Dar al-Shuruq, 1991.

23 Bull, *The Anarchical Society*, op. cit., p. 273.

24 On this simultaneity see Tibi, *The Challenge of Fundamentalism*, op. cit., chs 1 and 5, and also Tibi, *Islam between Culture and Politics*, op. cit., ch. 4.

25 E. Sivan, *Radical Islam. Medieval Theology and Modern Politics*, New Haven, CT: Yale University Press, 1985.

26 See B. Tibi, "Culture and Knowledge. The Fundamentalist Claim of de-Westernization," *Theory, Culture and Society*, 1995, vol. 12, no. 1, pp. 1–24.

27 On this subject see R. Litwak, *Rough States and US-Foreign Policy,* Washington, DC: Johns Hopkins University Press, 2000.

28 To be sure, Islamists do not talk about the "restoration of the Caliphate" as some "pundits" contend, but rather about the "Islamic system/*nizam Islami.*" For an equally authoritative and highly influential Islamist presentation of the concept of *al-Nizam al-Islami* see Salim Al-Awwa, *fi al-Nizam al-Siyasi li al-dawla al-Islamiyya*, Cairo: al-Maktab al-Masr, 1975, 6th reprint 1983. To be sure, Islamists no longer talk about the restoration of the Caliphate, but instead about this *nizam* ("system of rule") as this book shows.

29 M. Doran, "Somebody Else's Civil War," *Foreign Affairs*, 2002, vol. 82, no. 1, pp. 22–42.

30 The pioneer of relating migration to security is M. Weiner, *The Global Migration Crisis*, New York: HarperCollins, 1995, ch. 6. For an implementation of this approach on Islamic migration to Europe see B. Tibi, *Islamische Zuwanderung. Die gescheiterte Integration*, Munich: Deutsche Verlagsanstalt, 2002, in particular the Introduction. On Islamic fundamentalism in the diaspora see J. F. Revel, *Democracy Against Itself,* New York: Free Press, 1993, ch. 12; and in M. Teitelbaum and J. Winter, *A Question of Numbers. High Migration, Low Fertility and the Politics of National Identity,* New York: Hill & Wang, 1998, pp. 221–239.

31 See the detailed references in the second part of note 19 above.

32 See the references in note 17 above.
33 See M. Wolffsohn, "Falsche Lehren aus der deutschen Geschichte," *Frankfurter All-gemeine Sonntagszeitung*, 12 March 2006, p. 15.
34 On the religious legitimation of September 11th see Lincoln, *Holy Terrors*, op. cit.; on *jihad* see B. Tibi, "Islamism, National and International Security after September 11," in G. Baechler and A. Wenger (eds), *Conflict and Cooperation*, Zurich: Neue Zurcher Zeitung, 2002, pp. 127–152.
35 See the article by Philipott referred to in note 14 above.
36 See the allegation of "Une vaste conspiration judeo-chrétienne" by the Islamist Mohammed Y. Kassab, *L' Islam face au nouvel ordre mondial*, Algiers: Editions Salama, 1991, pp. 75–93. Not only Islamists, but also many prominent Germans (both Left and Right) continue to contend that September 11th was a US home-made conspiracy in a US imperial pursuit. This view is documented in dozens of German anti-American bestsellers. It is fortunate that the special issue *Verschwörung*/conspiracy of the news magazine *Der Spiegel*, 2003, vol. 37, contributed to dismantling these bestsellers, some of which are implicitly also anti-Semitic.
37 See the references in notes 13, 14, 16, and 18 above, as well as in G. Fuller and I. Lesser, *A Sense of Siege, The Geopolitics of Islam and the West*, Boulder, CO: West-view Press, 1995.
38 The two major books written by Sayyid Qutb are *Ma'alim* and *al-Salam al-Alami*, op. cit. For an interpretation of Qutb's political thought see the excellent book by Euben, op. cit.
39 On the Westphalian system, see L. Miller, *Global Order*, Boulder, CO: Westview Press, 1990, ch. 2; and on the challenge to it see Philipott (note 14 above) and more recently B. Tibi, *Political Islam, World Politics and Europe*, London: Routledge, 2007, in particular the Introduction and part 1.
40 Bull, *The Revolt Against the West*, op. cit., p. 223.
41 B. Tibi, *Der neue Totalitarismus. Heiliger Krieg und westliche Sicherheit*, Darmstadt: Primus, 2004, ch. 2 on Islamism, ch. 3 on *jihadism*. See also the TMPR article referenced in note 3 above.
42 J. Jansen, *The Dual Nature of Islamic Fundamentalism*, Ithaca and New York: Cornell University Press, 1997.
43 See M. Juergensmeyer, *Terror in the Mind of God. The Global Rise of Religious Violence*, Berkeley: University of California Press, 2000; and Juergensmeyer, *The New Cold War*, op. cit.
44 On this cultural analysis which is not a culturalism see the contributions by B. Tibi, *The Crisis of Modern Islam*, Salt Lake City, UT: Utah University Press, 1988; and the subsequent book, *Islam and the Cultural Accommodation of Social Change*, Boulder, CO: Westview Press, 1990, reprinted 1991.
45 The judgments on political Islam prematurely made as an explanation by G. Kepel, *Jihad-Expansion et le Déclin de l'Islamisme*, Paris: Gallimard, 2000, were defaulted by 9/11. For a contrast to Kepel see my introduction to the updated edition of my book *The Challenge of Fundamentalism*, op. cit.
46 On the notion of de-Westernization see Tibi, "Culture and Knowledge," op. cit.; on Westernization see T. van der Laue, *The World Revolution of Westernization*, New York: Oxford University Press, 1987. On globalization and culture see R. Robertson, *Globalization: Social Theory and Global Culture*, London: Sage, 1992, reprinted four times, new printing 1998. Robertson rightly criticizes those who overlook "the relative autonomy of culture."
47 R. Herzog *et al.*, *Preventing the Clash of Civilizations*, New York: St. Martin's Press, 1999. This book includes B. Tibi, "International Morality and Cross-cultural Bridging," pp. 107–126.
48 The traditional Shari'a includes numerous violations of human rights. The unacceptable discrimination of women and non-Muslims in the Shari'a acknowledged in the

36   B. Tibi

work of the Muslim reformist A. A. An-Na'im, *Toward an Islamic Reformation,* Syracuse: Syracuse University Press, 1990, ch. 7. On Islamic Shari'a, see B. Tibi, "Islamic Law/Shari'a, Human Rights, Universal Morality and International Relations," *Human Rights Quarterly,* 1994, vol. 16, no. 2, pp. 277–299.

49 See B. Buzan, *People, States and Fear. An Agenda for International Security Studies in the Post-Cold War Era,* Boulder, CO: Lynne Rienner, 1991.

50 On the traditional origins of the concept of *jihad* and on its current relevance see J. Kelsay, *Islam and War,* Louisville, KY: John Knox Press, 1993, ch. 5; and furthermore Kelsay's new book, *Arguing for Just War,* Cambridge, MA: Harvard University Press, 2007. See also J. T. Johanson, *The Holy War Idea in Western and Islamic Tradition,* University Park, PA: Pennsylvania State University Press, 1997.

51 See Sir Hamilton A.R. Gibb, *Studies on the Civilization of Islam,* Princeton, NJ: Princeton University Press, 1962, reprinted 1982.

52 On the movements conducting the addressed Sunni-Shi'a conflict carried out by Shi'a movements in Iraq after Saddam's fall see F. A. Jabar, *The Shi'ite Movements in Iraq,* London: Saqi, 2003. Earlier, A. Cockburn and P. Cockburn, *Out of the Ashes. The Resurgence of Saddam Hussein,* New York: HarperCollins, 1999, analyzed the Saddam era as Sunni rule.

53 Mandeville, op. cit., rightly coined the term *Reimagining the Umma',* and see Tibi, *Political Islam, World Politics, and Europe,* op. cit.

54 Kelsay, *Islam and War,* op. cit., p. 117.

55 See B. Tibi, *Der Krieg der Zivilisationen,* Hamburg: Hoffmann & Campe, 1995. An expanded edition, which includes a new chapter on Huntington's book *Clash of Civilizations,* published a year later (1996), was printed in 1998 and reprinted three times hereafter.

56 L. Martin (ed.), *New Frontiers in Middle Eastern Security,* New York: St. Martin's Press, 1999, Introduction.

57 Tibi, "Vom Debakel zur Tragödie. Die Hizballah frohlockt, der Iran ist gestärkt. Der Libanon-Krieg," *Der Tagessergel* (Berlin), 27 August 2007, p. 8.

58 Wolffsohn, op. cit.

59 See B. Nezar al-Sayyad and M. Castells (eds), *Muslim Europe or Euro-Islam?* Lanham, MD: Lexington Books, 2002; this volume includes B. Tibi, "Muslim Migrants in Europe: Between Euro-Islam and Ghettoization," pp. 31–52, and for a more recent conceptualization of Europeanizing Islam see my chapter in Katzenstein and Byrnes, op. cit.

60 B. Tibi, "Der importierte Haß. Der Antisemitismus ist in der arabischen Welt verbreitet," *Die Zeit,* 6 February 2002, p. 9. On Islamist anti-Semitism see also my chapter in J. Schoeps and K. Faber (eds), *Neu-alter Judenhass. Antisemitismus, arabisch-israelischer Konflikt und europäische Politik,* Berlin: Brandenburg Verlag, 2006, pp. 179–202. On this subject Professor W. Benz of the Humboldt University, Berlin, organized an international conference in December 2005 and published an edited volume on Islamist Anti-Semitism in 2007 (see herein the chapter by B. Tibi).

61 Ibid.

62 "Tolerating the Intolerable," *Newsweek,* 5 November 2001, p. 46.

63 K. Popper, *The Open Society and its Enemies,* London: Routledge & Kegan Paul, 1945; and my article "The Open Society and its Enemies Within," *Wall Street Journal Europe,* 17 March 2004, p. 10A.

64 B. Tibi, *The Totalatarianism of Jihadist Islamism,* op. cit.

65 See "The Fundamentalist Abuse of the Islam-Diaspora: Western Europe a Safe Haven," in B. Tibi, *Die fundamentalistische Herausforderung,* Munich: C.H. Beck, fully rewritten 4th edn, 2003, pp. 184–214.

66 S. Erlanger, "Extremists Found Safe Haven in Germany," *International Herald Tribune,* 6–7 October 2001, p. 3.

67 "Tolerating the Intolerable," op. cit.

68 Revel, op. cit.

69 On Euro-Islam see the references in note 59 above. The concept of Euro-Islam was first presented in Paris (1992) and later published there as B. Tibi, "Les conditions d'Euro-Islam," in R. Bistolfi and F. Zabbal (eds), *Islam d'Europe. Intégration ou insertion communitaire*, Paris: Editions de l'Aube, 1995, pp. 230–234. The Grand Mosque of Paris run by imam Dalil Boubakeur is one example of a successful Euro-Islamic institution backed by the secular French republic. See the report "Muslim and French and Proud to be Both" by Katrin Bennhold in *International Herald Tribune*, 16 March 2006, p. 2. In contrast, it is perplexing to see in post-Nazi Germany a state and society tolerating the totalitarian Islamists in the name of tolerance, thus drawing the wrong lessons from the shameful past (see the contestation by the Jewish historian Wolffsohn, op. cit.).

70 B. Tibi, "Between Communitarism and Euro-Islam. Europe, Multicultural Identities and the Challenge of Migration," in J. Docker and G. Fischer (eds), *Adventures of Identity. European Multicultural Experiences and Perspectives*, Tübingen: Stauffenberg, 2001, pp. 45–60.

71 Interview with B. Tibi published in *Focus*, 18 July 2005, no. 29, pp. 150–151.

72 B. Tibi, "The Quest of Islamic Migrants and of Turkey to Become European," *Turkish Policy Quarterly*, spring 2004, vol. 3, no. 1, pp. 13–28. See also B. Tibi, "A Migration Story: From Muslim Immigrants to European 'Citizens of the Heart?,'" *The Fletcher Forum for World Affairs*, 2007, vol. 31, no. 1, pp. 147–168.

73 On Islam and modernity see W. M. Watt, *Islamic Fundamentalism and Modernity*, London: Routledge, 1988; R. Fazlur, *Islam and Modernity. Transformation of Intellectual Tradition*, Chicago, IL: Chicago University Press, 1982; and B. Tibi, "Democracy and Democratization in Islam. The Quest of Islamic Enlightenment," in M. Schmiegelow (ed.), *Democracy in Asia*, New York: St. Martin's Press, 1997, pp. 127–146. On Islam and democratic peace, see Tibi, "From Islamist *Jihadism* to Democratic Peace? Islam at the Crossroads in Post-bipolar International Politics," Ankara Paper 16, London: Taylor & Francis, 2005.

74 See R. Chasdi, *Tapestry of Terrorism. A Portrait of Middle Eastern Terrorism 1994–1999*, Lanham, MD: Lexington Books, 2002; and P. Berman, *Terror and Liberalism*, New York: Norton, 2003.

75 See the work done at the EU Think Tank CEPS and edited by M. Emerson, *Democratization in the European Neighborhood*, Brussels: Center for European Policy Studies, 2005, esp. the chapter by B. Tibi, "Islam, Freedom and Democracy," pp. 93–117.

76 On this horror-Islam see Jean-Charles Brisard, *Zarqawi. The New Face of al-Qaeda*, New York: Other Press, 2005. There are better alternatives to it that can be promoted by Europe and the West, but (except some positive cases such as France's enlightened Imam Boubakeur) this does not happen. Moreover, political Islam has established itself in most EU states through the instrumental use of tolerance and civil rights.

77 The Culture Matters Project (CMP) was a research project directed by Professor Laurence Harrison at The Fletcher School for International Diplomacy, Tufts University in the years 2002 to 2004. The papers from the project are published in two volumes to which this author has contributed as a member of the project. See B. Tibi, "Cultural Change in Islamic Civilization," in L. Harrison and J. Kagan (eds), *Developing Cultures*, Vol. I, New York: Routledge, 2006, pp. 245–260; and B. Tibi, "Egypt as a Model of Development in the World of Islam," in L. Harrison and P. Berger (eds), *Developing Cultures*, Vol. II, New York: Routledge, 2006, pp. 163–180.

2 Islam from flexibility to ferocity

Ze'ev Maghen

Islam today in the minds of most Westerners – and not a few Easterners as well – is associated with fury, fierceness, fanaticism and intransigence. It is perceived to be a harsh and uncompromising faith, as deaf to the cries of the innocents slaughtered in its name as it is to the pleas for reform emanating from within its own walls. And although such a picture of glowering intractability is perhaps an unfair caricature of Islam as a whole, *fundamentalist* Islam – the brand of Islam that participates most actively in the "clash of civilizations" and consequently garners the greatest amount of coverage – may justifiably be portrayed as a stern, hidebound and merciless system, locked on an immutable course of conflict with any and all who do not accept its principles (indeed, its sovereignty). "Islam is not the bazaar, that it should be the object of negotiations and bargaining," Iran's Ayatollah Nateq-e-Nuri famously announced.[1] "Flexibility involves a compromise between two opposing positions," explained the late Ayatollah Beheshti, "but Islam's doctrine of monism (*tawḥīd*) can tolerate only *one* position."[2] Even Salman Rushdie's "Mahound" asserts that his religion is "an idea that does not bend."[3]

Matters were not always thus. Throughout most periods of Islam's 1400-year history and across the length and breadth of "the Abode of Islam," the Shariʿa (Islamic law) was in fact rarely enforced, such that the attempt on the part of today's Islamists to create full-blown Shariʿatic theocracies represents a major innovation. But this significant historical phenomenon is not our immediate concern today: our burden is rather to demonstrate that not only in practice, but also in accordance with the theoretical religious *ideal*, Islam was never – until very recently – a faith of unbending fanaticism.

Islamic tradition considers the Prophet Muhammad to be more than just the mouthpiece of Qurʾānic revelation; this aspect of his career – his duty to convey celestial messages to his flock – is not particularly impressive or interesting, and we have in fact only one or two descriptions of Muhammad receiving a divine communication in the entire classical literature. His most important role, a role which created almost single-handedly the vast corpus of Islamic law and lore, is as *uswa ḥasana*, the "Excellent Exemplar." The behavior of Muhammad, in other words, is supposed to be the model for all Muslims for all time, both as individuals and as a collective. If he was a diehard, unmovable zealot, so should today's Muslims be; if he was a soft, pliable, humane and merciful man, then they should be as merciful as he was. If he stuck to the letter of the law in all cases, not budging or deviating an inch from the divine rulebook, then today's *'ulama'* (Muslim clerics) should do likewise. If, however, he bent the rules with the best of them, always locating or manufacturing a loophole, then that should be the ideal to follow. So who was he? How did Muhammad behave in these matters?

The answer will come as a surprise to many, for it is decidedly in the direction of leniency. Few if any figures in history have been credited with the level of compassion and flexibility that Islamic literature ascribes to Allah's Apostle. Indeed, Muhammad easily deserves the title of Most Moderate Muslim of all time. His willingness to accommodate, readiness to retract, proverbial pliability and indomitable soft spot are a central motif of Islamic lore. He shortened congregational services for the sake of a mother with a difficult child (and canceled them without hesitation when it was too hot, cold or rainy), instructed a young man who found it hard to rise early to "pray whenever you get up," turned a blind eye to a warrior who wolfed down some common booty, regularly broke the fast of Ramadan before sunset (and urged others to do so as well), and asked for, and received, hundreds of divine "revisions" of previously enacted precepts that had in one way or another inconvenienced his flock. He threatened to thrash a maid-servant – who returned late from an errand – with a toothpick. He forgave the high treason of one of his followers – and the long-standing opposition of his fiercest enemy – on the eve of the invasion of Mecca (he compared his treatment towards the city to Joseph absolving his brethren). He granted amnesty to Waḥshī, the slave contracted by his enemy Abū Sufyān's wife Hind to assassinate his uncle Ḥamza, and eventually excused his erstwhile amanuensis 'Abd Allāh b. Abi Sarḥ, who had defected from Islam and called him an imposter. He even pardoned the Qurashite tribesman who had attacked his daughter and caused her to miscarry.[4]

Elaborating once on the many activities forbidden in Mecca's Sacred Precinct, Muhammad reached the subject of flora: "[N]either shall there be any gathering of shrubs or grasses in the *harem*," he proclaimed, "for such was forbidden by God himself on the day He created heaven and earth, and it will *remain* thus forbidden *forever*, from now until Resurrection Day!" Ibn 'Abbās interrupted, saying: "O Messenger of God – except for the Idhkhir bush, yes? For it is used by the people to ornament their persons and their houses?" "Except for the Idhkhir bush," replied Muhammad, without losing a beat.[5] A woman came to the Prophet complaining that she wished to allow a male friend to visit her, but this was prohibited by Islam because he was not a *mahram*, a close relative of hers. The Prophet advised her to turn the man into a "milk relative" by nursing him from her breast.[6] A Qur'ānic revelation came down demanding a fee for interviews with Muhammad; no one felt like paying the money except for his cousin 'Ali, so another revelation promptly arrived abolishing this requirement.[7]

This last anecdote brings us to the fact that in all his clemency, forbearance and pliability Muḥammad was merely engaging in *imitatio Dei*. "Allāh would not place a burden upon you," the Qurʾān regularly reassures the believers.[8] "Allah desires ease for you; He does not desire hardship for you."[9] "Allah desires to decrease your difficulties, for man was created weak."[10] Confronted with manifestations of human frailty, the God of Islamic tradition almost invariably "goes soft." After violating the law against sexual relations after sleep on Ramadan evenings, ʿUmar b. al-Khaṭṭāb, the number two man of Islam, made his way over to the Prophet's house, where he wept and confessed his misdeed. He begged forgiveness and went so far as to plead: "Might you find me some sort of indulgence, O Messenger of God (*hal tajidu lī min rukhṣa yā rasūl Allāh*)?" A new revelation, abolishing the onerous restriction, descended shortly thereafter: "From now on," this latest installment read, "have intercourse with your spouses and eat and drink until the white thread becomes distinct from the black thread at dawn."[11]

The seminal texts of Islam portray the Deity as a veritable "pushover." When al-Ḥārith b. Suwayd al-Anṣārī apostatized and fled to Byzantium, Allah delivered the following verses in a furious rage:

> How shall God guide those who lapse into unbelief after embracing the Faith, and after acknowledging the Apostle and receiving veritable truths? God does not guide the evil-doers! Their reward shall be the curse of God, of the angels and of all men; under it they will abide *forever*. Their punishment shall not be lightened, neither shall they under any circumstances be granted a reprieve.[12]

All possibility of pardon having been expressly denied, one would have expected our heretic to remain where he was. Instead, thereafter al-Ḥārith wrote to his folk, requesting them to:

> "Send to the Messenger of God and ask: Is there any repentance for me? (*hal lī tawba?*)." Immediately, we read, "Allah abrogated those verses, and revealed their counteractive conclusion: '...except for those who repent and mend their ways, for God is forgiving and merciful.'"[13]

The tone that Allah Himself had set in His capacity as archetypal and eminently malleable Mufti On High was subsequently taken up not just by his Apostle but by the ensuing generations of Muslim jurists and theologians, who worked hard to create a religio-legal system that they deliberately filled with loopholes, escape clauses and an overall elasticity. The Shariʿa was constructed by luminaries who had the image of their lenient Prophet always before their eyes, and this code was therefore designed from the start with a built-in ability to look the other way, shrug off misdemeanors and even felonies, and in general make life easy. Caliphs were supposed to enforce an empire-wide ban on wine; instead, many of them were so drunk themselves most of the time that they couldn't even sit on a chair, and yet the *fuqaha* ruled that they be forgiven;[14] people were supposed to fast during Ramadan, but this was hard during the long summer days, so the Shariʿa declared that even if just the tip of one's little finger hurt, one could forgo the fast;[15] Muslim armies were supposed to give Hindu polytheists the choice between Islam or death, but for the most part they didn't. For thirteen centuries, Muslims everywhere lived "Islam lite."

What happened to change all that? What turned a religion of flexibility and forgiveness into a religion of fierceness and ferocity? How did the faith founded by the man who tradition depicts as constantly kissing his children and rolling around on the floor playing camel with his grandchildren turn into a faith that sends children into minefields *en masse* or straps explosives to their bodies so they can die killing the offspring of others?

There are a great many answers we could advance to this question, perhaps the most important of which involves the major contribution of movements like Wahhabism, but I would like to suggest an alternative answer that does what it has been the fashion to do for a few decades now: blame the West. I would like to propose, more specifically, that the Middle Eastern encounter with Europe in the modern period has had one truly unexpected result. The Western tradition of scientific rationalism, hailing from Greek times and having revived considerably and made immense strides since the Renaissance, sought with all its considerable might to describe the world in logical terms, which is another way of saying in mathematical terms. By the end of the nineteenth century powerful attempts were being made to apply scientific principles to all walks of life. Fields like psychology, anthropology, sociology and "political science" strove to reduce our motivations and predilections to measurable formulae, and Marxism and Social Darwinism weighed in with lock-step, Hegelian theories of historical development. Things were falling into place, starting to make sense. No more blurry lines and rounded edges, but sharp lines and 90-degree angles. Humanity and its institutions are ultimately and ideally a machine – so we were told – and machines require precision.

In my reading of modern fundamentalist tracts and treatises, I have come across much evidence – most of it, albeit, in between the lines – that this new Western way of looking at things began to penetrate the consciousness of the educated classes in Middle Eastern countries by the end of the first half of the twentieth century. The Islamists were no exception. This is when a fascinating and monstrous hybrid began to grow. All of a sudden, the blurry lines and rounded edges that had forever characterized Islamic law and life were unacceptable. Mathematics was becoming the new global standard, and there is nothing flexible about math. How, one began to hear, can God's Perfect Law be subject to compromise? Where is the room to maneuver, one began to read, when the statutes are enshrined clearly, black on white for all to see? Shall we make a mockery of religion, asked the new men? Islam, they frowned, is no laughing matter! Precision, exactness, zeros and ones: a person either adheres to the law or he does not; he is either a saint or a sinner; there is no space in between.

Not for nothing do the Azharites regularly accuse the Islamists (at the same time as they become ever more "Islamist" themselves) of the ancient heresy of Kharejism: Taqī al-Dīn al-Nabhānī, founder of the conservative-revivalist Ḥizb al-Taḥrīr, writes that "either one punctiliously observes all the laws and sincerely believes in all the tenets of Islam, or he is an apostate whose blood not only may, but must, be shed."[16] The fiery Egyptian preacher 'Abd al-Ḥamid Kishk himself excoriates the *'ulama'* of al-Azhar for making an exception to the ban on alcohol in the case of medicines: he attacks them for their employment of traditional juristic methods like *istiḥsān* (choosing the best/easiest path) and *istiṣlāḥ* (taking public interest into account) and for their justification of mitigating circumstances, quotes the Qur'ānic verse forbidding alcohol consumption and asks, "Where does it say anything about mitigating circumstances?"[17] Life retreats before the inexorable juggernaut of the law. Compassion has no place, pity and mercy disappear. In this way, I would argue, did the fundamentalists – reacting not *negatively* but *positively* to this particular aspect of Western ideology – eliminate the flesh-and-blood finesse that had made Islam what it was and set it apart since its inception. In the place of that finesse and elasticity they have injected a strictness and a cruelty into the Muslim religion that it never knew before. What is so ironic about this, of course, is that true "fundamentalism" – the return to the roots and foundations of the Islamic religion as practiced in the time of the Prophet Muhammad and his immediate successors – is in fact bound up with nothing so much as a loosening up. Religious corner-cutting, legal laxity and a "laid-back" outlook on life were what pristine Islam was all about. May its days soon be renewed as of old.

Notes

1 Shahrokh-e-Forrokhzad, "Andishe-ya-Digar ya Andishe-ya Kohne: Nateq-e-Nuri dar Moqabel-e Professor Sorush," *Kayhan-e-Landan*, 2 July 1998.

2 Ebrahim-e-Emami, "Payam-e-Shahid-e-Beheshti," *Hamshahri*, 16 September 1993.

3 Salman Rushdie, *The Satanic Verses*, London: Viking Press, 1988, p. 268.

4 These examples are taken from A. Guillaume, *The Life of Muhammad: A Translation of Ibn Isḥaq's "Sirat Rasul Allah,"* Oxford: Oxford University Press, 1955.

5 Abū 'Abd Allāh Muḥammad b. Aḥmad al-Anṣārī al-Qurṭubī, *Al-Jāmi' li-Aḥkām al-Qur'ān*, Cairo: Al-Maktaba al-Tawfiqiya, 4: 195.

6 Aḥmad b. Ḥanbal, *Musnad, Bāqī Musnad al-Anṣār, Ḥadīth al-Sayyida 'Ā'isha*, 22979. See also Muslim, *Kitāb al-Riḍā', Bāb Riḍā'at al-Kabīr, passim.*

7 Tor Andrae, *Mohammed: The Man and His Faith*, trans. Theophil Menzel, London: George Allen & Unwin, 1936, p. 83.

8 Qur'ān, 5: 6.

9 Qur'ān, 2: 185.

10 Qur'ān, 4: 28.

11 Muhammad b. Jarīr al-Ṭabarī, *Jāmi' al-Bayān 'an Ta'wīl Āy al-Qur'ān*, Beirut: Dār al-Fikr, 1995, 2: 225.

12 Qur'ān, 3: 86–8.

13 Al-Tabarī, 3: 460–2; Qur'ān, 3: 89.

14 Thus the renowned tenth-century Muslim man of *belles lettres* al-Jāḥiẓ could claim that the reason the 'Abbāsid rulers screened themselves from their court was not to protect the courtiers from the blinding brilliance of their holy luminescence, but rather to conceal the fact that the caliphs were constantly inebriated.

15 Al-Tabarī, 2: 204.
16 Taqī al-Dīn al-Nabhānī, *al-Shakhsiyya al-Islāmiyya*, Beirut: Dār al-Umma, 1994, 2: 193. Kharejites were the most uncompromising of medieval Muslim sects.
17 'Abd al-Ḥāmid Kishk, *al-Nūr wa'l-Dastūr*, cassette recording of mosque sermon, *c*.1989.

3 An economic perspective on radical Islam

Arye L. Hillman

Introduction

The economic effects of radical Islam have been extensively studied through the consequences of terror inflicted on others. A substantial amount of literature on the topic includes the edited volume by Tilman Brück and Bengt-Arne Wickström.[1] In particular, Andrew Chen and Thomas Siems,[2] and Rafi Eldor and Rafi Melnik,[3] have studied how Islamic terror has affected capital markets. In another branch of investigation, James Yetman[4] and Franck *et al.*[5] have addressed the problems and moral dilemmas of defense against terror when terrorists in a population cannot be identified with certainty. Alan Kruger and Jitka Maleckova[6] have investigated the relationship between income and perpetration of terror (and conclude that low income is not a catalyst for terror). Tyler Cowen[7] and Steven Plaut[8] have proposed perspectives on the appropriate response to terror. Also Claude Berrebi and Esteban Klor[9] have studied how terror inflicted on a population affects election outcomes.

The focus of this chapter concerns a quite separate question, the economic consequences of radical Islam for *own* populations. Although the focus will be on own populations, the external orientation and objectives of radical Islam introduce consequences for populations in other societies.

Effects of *radical* Islam are superimposed on economic outcomes under *moderate* Islam. Addressing the economic consequences of radical Islam will oblige a consideration of outcomes under moderate Islam.

There is broad agreement that economic outcomes reflect attributes of societal institutions.[10] The institutions of the rule of law are a prerequisite for a civil society. Metin Coçgel *et al.*,[11] in a study that is part of a wider program of research on the economic history of the Ottoman Empire, describe how Ottoman rulers were restrained by the rule of law, although the legal system was often subjugated to the wishes of the ruler, who also controlled public finance. As in the West, hereditary rule provided political stability under Islam. Indeed, historically, Islam dominated the West in intellectual and scientific pursuits. Over time, societies under Islam underwent economic decline and were in due course overtaken by the West in economic achievement.

The historical question as to why Islam declined has been extensively studied, in particular by Timur Kuran,[12] whose works will be discussed below. The historically based explanations for the economic decline of Islamic societies describe influences through Islamic legal principles and other aspects of traditional Islamic society, and provide links to contemporary outcomes through persistence of institutions. Yet relatively little attention has been directed at understanding the contemporary relationship between Islam and economic development. By comparison, numerous studies have, for example, sought explanations for failures of economic development in sub-Saharan Africa.[13] As observed by Martin Paldam[14] and others, the most prominent development successes in recent decades have been in East Asia. The East Asian experiences, and more recently economic growth in China and India, motivate the question as to why other contemporary societies have not been able to emulate their development successes. These East Asian successes have, moreover, taken place without natural resource wealth.

Data presented below indicate that the presence of natural resources, or more particularly oil wealth, in Arab and other Islamic societies can provide high incomes but oil wealth has not resulted in Western standards of economic growth. Where oil is not present incomes are low, as has been economic growth. Whether or not natural resource wealth is present, human development indicators in Islamic societies show lower standards of health and education than are predicted by income levels.

The economic and human development outcomes in Islamic societies provide the base from which to evaluate the consequences of radical Islam. Radical Islam introduces a conjunction between supreme values and rent-seeking behavior that has not been recognized or has not been given prior emphasis when explanations have been sought for economic outcomes. By ranking objectives hierarchically, supreme values disallow trade-offs and distractions that would compromise the achievement of unattained priority goals. The supreme values that guide radical Islam subordinate economic achievement to religiously ordained geopolitical goals.

A priority objective, as in the original Arab conquests, is increasing the domain of Islam. Lands previously conquered and subsequently lost to Islam are required to be reconquered – and, in the end, all lands and people are required to submit to Islam. In contemporary times, not all Islamic rulers and states actively abide by the supreme values. To do so would require an ongoing active state of war against non-Islamic societies. Radical Islam does, however, actively seek the priority supreme-value objectives.[15]

In the quests to achieve the supreme-value objectives, economic progress is forgone. Economic progress is also reversed where it is achieved. Two contemporary natural experiments, described below, exemplify the decisions required by the supreme values to forgo and to reverse economic progress.

In the forgoing and reversal of economic progress, radical Islam imposes economic self-deprivation on own populations. Economic analysis categorizes self-imposed economic deprivation aimed at achieving distributional objectives as rent-seeking. In the usual representations, rent-seeking occurs in the course of the internal distributive quests that take place within a society. Rent-seeking in the case of radical Islam is *externally* directed at changing institutions and belief systems of other societies. The social loss due to rent-seeking is expressed in internal economic deprivation. The rent or benefit is sought through attainment of the priority supreme-value geopolitical objectives.[16]

Willingness to give one's life in defense of one's people and country has been considered meritorious in numerous societies. For example, the children's verse of the *La Marseillaise* is an exhortation to children to be prepared to die for France.[17] Under post-heroic Western values, people expose themselves to the likelihood of harm or death in times of war and conflict. However, death is not actively sought – neither for oneself nor for one's own fellow population or for other non-combatant civilian populations. Radical Islam randomly takes lives and maims people in populations that have not submitted to Islam or that adhere to another variant of Islam. The lives of own adherents are also required to be willingly forgone. Departure from this world as a *shahid* or martyr has ultimate merit. Laurent Murawiec[18] documents how, in ceremonies that honor the impending meritorious behavior, martyrs participate in the celebrations of their own deaths and so "die before they die." Debasement of the worth of one's own life is expressed in the proclamation that "we love death more than you love life"– a preference that derives from rewards promised and believed to be delivered after "death." The forgoing of one's own life extends self-deprivation beyond the quality of life to the end of one's own life. The logical consistency in the value and belief system is that the immediacy of benefits in the afterlife is enhanced by self-deprivation in this life.[19]

There are semantic issues and issues of categorization to be addressed before we proceed further. The term "Islamic" can be used to refer to traditional Arab society. Yet Islam and also radical Islam are not exclusively Arab. Nor correspondingly has Islamic terror emanated exclusively from Arab societies. The Arab conquests and the spread of Islam introduced elements of Islamic values and institutions to different degrees into the non-Arab Muslim world. In some cases institutions of the state are secular, as in contemporary Turkey, as well as in Tunisia and in the Turkic societies of Central Asia.[20] However, secular institutions of the state are consistent with populations for whom more traditional Islamic values guide personal and family behavior. Populations are also not homogeneous. Lebanon has been a special case of a multicultural secular state where radical Islam has become embedded with its own separate institutions. Ideally, in considering radical Islam, we would want data for the radical Islamic state-within-a-state in Lebanon. The fragmentation of society is not reflected in the data for Lebanon.

After presentation of the data, we shall turn to explanations of the outcomes. A brief general overview will be provided of the role of institutions in economic growth and of competing explanations of resources and geography. We shall then consider the historically-based explanations for economic outcomes under Islam. Here we shall draw on the writings of Timur Kuran. We shall then proceed to the perspective founded in the conjunction of supreme values and rent-seeking. Issues of cultural relativism, which are inevitable in a study such as this, are addressed. The conclusion notes the challenges radical Islam poses for aid donors and development agencies seeking to increase income and economic growth, and the security challenges when supreme values disallow conciliation and compromise.

Comparative data

Empirical studies reveal a consistent pattern of outcomes associating Muslim societies with low income and low economic growth. Rachel McCleary and Robert Barro[21] review studies of the relationship between religion and economic outcomes and find that, of all belief systems, only the Muslim share of the population is significant in regressions explaining economic growth, and the coefficient is negative.[22] Rather than summarizing once more the empirical evidence from regression analysis, we can look more directly at outcomes.

Per capita income comparisons

The World Bank provides comparative data on per capita incomes based on exchange rate conversion and correction for purchasing–power parity. The more indicative statistics are the latter. Tables 3.1 and 3.2 show both measures.

Table 3.1 shows 2004 per capita income for a sample of countries, together with country rankings. The US, UK and Australia are high-income countries, Mexico is medium-income, and China is low-income by the exchange rate measure but medium-income by the purchasing–power parity measure. Sub-Saharan Cameroon, Kenya and Sierra Leone represent low-income countries.

Table 3.1 Reference countries

	2004 per capita income in US dollars	*Rank*	*2004 per capita income purchasing– power parity*	*Rank*
US	41,440	5	39,820	3
UK	33,630	13	31,340	14
Australia	32,220	21	30,610	22
Mexico	6,790	70	9,640	80
China	1,500	129	5,890	108
Cameroon	1,010	147	2.150	163
Kenya	480	171	1,130	187
Sierra Leone	220	199	780	202

Source: http://sitesources.worldbank.org/DATASTATISTICS/Resources/GNIPC.pdf.

Note
The per capita income data that follow are for the years 2003 and 2004. The same or similar outcomes are present in the data in any other year in recent years. There is a consistent pattern beyond the cross-section for the year chosen.

Table 3.2 shows per capita income for Arab states with oil. Also included is non-Arab but radical Islamic Iran. The United Arab Emirates and Kuwait have high incomes. The per capita income of oil-rich Saudi Arabia is some half of that of the Gulf States. The other states have lower incomes but incomes by purchasing–power parity that place them in the middle-income range (e.g. Mexico and China in Table 3.1).

Table 3.3 compares three groups of countries that do not have natural

Table 3.2 Arab oil states

	2004 per capita income in US dollars	Rank	2004 per capita income purchasing–power parity	Rank
UAE	23,770	31	24,090	42
Kuwait	22,470	33	21,610	43
Saudi Arabia	10,140	55	13,810	61
Libya	4,400	81	n/a	n/a
Iran Islamic Rep*	2,320	109	7,530	92
Algeria	2,270	113	6,329	105

Note
* Non-Arab.

Table 3.3 Arab non-oil, non-Muslim Mediterranean countries, secular Muslim

	2004 per capita income in US dollars	Rank	2004 per capita income purchasing–power parity	Rank
Arab non-oil				
Jordan	2,190	117	4,770	128
Morocco	1,570	128	4,250	131
Egypt	1,250	133	4,200	134
Syria	1,230	134	3,500	139
West Bank and Gaza	1,120	135	n/a	n/a
Yemen	550	167	810	197
Non-Muslim Mediterranean				
Italy	26,280	28	28,020	28
Spain	21,530	34	24,750	33
Israel	17,360	39	23,770	37
Greece	16,730	42	22,230	41
Secular Muslim/significant non-Muslim populations				
Turkey	3,750	89	7,720	90
Tunisia	2,650	102	7,430	94
Lebanon	6,010	73	5,550	117

resource wealth.[23] Arab states have per capita incomes substantially below neighboring non-Muslim Mediterranean countries.[24] The purchasing–power parity adjusted incomes of the non-Muslim Mediterranean countries approximate those of the high-income oil-rich Arab states. Middle-income Lebanon has a significant non-Muslim population but also harbors radical Islam.[25] Tunisia is quite secular. The constitution of Turkey detaches the institutions of the state from Islam.

Table 3.4 shows comparisons in South Asia. Primarily Muslim Malaysia and Muslim Indonesia have considerably lower incomes than neighboring non-Muslim Singapore. The per capita income of Malaysia, which has a large Chinese non-Muslim minority, is substantially higher than that of Indonesia, which has natural resource wealth and where non-Islamic minorities are smaller. India and its Muslim neighbors Pakistan and Bangladesh are among the poorest countries in the world. Using the purchasing–power parity measures, Indian per capita income is 44 percent higher than that of Pakistan and 58 percent higher than that of Bangladesh.[26]

Comparisons of economic growth

Economic theory predicts "convergence" in economic growth of incomes across countries. Populations in high-income countries that are on the frontiers of knowledge are limited to benefits from the creation and application of *new* knowledge. Populations in countries not on the frontiers of knowledge have lower incomes but should be able to benefit from higher growth through application of knowledge that already exists.[27]

In Figure 3.1, the vertical axis shows the natural logarithm of gross domestic product (GDP) per capita at purchasing–power parity over the period 1950 to 2005. The horizontal axis shows time. Data is presented for the country average of four groups of countries: a group of 26 Western European countries, a world average based on 133 countries, and respective oil and non-oil Arab states.[28] The slope of the line for a country group indicates growth or decline in the *value* of

Table 3.4 South Asia

Singapore and neighbors	2004 per capita income in US dollars	Rank	2004 per capita purchasing–power parity	Rank
Malaysia	4,520	79	9,720	78
Indonesia (oil)	1,140	137	3,480	140
Singapore	24,760	29	27,370	29
Subcontinent				
Pakistan	600	161	2,170	157
Bangladesh	440	174	1,970	164
India	620	159	3,120	144

per capita output. *Value* is emphasized, because output may not change but per capita GDP responds to changes in prices. The price of oil is particularly significant for the GDP per capita of Arab oil countries. Where the slope in Figure 3.1 is positive, (the natural logarithm of) GDP per capita has increased and so growth has been positive. Where the slope is negative, GDP per capita has declined, indicating negative growth or contraction. The change in the slope of the line indicates the growth rate.[29]

Consistent with the previous per capita income data, the Western countries in Figure 3.1 are shown to have had the highest levels of per capita output over time, followed by the Arab oil countries. Per capita output of non-oil Arab states has approximated the world average. All country groups experienced growth over time, with the exception of the Arab oil states between the late 1970s and 1995. Growth for the world at large has been below the Western European average, with small divergence; hence the world at large did not use the technology and knowledge gap in order to catch up with Western European incomes. As with levels of output per capita, the pattern of economic growth of non-oil

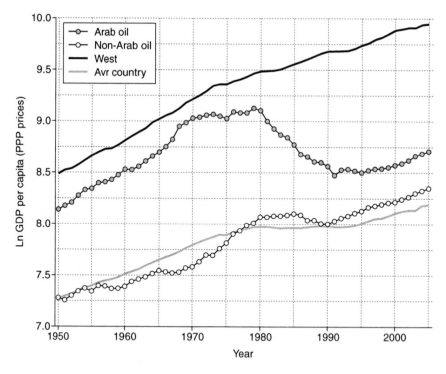

Figure 3.1 Growth and convergence.

Note
All averages are based on the Maddison dataset (Angus Maddison, 2003), updated to 2005 using the World Bank WDI data. All averages are unweighted. The average country covers 133 countries with consistent data. Ln refers to natural logarithm.

Arab states closely follows the pattern for the world at large. Growth of Arab oil states was above the world average but slightly below the Western European average up until to the late 1970s. Growth was therefore positive but convergence to Western European income levels was not taking place. In the late 1970s growth in the Arab oil states became negative, indicating divergence. In 1995 positive growth resumed.

Human development indicators

Table 3.5 shows data on mortality under age 5, life expectancy at birth, secondary school enrolment, the ratio of boys to girls in primary and secondary schooling, and the literacy rate for selected countries. The UN Human Development Index averages components of these and other indicators. Non-oil Muslim countries tend to have greater infant mortality than do Western countries and slightly lower life expectancy. Secondary school enrolment also tends to be lower. Literacy rates are high, and with the exceptions of Egypt and Syria, girls tend to attend school at the same rates as boys. Whether an Arab country has oil was shown to affect per capita income significantly (see Tables 3.2 and 3.3). Oil wealth however is not of the same significance in improving outcomes measured by the Human Development Index.

Table 3.6 presents summary data for groups of countries on: GDP per capita (purchasing–power parity), the Human Development Index, and components of development measured by life expectancy at birth, the adult literacy rate and gross school enrolment. Rankings of GDP per capita and the Human Development Index for all country groups would be perfectly correlated were it not for the low values of the Human Development Index for the Arab states. The same divergence from perfect correlation with ranking by income is shown in life expectancy at birth, the adult literacy rate and school enrolment.

Summary of the data

Oil wealth is a necessary condition for Arab states to have high per capita incomes. Under similar geographical conditions, Arab or Muslim states without oil wealth have substantially lower per capita incomes than neighboring non-Islamic states that also lack oil or other natural resource wealth. More secular Muslim countries without oil wealth have higher incomes than more traditional non-oil Arab states. Convergence of growth rates did not occur in either the oil or non-oil Arab states, with the Arab oil states faring less well overall with regard to growth than the non-oil states. Arab and Muslim states have also had lower indicators of human development than predicted by the ranking of country groups by per capita income. Oil wealth has had asymmetric effects on incomes and human development indicators such as life expectancy, the adult literacy rate and school enrolment. Incomes are significantly increased by oil wealth in Arab societies. Similar gains are not expressed in the values of human development indicators.[30]

Table 3.5 Selected development indicators, selected countries

2004	Mortality rate under age 5	Life expectancy	School enrolment secondary	Ratio girls to boys in schooling	Literacy rate	Human Development Index 2003	
						Value	Rank
High income							
Australia	5.5	79.9	153.8*	98.5*	99.0	0.955	3
US	7.6	77.4	94.5*	100.0	99.0	0.944	10
France	4.6	80.2	110.0*	100.2*	99.0	0.938	16
Greece	4.9	78.9	95.6	100.9	97.5	0.912	24
Israel	5.9	79.4	92.8*	99.0*	97.1	0.915	23
Singapore	3.3	79.3	n/a	n/a	92.5	0.907	25
Middle income							
Mexico	27.6	75.1	78.8*	101.9	91.0	0.814	53
China	31.0	71.4	70.3*	98.5*	90.9	0.755	85
Turkey	32.0	69.9	85.3*	85.1*	97.7	0.750	94
Oil							
UAE	7.6	78.9	66.4	101.6	n/a	0.849	41
Saudi Arabia	26.6	72.3	67.8	92.3	79.4	0.772	77
Iran	40.3	70.8	81.9	100.0	77.0	0.736	99
Non-oil							
Malaysia	12.4	73.5	69.3**	104.5**	88.7	0.796	61
Jordan	26.8	71.8	88.3*	101.3*	89.9	0.753	90
Syria	16.4	73.6	63.2	93.8	79.6	0.721	106
Indonesia	38.4	67.4	61.8*	98.2*	90.4	0.697	110
Egypt	36.2	70.2	86.9*	94.0*	57.7	0.659	119
Sub-Saharan Africa							
Cameroon	149.4	46.0	43.8	86.7	67.9	0.487	148
Kenya	119.3	48.3	48.0	94.1	73.6	0.474	154
Sierra Leone	282.5	41.1	n/a	n/a	35.1	0.298	176

Sources: http://web.worldbank.org/WBSITE/EXTERNAL/DATASTATISTICS/0,,contentMDK:20535285~menuPK:1192694~pagePK:64133150~piPK:64133175~theSitePK:239419,00.html. http://hdr.undp.org/statistics/data/indicators.cfm?x=1&y=1&z=1. Data not available from the above source (literacy rate for Australia, US, France, Greece, Egypt; mortality rate under age 5 Iran) has been supplemented by data from https:/cia.gov/cia/publications/factbook/geos/eg.html#People.

Notes
** 2000, * 2003.

Table 3.6 Development indicators and income, average for country groups, 2003

	GDP per capita (ppp)	Human Development Index	Life expectancy at birth	Adult literacy rate (proportion aged 15 and above), %	Gross school enrolment, all levels, %
Sub-Saharan Africa	1,856	0.515	46.1	61.3	50
South Asia	2,897	0.628	63.4	58.9	56
East Asia and the Pacific	5,100	0.768	70.5	90.4	69
Arab states	*5,685*	*0.679*	*67.0*	*64.1*	*62*
Latin America and the Caribbean	7,404	0.797	71.9	89.6	81
Central and eastern Europe and CIS (former communist)	7,939	0.812	68.1	99.2	83
OECD	25,915	0.892	77.7		89
High-income OECD	30,181	0.911	78.9	98.9*	95

Source: Developed countries, from http://portal.unesco.org/education.

Note

*As Table 3.5.

Institutions and economic outcomes

Explanations for different economic and human development outcomes as expressed in the above data may be categorized into (1) resource availability including investment, (2) geographic location, and (3) "institutions." The explanations that stress resource availability underlie the quest to achieve economic development through foreign aid programs. Geographic location has consequences through climate and access to markets. Location can also be beneficial if neighboring countries have favorable institutions. Institutions in themselves, however, have been identified as the primary determinants of societal economic achievement.[31]

Institutions affect personal and political behavior through incentives, conventions and social norms. In turn, institutions are influenced by history, traditions and the presumptions of appropriate behavior expressed in culture and belief and value systems. Institutions determine whether there is democratic and accountable government, or authoritarian and despotic rule with corruption and benefit for a privileged few. Institutions also determine the scope of individual opportunity through social mobility, as expressed in access to education and health care, attitudes to free markets and free trade, and access to credit and resources. The role of institutions in economic development has a historical context, for example, with respect to why the Industrial Revolution began when and where it did, and why it bypassed some societies.

Rent-seeking associated with institutions has been identified as inhibiting economic growth in different ways.[32] If insufficient resources were the sole impediment to economic development, aid would be successful in achieving economic growth. However, aid has been ineffective in fostering economic growth.[33] Evidence points to the role of rent-seeking when aid provides rents to be contested.[34] Whether natural resource wealth invites the contestability of rent-seeking also depends on institutions.[35] The data presented above confirms that societies have achieved economic growth and high income with little or no natural resource wealth, and that populations in countries in similar geographic locations and with similar natural resources have fared quite differently in economic outcomes. The evidence that natural resource wealth and advantageous geography are neither sufficient nor necessary for high income and economic growth substantiates the primary role of institutions and associated rent-seeking behavior in economic development.

Attributes of institutions are reflected in discretionary behavior of rulers. Incentives have been noted for autocratic rulers to resist economic development because higher incomes and improved standards of health and education are anticipated to bring demands for democratic accountability and political participation. There are incentives to resist the elimination of poverty because maintained poverty provides ongoing foreign aid flows. The poor are held as "hostages" to secure foreign aid.[36] In both instances, rents are sustained at the expense of the well-being of the population.

These observations regarding institutions are drawn primarily from the study of economic development in sub-Saharan Africa. Similar observations about institutions, including roles of rent-seeking in various forms, have been made about economic progress in the transition from socialism to a private property market economy.[37]

Since institutions and associated incentives including rent contestability are prominent in explanations of economic outcomes in other societies, what is the role of institutions in explaining economic development in Islamic societies? In the quest for answers, we begin by drawing on the writings of Timur Kuran, who has proposed a number of traditional and historically based explanations for economic outcomes under Islam. We shall then supplement Kuran's explanations with explanations framed more in terms of public choice-oriented concepts. We begin with moderate Islam while noting that manifestations of contemporary radical Islam are reflected in the values and objectives of historical traditional Islam.

Islamic legal and ethical principles

Kuran points to inhibitions on economic development due to Islamic legal principles that disallow payment of interest, businesses as judicial entities, and insurance. He notes also that economic growth was deterred by Islamic trusts. The purpose of the trusts was to provide legal entities that would protect private property rights against the intent of appropriation by rulers. Legally designated objectives of the trusts however prevented resource reassignment in response to changing priorities and opportunities. Since change in the allocation of resources of the Islamic trusts could only be informal, a tradition of bribery and corruption came to be established, as means were sought to circumvent the legal impediments to changes in the ways that the assets of trusts could be used. Kuran also notes the adverse consequences of an inheritance system that fragmented wealth and disrupted business partnerships. He points out that the Islamic legal system did not necessarily apply to the Jews and Christians living under Islam, and, as a consequence, Jews and Christians came to dominate economic activity in Islamic societies.[38]

Ethically based principles are not necessarily expected to promote personal material gain. This is particularly so when personal wealth acquired through productive effort is deemed non-meritorious so that guilt feelings are imparted by personal economic success. The ethical response to the guilt is to contribute to charity. Guilt resulting from economic success is consistent with Max Weber's distinction between "publican" and "pharisaic" religions. For example, as noted by Mariano Grondona,[39] in the former cases which include Islam, the economically successful are perceived, and are made to perceive themselves, as ethically inadequate while the poor and economically unsuccessful are given comfort in the ethical merit of their personal circumstances. By contrast, in the latter cases, economic success is a sign of worthiness, and it is the poor who are made to feel ethically inadequate.[40]

Kuran's evaluation is that an economic system based on Islamic principles can be "criticized extensively for its incoherence, incompleteness, impracticality, and irrelevance."[41] The principles, however, are not consistently applied in contemporary Islamic societies. As in the past, means are found of redefining economic transactions to establish consistency with Islamic principles, in particular through Islamic banking. Islamic legal principles do not directly explain contemporary economic outcomes under Islam.

Islam initially accommodated the openness of societies it conquered, and flourished intellectually while Europe languished in the Dark Ages. Subsequent closure to new knowledge followed. Kuran[42] has pointed to the adverse effects on economic growth of impediments to new knowledge and to independent thought. Richard Easterlin[43] correspondingly draws attention to evidence that modern education of a broad segment of the population is a requisite for a society's ability to absorb new information and technology. An education system that stresses rote-learning of religious tracts is not conducive to advances in scientific knowledge. While the Industrial Revolution bypassed Islamic societies, there has also been no significant industrialization in contemporary times. The low rates of economic growth in oil-rich states are consistent with impediments to access to new knowledge. New knowledge could have been embodied in investment, with accompanying human adaptation. As has been shown in the data, convergence to Western growth rates did not take place. The hereditary rulers in the Arab oil states did not use income from oil wealth for knowledge-based and technology-embodied investment.[44] Why did the potential beneficiaries of growth not succeed in introducing growth-promoting change? An impediment to change is the inhibition of public discourse that would permit dissemination of information about the benefits of a more open approach to new knowledge. These inhibitions take the problem of impediments to new knowledge one step back, to impediments to knowledge about the consequences of new knowledge.

The above framework based on Kuran's writings provides important insights for understanding economic outcomes under Islam. An alternative and supplementary direction of analysis focuses on insights from the theory of the rent-seeking society and the relation between rent-seeking and supreme values.

Rent-seeking

In Islamic societies, in common with other societies, wealth and power have historically been concentrated in the hands of an absolute ruler and associated elites. The concentrated wealth attracts resources to contestability – if the means of contestability are available. As elsewhere, the institutions of Islamic societies have also sought to protect property rights of rulers through hereditary succession.[45] In the case of Islam, since the ruler follows the principles of Islam, rebellion against the ruler is rebellion against Islam itself.

The objective of pre-empting internal rent-seeking directed at the ruler's wealth has not always been achieved. Rebellions have occurred over the course of time. Internecine contestability of succession has often been a consequence of rulers' large numbers of wives and children.[46]

Where contestability is possible, the wealth of the ruler is threatened by private wealth *not* in the hands of the ruler, because of the prospect for use of private wealth in rent-seeking quests to augment the ruler's wealth. Institutions that are intended to sustain the ruler deter competing private wealth creation, which would occur with the creation and adoption of new technology. Impediments to growth thus arise as the consequence of the objective of protecting the wealth of the ruler.

In European societies, absolute monarchy was historically compromised through concessions made by reigning monarchs. As noted by Roger Congleton,[47] where it survived, monarchy in Europe came to be limited by constitutional provisions that are consistent with and evolve into eventual democracy. The same liberalizing trends did not occur in Arab societies. Rather, absolute hereditary authoritarian rule persisted up until contemporary times.[48] Vani Borooah and Martin Paldam[49] have studied institutions in 171 countries between 1972 and 2004 and found that Islam is a primary reason for the absence of democracy.

Persistence of autocracy has consequences for corruption beyond the historical role of the Islamic trusts in fostering corruption noted by Kuran.[50] Corruption is facilitated when the political accountability of democracy is absent.[51] In authoritarian regimes, permissible corruption is a means of sustaining loyalty to the regime by providing privileged sources of income within the government bureaucracy.[52]

William Easterly, Jozef Ritzen and Michael Woolcock[53] have measured social cohesion in terms of ethnic fractionalization and equality in income distribution, including the indicator of the presence of a middle class with a substantial share of national income. They use their measure to confirm empirically the benefits of social cohesion expressed in institutions that are conducive to growth. Muslim countries or countries with large Muslim populations are identified as among the least socially cohesive.

David Landes[54] observed how, historically, it was expeditious in Islamic societies to hide personal wealth. The unostentatious facades of houses hid more valuable internally ensconced private wealth. This shows a lack of trust, expressed in insecurity of personal property rights. We recall that the reason for the existence of Islamic trusts was to protect property rights from incursion by rulers. The need to hide personal wealth from the ruler is consistent with the incentive of the ruler to pre-empt the presence of competitive wealth that could be used to contest the ruler's own wealth. A rent-seeking society centers on how much wealth can be acquired through rent-seeking, and for use in rent-seeking.

Barbara Crossette[55] has observed the absence of trust regarding gender relations. She explains female genital mutilation and denial of sexual satisfaction for women as reflecting lack of trust of women by men. Lack of trust is also expressed in prohibitions on women being in the company of men from outside the extended family. The restrictions on women impede labor market participation, which reduces income. When social mobility and incomes are low, gender relations provide compensating benefits or rents for males through polygamy and male dominance within the extended family. Financial independence through personal income earned by women would compromise male dominance. Disallowing participation of women in labor markets is also consistent with the ruler's objective of restraining creation of competitive private wealth. Literate mothers promote literacy in children and increase children's future productiveness and future income. If girls are not destined to earn market income, there are disincentives for educating girls. Again, incomes are kept low across generations, and the creation of private competitive wealth is contained.

Externally directed rent-seeking

It is an enlightened concept that a society should seek economic improvement through individual productive activity, comparative advantage and market exchange. Much of human experience is a history of quests for enrichment at the expense of others through conquest and appropriation. In a Nietzschean context, as I have described elsewhere, the strong seek to enrich themselves by taking from the weak.[56]

Islam divides the world into the domain of Islam and the domain of the sword; that is, the domain yet to be conquered by the sword. If the pre-Islam tribes of Arabia were predatory with respect to one another, and if Islam disallowed continued predation among the tribes themselves, then, following the demise of the local Jews and the removal of their possessions and property, the predation would have to continue elsewhere, through wider Islamic conquests.[57] The predation is externally directed rent-seeking. A gain to the ruler is through distraction from internal rent-seeking. In other instances, Islam met barriers to continued conquest and expansion. At the battle of Poitier, at the gates of Vienna and elsewhere, the advances stopped. Conquered land was lost in various locations including the Iberian Peninsula, the Balkans, Sicily, and, in the twentieth century, through the partition of India and the establishment of the State of Israel. Since loss of land previously conquered by Islam can only be temporary, the losses set in place injunctions of reconquest. Contemporary radical Islam adheres to the supreme-value injunction of reconquest – and also new conquest.

Radical Islam

Expression of the supreme values is found in the declaration by Hamas Foreign Minister Mahmoud Al-Zahar of the government of the Palestinian Authority when he stated that, "Even if the US gave us all its money in return for recognizing Israel and giving up one inch of Palestine, we would never do so even if this costs us our lives."[58] In another expression of the supreme values, the Hamas leader Khaled Mashaal has stated, "We do not promise our people to turn Gaza into Hong Kong or Taiwan, but we promise them a dignified and proud life behind the resistance in defense of their honor, their land and their pride."[59] Both declarations substantiate that economic improvement for the population is subordinate to the priorities of the supreme-value system.

Kuran has posed the question,

> If the critics of Islamic economics are right, and its capacity for improving economic performance is at best marginal, what explains its existence and popularity? ... Why would anyone believe that Islamic economics is capable of raising productivity, stimulating growth, or reducing inequality?[60]

His answer is as follows:

> These questions mask an essential, if paradoxical fact: the main purpose of Islamic economics is not to improve economic performance ... Its real purpose is to help prevent Muslims from assimilating into the emerging global culture whose core elements have a Western pedigree.... A complementary objective of Islamic fundamentalism has been to weaken the prevailing commercial and industrial ties between the Muslim world and the West, in order to protect Muslims from un-Islamic influences.[61]

The intent is therefore separation. Western economic theory, with origins in Adam Smith and classical economists like David Ricardo, points in contrast to the mutual gains from voluntary exchange in markets. As Kuran explains, radical Islam seeks to ensure that influences undesirable to Islam do not permeate through the contacts of market exchange. Although mutually beneficial by usual Western economic criteria, trade would also benefit the adversary in the yet unconquered or to be reconquered world of the sword. The supreme values would be contradicted. Two natural experiments, which occurred almost simultaneously, are illustrative of the supreme values.

Towards the end of the summer of 2005, all areas of the Gaza strip were transferred to the jurisdiction of the radical Islamic government of the Palestinian Authority. Under the supervision of the World Bank, and with the former president of the World Bank taking charge, the property of Jewish farmers was transferred to the Palestinian farmers.[62] The transferred assets, which consisted principally of agricultural greenhouses, were in the end not put to productive use. Terror sponsored by the radical Islamic government resulted in closing off the border crossing with Israel through which produce from the Palestinian farmers was to be shipped to market. Denial of market access *by their own government* led the Palestinian farmers to abandon the farms in late May 2006. Productive activity in the farms ceased, with a loss of income for the local Palestinian population.[63] With the cessation of productive activity, externally directed rent-seeking resumed priority. War was initiated with Israel in summer 2006, through kidnapping and armed assault, and missile attacks were directed at Israeli towns. As was to be anticipated, suffering among the Palestinian population increased. Added to the self-deprivation that had occurred through the cessation of productive activity was the deprivation and loss of life incurred as the Israel Defense Forces responded by attempting to free the kidnap victim and to end the missile attacks.[64]

Whereas Hamas is a Sunni radical Islamic organization, radical Islamic Hezbollah (the Army of God) is Shiʿa. The Shiʿa variant of radical Islam was consistent in exhibiting the same behavior as the Sunni radical Islam. By the summer of 2006, Lebanon had undergone economic reconstruction and semblances of economic normalcy had returned. Resources were being used for economic improvement and incomes had increased. That summer, the Hezbollah, a state-within-a-state in Lebanon but also a member of the coalition government, likewise initiated conflict with the state of Israel by the same means of kidnapping and armed incursion across recognized boundaries and missile attacks on towns in Israel.[65] The consequence was war. Economic progress for the local populations in Lebanon ceased and previous economic gains were destroyed.

The nuclear weapons program of Iran was acquired by a supreme-value objective of radical Islam. As the data have shown, notwithstanding natural resource wealth, the population of Iran is quite poor. Income from natural resource wealth that could have been used for the economic improvement of the population was used in externally directed external rent-seeking with the intent of changing institutions in other societies, through the threat of destroying or taking what others outside the belief system have.

Demographic contestability

Contemporary conquering and reconquering through violent actions are the means of radical Islam. The advent of change can be non-violently awaited. A non-violent form taken in awaiting change is demographic contestability. Demographic contestability is a sensitive issue due to the social consequences and collective intent imputed from the conjunction of personal fertility choices.[66] The question is whether democracy can be used to change institutions by majority voting, including ending democracy itself.[67] The political turnover in office necessary for sustained democracy requires political competition to present voters with choices among alternative policies or candidates with different competencies. If a part of the population votes exclusively according to religious identity rather than by comparing policies and political competencies, democracy will no longer be sustainable when that segment of the population becomes the majority of voters.

The opportunity cost of demographic contestability is lowered if women do not participate in labor markets. Non-participation in labor markets and high fertility reduce per capita or family incomes. The host welfare state may however maintain living standards.

Home-societal disincentives for personal productive activity and personal wealth creation may be sustained by intergenerational cultural transmission in immigrant populations. With norms and conventions – and culture – sustained, the beneficiaries of the welfare state who have come from outside do not undertake productive activity to create personal wealth. Norms of non-contestable wealth combine with the perception of the welfare state as expressing the traditional merit of charity to those who have less.

The welfare state relies on productive activity to provide the tax base for redistribution. Demographic trends of declining fertility and increased longevity among local historically original populations pose problems of fiscal sustainability of welfare state commitments. Demographic contestability hastens the advent of non-viability of the institutions of the welfare state – and eventually achieves the demise and replacement of the institutions of the Western welfare state.[68]

Contestability and passivity

Contestability suggests a contest. The theory of rent-seeking describes the rent-seeking contests. Contestability may be met with passivity from those whose property – and freedom, for example, in the way women dress – provides the rents that are contested. The sources of that passivity make an interesting study. Passivity can be due to hyperbolic discounting. The influence of cultural relativism can also be present.

Cultural relativism

Since the writings of Max Weber,[69] there has been an awareness that belief and value systems have economic consequences. Weber's insights are expanded in the modern literature on the economic consequences of religion.[70] The effects of belief and value systems are reflected in culture, which in turn is mirrored in institutions.[71] We have observed that different aspects of culture appear to have a role in explaining economic outcomes under Islam. The differences in criteria across cultures for evaluation of personal and societal success introduce cultural relativism.[72]

Cultural relativism might preclude an investigation such as the one in this chapter. The position can also be taken, as eloquently expressed by Lawrence Harrison,[73] that cultural relativism should not be permitted to restrict intellectual inquiry. In particular, this position might be taken when a culture harms people or condemns them to economic deprivation. Acceptance of cultural relativism would also presuppose that adherence to the value system is voluntary. For women, subjugation through gender dominance can make personal preferences unclear. Proponents of cultural relativism likewise confront the need to account for effects on personal security of those outside of the belief system. When a culture seeks to compel imposition of its value system and harms people who do not accept the imposition, cultural relativism is a denial of the right of self-defense for those who are threatened with harm.

Conclusions

Arab and other Muslim societies without oil have lower incomes than do non-Muslim neighbors who are similarly without natural resource wealth. Growth has not closed income gaps, including in oil states where resources for investment have been available from oil revenues. Absence of convergence of growth indicates that innovations and new technologies available from the outside have not been used to advantage. Human development indicators show outcomes for populations inferior to those predicted by per capita income. From these initial circumstances of moderate Islam, the supreme values of radical Islam deprioritize economic achievement and impose self-deprivation on own populations. Theories of economic development presuppose that intended beneficiaries seek economic improvement. The theories lose applicability when supreme values require economic self-deprivation and when ongoing life has no value. The supreme values require all available resources to be directed to the priority objectives. Aid donors and international agencies then cannot be expected to achieve development objectives. The aid resources provided will not be used for economic development.

Were there not significant consequences for other societies, an appeal to cultural relativism could allow acceptance that voluntarily chosen supreme values deprioritize economic progress. More difficult for cultural relativists might be gender relations and the diminution of the worth of ongoing life within the society. These are nonetheless internal consequences of a belief and value system that cultural relativism would ask those outside the belief and value system not to judge. The supreme values, however, have security consequences through the change sought in other societies.

Are impediments to compromise with other societies insurmountable? A civil constitution could seek to change institutions of radical Islam but would require the voluntary relinquishment of the supreme values of the belief and value system. A change in values could be sought through education but, when the value system is embedded in the content of education, education reinforces the supreme values and does not promote tolerance. Radical Islam can accommodate temporary compromise or truce if, in the longer perspective, the likelihood of the achievement of the supreme-value objectives is thereby enhanced. As long as other societies remain unwilling to accept the supreme values (and it is a supreme value of radical Islam that the supreme values should become universal), it seems that the challenge will remain for longer run conciliation between radical Islam and the societies whose institutions (and beliefs) radical Islam seeks (or is required by its own values) to change.

Acknowledgment

An earlier version of this chapter was presented at the conference on Radical Islam: Challenge and Response organized by the Begin-Sadat (BESA) Center for Strategic Studies at Bar-Ilan University, May 24–25 2006. It has been reprinted with the kind permission of Springer Science and Business Media from Arye Hillman, "Economic and Security Consequences of Supreme Values," *Public Choice*, June 2007, vol. 131, nos 3–4.

Notes

1 T. Brück and B. Wickström (eds), Special Issue on The Economic Consequences of Terror, *European Journal of Political Economy*, June 2004, vol. 20, no. 2, pp. 291–515.

2 A.H. Chen and T.F. Siems, "The Effects of Terrorism on Global Capital Markets," in Brück and Wickström, op. cit., pp. 349–366.

3 R. Eldor and R. Melnik, "Financial Markets and Terrorism," in Brück and Wickström, op. cit., pp. 349–366, 367–386.

4 J. Yetman, "Suicidal Terrorism and Discriminatory Screening: An Efficiency–Equity Trade-off," *Defense and Peace Economics*, 2004, vol. 3, no. 3, pp. 221–230.

5 R. Franck, A.L. Hillman and M. Krausz, "Public Safety and the Moral Dilemma in the Defense Against Terror," *Defense and Peace Economics*, October 2005, vol. 16, no. 5, pp. 347–364.

6 A.B. Kruger and J. Maleckova, "Education, Poverty and Terrorism: Is There a Causal Connection?," *Journal of Economic Perspectives*, fall 2003, vol. 17, no. 4, pp. 119–144.

7 T. Cowan, "Road Map to Middle Eastern Peace? A Public Choice Perspective," *Public Choice*, January 2004, vol. 118, pp. 1–10.

8 S. Plaut, "Misplaced Applications of Economic Theory to the Middle East," *Public Choice*, January 2004, vol. 118, pp. 11–24.

9 C. Berrebi and E. Klor, "On Terrorism and Electoral Outcomes," *Journal of Conflict Resolution*, 2006, vol. 50, no. 6, pp. 899–925.

10 Nobel laureate Douglass North, in *Structure and Change in Economic History*, New York: W.W. Norton, 1981, and subsequently many others have pointed out that incentives associated with institutions are the primary determinants of whether economic progress takes place.

11 M. Coçgel, R. Ahmed and T. Miceli, "Law and State Power: The Institutional Roots of the Strong State in Islamic History," University of Connecticut, Department of Economics Working Paper series, 2007–01. At www.econ.uconn.edu/working/ 2007–01.pdf (accessed 27 February 2007).

12 Tim Kuran is Professor of Economics and Law and King Faisal Professor of Islamic Thought and Culture at the University of Southern California.

13 The extensive literature on economic development in sub-Saharan Africa includes Paul Collier and Jan Gunning, "Why Has Africa Grown So Slowly?," *Journal Economic Perspectives*, summer 1999, vol. 13, no. 3, pp. 3–22; C.K. Rowley, "Political Culture and Economic Performance in Sub-Saharan Africa," *European Journal of Political Economy*, March 2000, vol. 16, no. 1, pp. 133–158; W. Easterly, *The Elusive Quest for Growth: Economists Adventures and Misadventures in the Tropics*, Cambridge, MA: MIT Press, 2001. See also my 2002 overview of Easterly, op. cit., 2001. R. Paap, P. Hans Franses and D. van Dijk, "Does Africa Grow Slower than Asia, Latin America, and the Middle East? Evidence from a New Data-based Classification Method," *Journal of Development Economics*, August 2005, vol. 77, issue 2, pp. 553–570, documents the diversity of growth experiences in sub-Saharan Africa and provides comparisons with other regions, including the Middle East.

14 M. Paldam, "Economic Freedom and the Success of the Asian Tigers: An Essay on Controversy," *European Journal of Political Economy*, September 2003, vol. 19, no. 3, pp. 453–477.

15 As Peter Bernholz observes in "Supreme Values, Tolerance, and the Constitution of Liberty," in G. Radinsky and H. Bouillon (eds), *Values and the Social Order, Values and Society*, vol. 1, Brookfield, VT: Avery Publishing, 1995, pp. 235–250, and in "Supreme Values as the Basis for Terror," *European Journal of Political Economy*, June 2004, vol. 20, no. 2, pp. 317–334, supreme values have historically not been exclusive to Islam. Societies with supreme-value systems have included the

Anabaptists, other variants of Christianity at various times such as during the Spanish and Portuguese inquisitions, the Nazi regime in Germany and regimes in collaborating European societies, and communist regimes.

16 The social loss due to rent-seeking because of unproductive resources to seek distributional objectives was pointed out by Gordon Tullock, "The Welfare Costs of Tariffs, Monopolies and Theft," *Western Economic Journal*, 1967, vol. 5, pp. 224–232. Anne O. Krueger introduced the terminology in "The Political Economy of the Rent-Seeking Society," *American Economic Review*, 1974, vol. 64, pp. 291–303. See also Tullock, *The Economics of Special Privilege and Rent Seeking*, Boston, MA: Kluwer, 1989. For an introduction and overview of the concept of rent-seeking, see my book, *Public Finance and Public Policy: Responsibilities and Limitations of Government*, New York: Cambridge University Press, 2003, ch. 6.3.

17 The last verse of the French national anthem is called the children's verse, and was intended to be sung by children only:

Into the fight we shall enter
When our fathers are dead and gone
We shall find their bones laid down to rest
With the fame of their glories won (repeat)
Oh, to survive them care we not
Glad are we to share their grave
Great honor is to be our lot
To follow or to venge our brave
To arms...

I thank Pierre-Guillaume Méon for bringing this verse to my attention.

18 Laurent Murawiec, "Deterring Those who are Already Dead?" Chapter 10, this volume.

19 In a focus on the benefits of sexual favors, the value of ongoing life is diminished when "death" is believed to bring access to the 72 virgins who await a *shahid*.

20 On the latter societies, see R. Pomfret, *The Economics of Central Asia*, Princeton, NJ: Princeton University Press, 1995.

21 R.M. McCleary and R.J. Barro, "Religion and the Economy," *Journal of Economic Perspectives*, spring 2006, vol. 20, no. 2, pp. 49–72.

22 See McCleary and Barro, op. cit., 2006, table 4, p. 67.

23 Syria has oil but not in the quantities of other Arab oil-extracting states.

24 The purchasing–power parity measures leave the rankings of Morocco, Egypt and Syria more or less unchanged; Tunisia's rank increases; the ranks of Jordan and Yemen decline.

25 Egypt has a substantial Copt minority.

26 In India, there is a substantial middle class with incomes not derived from quasi-feudal landownership. See D. Rodrik and A. Subramanian, "From 'Hindu Growth' to Productivity Surge: The Mystery of the Indian Growth Transition," *IMF Staff Papers* 2005, vol. 52, pp. 193–228.

27 Convergence refers to rates of economic growth, and not necessarily to income levels. Conditional on initial low incomes, growth is predicted to be higher in low-income countries than in high-income countries. In the formal expositions, convergence is also shown to be conditional on steady state characteristics. The so-called Dutch disease describes expansion of the natural resource sector at the expense of other sectors; oil extraction does not, however, appear to have attracted domestic resources from other sectors. The other sectors were not there to begin with. Employment of expatriates has been prominent in oil-rich Arab states.

28 Arab non-oil countries included here are Jordan, Lebanon, Syria, Yemen, Egypt, Morocco and Tunisia; Arab oil countries are Algeria, Bahrain, Iraq, Libya, Kuwait, Oman, Qatar, Saudi Arabia and the UAE.

29 That is, formally, denoting by *y* the natural logarithm of GDP per capita output:

$$\frac{d \ln y}{dt} = \frac{\dot{y}}{y}.$$

30 The description of outcomes is consistent with the econometric evidence. M. Noland, "Religion, Culture and Economic Performance," *World Development*, August 2005, vol. 33, no. 8, pp. 1215–1232, concludes however from regressions that Islam, if anything, is conducive to growth. One of Noland's findings is that Jewish, Catholic and Protestant population shares negatively affect per capita income growth. Less puzzling is Noland's finding that closeness to Mecca of a national capital weighted by Muslim population share increases a country's total factor productivity: since oil or natural resource wealth increases total factor productivity, this finding by Noland appears to reflect the geographic concentration of oil and of Islamic populations around Mecca.

31 Confirmation of the role of institutions in economic development is provided by a substantial literature including D. Rodrik, A. Subramanian and F. Trebbi, "Institutions Rule: The Primacy of Institutions Over Geography and Integration in Economic Development," Discussion Paper No. 3643, 2002, Center for Policy Studies, London: Center for Economic Policy Research; E.L. Glaeser, R. La Porta, F. Lopez-de-Silanes and A. Shleifer, "Do Institutions Cause Growth?," *Journal of Economic Growth*, September 2004, vol. 9, no. 3, pp. 271–303; and D. Acemoglu, S. Johnson and J. Robinson, "Institutions as the Fundamental Cause of Long-run Growth," NBER Working Paper No. 10481, 2004, Cambridge, MA: National Bureau of Economic Research.

32 The consequences of rent-seeking for economic growth have been studied by M. Rama, "Rent Seeking and Economic Growth: A Theoretical Model and Some Empirical Evidence," *Journal of Development Economics*, October 1993, vol. 42, no. 1, pp. 35–60; K.M. Murphy, A. Shleifer and R.W. Vishny, "Why is Rent Seeking So Costly for Growth?," *American Economic Review Papers and Proceedings*, 1993, vol. 83, pp. 409–414; and K.R. Pedersen, "The Political Economy of Distribution in Developing Countries: A Rent-seeking Approach," *Public Choice*, June 1997, vol. 98, nos 3–4, pp. 351–373.

33 The empirical studies on the effectiveness of aid have been compiled and studied by H. Doucouliagos and M. Paldam. "The Aid Effectiveness Literature: The Sad Result of 40 Years of Research," University of Aarhus working paper, 2005. Available www.econ.au.dk/vip_htm/mpaldam/Papers/Meta-meta_8.pdf.

34 See J. Svensson, "Foreign Aid and Rent Seeking," *Journal of International Economics*, August 2000, vol. 51, no. 2, pp. 437–461.

35 See H. Mehlum, K. Moene and R. Torvik, "Institutions and the Resource Curse," *Economic Journal*, January 2006, vol. 116, pp. 1–20.

36 The disincentives for development due to political participation of a middle class have been studied by Yariv Welzman, "Corruption, Poverty, and Political Exclusion," paper presented at the 14th Silvaplana Workshop on Political Economy, Silvaplana, Switzerland, 2005. On the hostage problem, see William Easterly, op. cit. and my review of Easterly, op. cit., 2001, A.L. Hillman, "The World Bank and the Persistence of Poverty in Poor Countries," *European Journal of Political Economy*, November 2002, vol. 18, no. 4, pp. 783–795.

37 See A. Gelb, A.L. Hillman and H.W. Ursprung, "Rents as Distractions: Why the Transition from Socialism is Prolonged," in N.C. Baltas, G. Demopoulos and J. Hassid (eds), *Economic Interdependence and Cooperation in Europe*, Berlin: Springer, 1998, pp. 21–38; and, for example, papers in Nauro F. Campos and Jan Fidrmuc (eds), *Political Economy of Transition and Development: Institutions, Politics and Policies*, Dordrecht: Kluwer Academic, 2003.

38 See T. Kuran, "Why the Middle East is Economically Underdeveloped: Historical

Mechanisms of Institutional Stagnation," *Journal of Economic Perspectives*, summer 2004, vol. 18, no. 3, pp. 71–90.

39 M. Grondona, "A Cultural Typology of Economic Development," in L.E. Harrison and S.P. Huntington (eds), *Culture Matters: How Human Values Shape Economic Progress*, New York: Basic Books, 2000, pp. 44–55.

40 The comparison is usually made for Protestant and Catholic variants of Christianity. See Grondona, op. cit.

41 Kuran, "The Discontents of Islamic Economic Morality," *American Economic Review*, March 1996, vol. 86, no. 1, pp. 438–442.

42 Kuran, "Islam and Underdevelopment: An Old Puzzle Revisited," *Journal of Institutional and Theoretical Economics*, March 1997, vol. 153, pp. 41–71.

43 R. Easterlin, *The Reluctant Economist*, New York: Cambridge University Press, 2004, pp. 57–73.

44 The distinction here is once more between the creation and adoption of new technology. Technological creativity is a foundation for societal wealth and resistance to technical growth impedes growth; see J. Mokyr, *The Gifts of Athena: Historical Origins of the Knowledge Economy*, Princeton, NJ: Princeton University Press, 2002, ch. 6. On inhibitions to growth because of impediments to technology adoption, see also S.L. Parente and E.C. Prescott, "Barriers to Technology Adoption and Development," *Journal of Political Economy*, 1994, vol. 102, pp. 298–321. As noted when considering convergence of growth, adoption of new pre-existing technology is an easier task than creation of new knowledge. The changes in economic growth rates for Arab oil states in Figure 3.1 reflect changes in oil prices and not growth due to creation or adoption of new knowledge.

45 On hereditary succession, see J.M. Buchanan, "Rent Seeking, Non-compensated Transfers, and Laws of Succession," *Journal of Law and Economics*, April 1983, vol. 26, pp. 71–85.

46 Conflicts have at times been particularly violent, and the consequence has been "failed states," as in contemporary times in Algeria, Lebanon, Yemen, Somalia, Iraq, and the areas of jurisdiction of the Palestinian Authority.

47 R. Congleton, "On the Durability of King and Council: The Continuum between Dictatorship and Democracy," *Constitutional Political Economy*, September 2001, vol. 12, no. 3, pp. 193–215, and "From Royal to Parliamentary Rule without Revolution: Credible Commitments and the Market for Power within Divided Governments," Working Paper, Public Choice Center, George Mason University, 2006.

48 On the Arab regimes, see M. Noland, "Explaining Middle Eastern Authoritarianism," Working Paper No. 05–5, Institute for International Economics, Washington DC, 2005. Where there has not been formal hereditary monarchy, hereditary rule has often been de facto (e.g. in Syria). In Iraq under Saddam Hussein, a son was the designated successor. In Egypt a son of the president has been proposed as the successor. In democratic societies as well, there have been political family dynasties. A criterion for the presence of democracy is an identifiable leader of the opposition not in jail or exile who could credibly replace the head of government when new elections are held. This criterion is, for example, satisfied in Turkey. Democratic institutions allowing contestable political office have also been present in other Muslim non-Arab states, including Iran, Bangladesh, Pakistan, Malaysia and Indonesia. In Algeria, an election that would have brought radical Islam to political office was cancelled in the second round in 1991 (there are estimates that some 100,000 people died in violent conflict in Algeria in the two decades up to 2000). Available at http://news.bbc.co.uk/1/hi/world/middle_east/country_profiles/811140.stm (accessed 28 February 2007). Algeria has considerable natural resource wealth.

Often, elections in Arab societies offer partial democracy. As a contemporary example, in Kuwait a woman was appointed minister of planning and administrative development in 2005, against Islamist opposition. Available at http://news.bbc.

co.uk/1/hi/world/middle_east/4111234.stm (accessed 28 February 2007). Women had been given the right to vote a month previously and also voted in elections that took place in 2006. Primary political power, however, remained with the hereditary ruler, who appointed the 15 members of the cabinet, who in turn joined the elected assembly of 50. Attempts have been made to impose democracy in Afghanistan and Iraq. Elections in 2006 in the areas of jurisdiction of the Palestinian Authority resulted in a radical Islamic regime.

49 V.K. Borooah and M. Paldam, "Why is the World Short on Democracy? A Cross-country Analysis of Barriers to Representative Government," *European Journal of Political Economy*, December 2007, vol. 23, no. 4.

50 Kuran, op. cit., 2004.

51 Accountability is to be distinguished from transparency in governance. Accountability relates to opportunities expressed in institutions for the population to change governments, through government being accountable to voters. Transparency describes the provision of information about the internal functioning of government including budgetary allocation decisions. Roumeen Islam, "Does Better Transparency Go Along with Better Governance?," *Economics and Politics*, July 2006, vol. 18, no. 2, pp. 121–167, uses a measure of government transparency to confirm that greater transparency in government is associated with enhanced quality of institutions of governance.

52 For a discussion of the causes and consequences of corruption, see V. Tanzi, "Corruption Around the World: Causes, Consequences, Scope, and Cures," *IMF Staff Papers*, December 1998, vol. 45, no. 4, pp. 559–594. Empirical studies include M. Paldam, "The Big Pattern of Corruption. Economics, Culture and the Seesaw Dynamics," *European Journal of Political Economy*, June 2002, vol. 18, no. 2, pp. 215–240. A ranking of countries according to corruption is provided by Transparency International. Available at: www.transparency.org/cpi/2005/cpi2005_infocus.html (accessed 28 February 2007).

53 W. Easterly, J. Ritzen and M. Woolcock, "Social Cohesion, Institutions and Growth," *Economics and Politics*, July 2006, vol. 18, no. 2, pp. 103–120.

54 D.S. Landes, *The Wealth and Poverty of Nations*, New York: Norton, 1999.

55 B. Crossette, "Culture, Gender and Human Rights," in L.E. Harrison and S.P. Huntington (eds) op. cit., pp. 178–188.

56 See my paper, "Nietzschean Development Failures," *Public Choice*, June 2004, vol. 199, nos 3–4, pp. 263–280, on economic consequences of Nietzschean relations.

57 See Bernholz, op. cit., 2004, for elaboration. As Kuran has stressed in private communication, conversion to Islam was often voluntary. Nonetheless, for those who were not of the People of the Book (Jews and Christians), the alternative to conversion was in principle death. The survival of the Hindu population of India under Muslim rule demonstrates that this injunction was not always followed.

58 *Website of Honest Reporting*. Available at www.honestreporting.com/.

59 *Jerusalem Post*, 7 April 2006.

60 Kuran, op. cit., 1996, p. 438.

61 Ibid., p. 439.

62 The primacy of private property rights makes it appropriate to stress that the Jewish farmers had established their agricultural hothouses on sand-dunes that had not previously been used productively and to which there were no prior private property rights.

63 The agricultural hothouses had employed 6,000 people, twice the number that had been employed by the Jewish farmers; *Jerusalem Post*, 22 May 2006.

64 On economic outcomes in the jurisdiction of the Palestinian Authority, see the World Bank, "Growth in the West Bank and Gaza: Opportunities and Constraints," West Bank and Gaza Country Economic Memorandum, Washington DC, 2006. The World Bank documents how external focus has resulted in lack of economic progress and how low incomes in the areas under the jurisdiction of the government of the

Palestinian Authority declined further under radical Islam. Other claims apportion blame to the Israeli "occupation." This chapter is not concerned with the important topic of disinformation. The World Bank makes it clear that the Palestinian Authority has been an autonomous regime since the Oslo Accords of 1992, with a head of state, a head of government and a finance minister, and copious aid resources.

65 In 2000 Israeli Defense Forces, which had been in Lebanon to pre-empt attacks on the Israeli civilian population, withdrew under the auspices of a UN resolution to a recognized international boundary with Lebanon. The UN resolution required the Lebanese government to exercise sovereignty and to police border areas. The border areas were, however, occupied by the armed forces of the radical Islamic group Hizballah.

66 Demographic contestability has been discussed and investigated against the background of differential fertility in India. See A.M. Basu, "The Politicization of Fertility to achieve Non-demographic Objectives," *Population Studies*, March 1997, vol. 51, no. 1, pp. 5–18; and V.K. Borooah, "The Politics of Demography: A Study of Inter-community Fertility Differences in India," *European Journal of Political Economy*, September 2004, vol. 20, no. 3, pp. 551–578. Institutional issues include legal polygamy and the ease of Muslim divorce. J. Johnson-Hanks, "On the Politics and Practice of Muslim Fertility: Comparative Evidence from West Africa," *Medical Anthropology Quarterly*, 2006, vol. 20, pp. 2–30, has studied relative fertility in seven West African countries and finds that, where Muslims are a majority, fertility is lower among Muslim than among non-Muslim women, but the contrary is the case where Muslims are a minority in the population.

67 On the use of majority voting for redistribution, see G. Tullock, "Problems of Majority Voting," *Journal of Political Economy*, 1959, vol. 67, pp. 571–579.

68 On the threats to viability of the European welfare state, see e.g. Hans-Werner Sinn, "The Selection Principle and Market Failure in Systems Competition," *Journal of Public Economics*, 1 November 1997, vol. 66, no. 2, pp. 247–274; Sinn, "Migration, Social Standards and Replacement Incomes: How to Protect Low-income Workers in the Industrialized Countries Against the Forces of Globalization and Market Integration," *International Tax and Public Finance*, August 2005, vol. 12, no. 4, pp. 375–393; and P. Nannestad, "Immigration as a Challenge to the Danish Welfare State?," *European Journal of Political Economy*, September 2003, vol. 20, no. 3, pp. 755–767, among others.

69 M. Weber, *The Protestant Ethic and the Spirit of Capitalism*, New York: Scribner, 1958, and other writings.

70 See L.R. Iannaconne, "Introduction to the Economics of Religion," *Journal of Economic Literature*, September 1998, vol. 36, no. 3, pp. 1465–1495, for an overview on religion and economic behavior. Empirical studies of economic consequences of religion include M. Paldam, "Corruption and Religion: Adding to the Economic Model," *Kyklos*, May 2001, vol. 54, nos 2–3, pp. 383–413; L. Guiso, P. Sapienza and L. Zingales, "People's Opium: Religion and Economic Activities," NBER Working Paper no. 9237, National Bureau of Economic Research, Baltimore, MA: Johns Hopkins University, 2002; R. Barro and R. McCleary, "Religion and Economic Growth Across Countries," *American Sociological Review*, August 2003, vol. 68, no. 4, pp. 760–781, and "Which Countries Have State Religions?," *Quarterly Journal of Economics*, 2005, vol. 120, no. 4, pp. 1331–1370.

71 On culture and economic development, see D. Landes, op. cit., the papers in the edited volumes by L. Harrison and S. Huntington, op. cit., and V. Rao and M. Walton (eds), *Culture and Public Action: Understanding the Role of Culture and Development Policy in an Unequal World*, Stanford, CA: Stanford University Press, 2004. G. Tabellini, "Culture and Institutions: Economic Development in the Regions of Europe," CESifo Working Paper No. 1492, 2005, Munich, concludes that aspects of culture explain regional development disparities in Europe.

72 Cultural relativism is the position where we cannot or should not judge the values of

others. There is a relation to political correctness as an impediment to intellectual enquiry. See my paper "Political Economy and Political Correctness," *Public Choice*, September 1998, vol. 96, nos 3–4, pp. 219–239.

73 L. Harrison, "Why Culture Matters," in L. Harrison and S.P. Huntington, op. cit., pp. xvii–xxxiv.

Part II

The Islamist challenge

Case studies

4 The rise of *jihadi* trends in Saudi Arabia

The post Iraq–Kuwait war phase

Joseph Kostiner

Introduction

Jihadi trends in the Saudi Kingdom resulted from an interplay of two historical processes: the evolution of Wahhabi Islam, which often espoused a violent response to both non-Wahhabi and its own Wahhabi believers, and the building of the Saudi state, of its institutions and internal power structure, which had a restraining and institutionalizing effect on radical Islam in the Kingdom.

The Saudi Arabian Kingdom rests on underpinnings established in 1744 as an alliance between the Saudi tribal chieftain Muhammad Ibn Saud and the clergyman Muhammad Ibn ʿAbd al-Wahab. The new state's goals drew on the teachings and preachings of Ibn ʿAbd al-Wahab. As a state ideology, Ibn ʿAbd al-Wahab's principles had a distinct message of violence and aggression. The following items attest to this fact.

The fight against *shirk* (or polytheism; a mix of paganism with monotheism) which aimed to eradicate the tendency of Muslims to associate godly and human traits in their prayer and daily conduct. According to the Wahhabi doctrine God's oneness (*tawhid*) must be kept, and the association of God's name with human conduct was strictly forbidden. Therefore, the Saudis undertook to "purify" Islamic conduct and Islamic sites, and to persecute people found guilty of such a sin until death. The *jihad*, or holy war, against impure Muslims, against infidels, or non-Muslim unbelievers, became binding norms. Through different periods in the late eighteenth, early nineteenth and early twentieth centuries, the Saudi state embarked on aggressive campaigns raiding neighboring states.[1]

The heavy reliance on the Shariʿa, the Islamic law, as the actual state constitution and exclusive moral guide for society, is also manifested in violence. People have been punished for their crimes in the most literal way: hanging, stoning and amputation of limbs. Those who seem to cease following the Shariʿa properly may be declared by clerics to be committing *takfir* (turning to sin and unbelief, a principle initiated by the pious sage Muhammad Ibn-Taymiyya (d. 1328)), which may lead to their extermination. In the twentieth century, a special body, named in the West as the "moral police" (In Arabic: *Hayʾat al-Amr Bilmarʿuf wal-Nahi ʿan al-Munkar*, "The organization for enjoining the good and denying the forbidden") was established to control people's public behavior. The members of this corps were allowed to publicly apprehend men and women who failed to dress modestly or to join in public prayer, and then to beat and humiliate them.[2]

The inclination of the Wahhabis to see themselves as superior to other Muslim denominations, and their own sites and prayers as the most "purified" among all Muslims, led them both to disregard other Muslim communities and to seek to subjugate them. However, the defeat in 1818 of the first Wahhabi–Saudi state by an Egyptian force, and the failure of the second state (1821–1891) to root itself and avoid deteriorating into an internal war, attested to the collapse of the central authority of both the supreme ruler and the supreme clerics, and consequently left the Saudis with no authority to decide when and where to carry out a *jihad*. As a result, tribal groups raised their own preachers and made their separate interpretations and decisions about raiding and spreading their religion. Even when a new ruler, Abd al-ʿAziz "Ibn Saud," the founder of the third and incumbent Saudi Kingdom, who reigned from 1902 to 1953, initiated the *Ikhwan* movement around 1912 and arrayed the main Saudi tribal groups as a standing army, they continued to raid beyond the limits which Ibn Saud set. The *Ikhwan* symbolized a wild outgrowth of the Saudi–Wahhabi state, hardly controllable by its authorities, and a danger to its neighbors.[3]

Nonetheless, in the twentieth century, notably under Ibn Saud and later under his sons King Faysal (r. 1962–1975) and Khalid (r. 1975–1982), the Saudi state learned to control and contain the violence it had used. Several reasons account for that process. The *Ikhwan* were destroyed militarily and subjugated during 1929 and 1930, and Saudi Arabian groups ceased raiding its neighbors; in fact, the Saudi leaders actually stopped using force in its regional and international affairs. As part of state-building, Ibn Saud shifted the focus of his state interests to hosting the annual pilgrimage to Mecca, in addition to finding and profiting from oil. As part of launching a process of state centralization, Ibn Saud sought to control the "wild" tendencies of Wahhabism. Under King Faysal, a supreme council of clerics was established, and the authority to make binding religious rulings was vested in it. Some of the principle clerics married into the royal family and effectively functioned as moral advisers to the king and the main ministers. Religion was thereby incorporated into the high echelons of the Saudi state, but it was also put under its control.[4]

Since the 1960s, the growing oil income has also served to contain Islamic extremism. The government allocated the emerging business opportunities (in sectors such as banking, insurance, advertising, construction and public administration) to those leading families and tribal clans that had been trusted by the royal leaders and the government. We may call this system "Faysal's Order," named after the king who had inaugurated it. Thus, supreme public and private business positions were held by a "loop" of elite families who acted as patrons to lower-ranking "clients," namely families of the lower classes. Under this system of financial distribution, the government was able to control the economy and deprive potential opposition of financing capability.[5] Moreover, the government thereby gained control over all important tribes and families. These circumstances were not conducive to the rise of religious fanatic opposition. There were only sporadic outbursts of religious-based violence, such as the capturing on 20 November 1979 of the Grand Mosque in Mecca by a group of fanatics. In this case, the compound was recaptured after three weeks, and the perpetrators were sentenced to various punishments.[6] This was an exception to a relatively long period of calm in the area of religious radicalism.

The rise of extremist opposition: causes and motives

Several reasons explain the rise of Islamic extremist opposition groups in Saudi Arabia since the early 1990s.

New socio-economic conditions

In the twenty-first century, Saudi Arabia's population grew to approximately 24 million, including about 18 million Saudi citizens and about five million foreign workers. Approximately 50 percent of the Saudis are below the age of 18. During the period in question, the Saudi Kingdom had an annual average budget deficit of about $57 billion when the average price of oil dropped to less than $25 per barrel (and sometimes to less than $20 per barrel) from $41 in 1981. As a result, the per capita income dropped from $17,000 in 1981 to $6,975 in 1993. Several major problems resulted.

One must bear in mind that "Faysal's Order" was crafted when the size of the Saudi population was between seven and eight million, while Saudi citizens numbered fewer than five million and the rest were foreign workers. Given the fact that the general Saudi population has tripled since that time, it is unlikely that the royal patronage and allocation of jobs and business opportunities, incorporated within Faysal's Order, could be made to extend to 19 million Saudi citizens. Hence, more and more Saudis found themselves out of the "loop of patronage." Unlike in the 1970s, since the 1990s many Saudis of the lower classes were not clients of the elite families' patronage and did not feel obligated to them; thus they were more likely to point out the flaws of the regime and to criticize the royal family more than ever before.

Official reports noted an unemployment rate of about 15 percent among 18- to 25-year-olds. Unofficially, it was often argued to be closer to 30 percent. In 2003, experts estimated that the regime would need to create about 200,000 jobs per year, which would necessitate about $40 billion per year in new investments. This did not seem to be an achievable objective.[7]

Since Faysal's time, an attempt has been made to balance the modern secular curricula, the consumer lifestyle and the technological changes with religious measures, with the goal of turning the students into more pious elements and bestowing on the government an image of preserving the proper Wahhabi values. The government's attempts to co-opt Islamic extremists following the Grand Mosque incident of 1979 further induced such policies. Anthony

Cordesman analyzed polls of Saudis in 2002, and noted that over 60 percent were worried about Saudi youth turning to Western values and morality.[8] The government, therefore, developed university studies in religion, Shari'a and theology ('*aqida*), and encouraged students to engage in such studies. Many, indeed, chose that pattern: they became engineers, lawyers or physicists who were also religious experts. They lacked the official diplomas (*ijaza*) of a clergy-man ('*alim*) but, in the Islamic (and Jewish) tradition, they could become preachers and lay specialists sufficiently versed in the Qur'ān and Wahhabi texts to argue religious issues and participate in religious discourses. An entire gener-ation of academics and students adopted this mode. The use of Ibn Taymiyya's *takfir* arguments thus achieved new popularity.

As part of its efforts to fight radical Arab nationalist (notably Nasserist) influ-ences in the Arab world, the Saudi government opened its gates to Islamist radical intellectuals. Saudi universities then employed some foreign Muslim-Arab lecturers to reinforce their academic faculties. Muhammad Qutb (the brother of Egyptian religious extremist Sayyid Qutb, who was sentenced to death in Egypt in 1966), the Palestinian extremist 'Abdullah Azzam (later a founder of al Qaeda), as well as a Yemeni extremist leader of the Muslim Broth-erhood, 'Abd al-Majid al-Zindani, came to teach in Medina and Riyadh. They created an aura of interest in the fate of the other Islamic groups: the Palestini-ans, the Iranians, the Afghans, the Central Asian and the Balkan Muslims.

They also brought concepts originating in Muslim Brotherhood thought, such as the need to replace any lax Islamic regime with a fundamentalist Shari'a-based regime, and to regard it as a binding duty to fight such sinful regimes or infidel powers which dominate Muslim peoples. They imported into Saudi Arabia the hatred of Western culture and society. Ideas from fundamentalists such as Hasan al-Turabi from Sudan, 'Ali al-Tantawi from Egypt, and Yusuf al-Qaradawi from Egypt and later on from Qatar, were disseminated into the Kingdom. Thus the mode of criticizing the United States as an infidel power and the Saudi regime as its collaborator, typical of some academics and students, turned into an extremist, religious message, reinforced by Muslim Brotherhood ideas from outside the Kingdom.[9] These balancing acts were accompanied by the government's acquiescence to the growing impact of the religious establish-ment on Saudi society. Clergymen influenced the high schools' and universities' curricula, the media, and shaped concepts of education, ethics and the position of women. The "moral police" were most active in enforcing public conduct. Hence, the government responded to the infiltration of Western social and cul-tural influences by increasing official and popular adherence to strict religious law and by complying with the growing impact of religious elements on public life. Clerics and journalists viewed the infiltration of Western values as a "spir-itual raid" (*ghazu fikri*), or a "Christian Crusade" against Islam, which must be met by an appropriate counter-action. Hatred of Western values, the use of dated teaching materials and methods, and the control of academic studies by Wahhabi theology thus prevailed. These developments proved conducive to the rise of Islamic extremism: the impact of Islamic rhetoric and Shari'a-based norms grew in the public sphere, where many young self-styled theologians were ready to promote such ideas.[10]

One of the other means by which the government tried to appease the strict Islamists was the encouragement of young Saudis to travel to Afghanistan to fight the invading forces of the Soviet Union. Starting in 1979 and throughout the 1980s, thousands of Saudis volunteered to go on this mission (as many as 25,000 Saudis may have received military training or experience abroad since 1979, according to Saudi intelligence).[11] This venture was depicted as *jihad* for Islam and Allah. While the actual periods of training and fighting for most of them seldom lasted longer than the summer holidays and many never made it across the border from Pakistan to Afghanistan, for those who actually fought, the experience was profoundly transformative. The notion of fighting a foreign superpower in the name of Islam, and winning, as was the case against the Soviet Union in Afghanistan, and the guerrilla tactics by which the fighters defeated the Soviet Union, became symbols for future action by the "Afghani" Saudis. They saw themselves as *mujahidin*, with a fanatic and violent worldview. This is also where their "home base" (in Arabic, al Qaeda), in Afghanistan, turned into the iconic name of their organization.

Another factor which attenuated the restraint on violent Wahhabi activities was the tainted image of the royal leaders. In the 1990s new issues of criticism concerning deficiencies in the Royal Family came to dominate the public views, and were expressed in new modes of activity. The fact that the Royal Family had failed to devise a successful strategy to stop Iraq's invasion of Kuwait and a possible attack into Saudi territories, despite all the money that had been invested in new weapons, which resulted in King Fahd's invitation to Western forces in August 1990 to defend the Kingdom from an Iraqi invasion, further eroded their image as beneficiaries of invincibility and political wisdom. A new image was attached to the royal leaders, attributing to them administrative malfeasance, nepotism and preferential appointments that discriminated against many Saudis who were "outside the loop." They were also accused of corruption and leading a hedonistic lifestyle. The fact that the three supreme leaders, King Fahd (b. 1921), his half-brother Crown Prince ʿAbdullah (b. 1923), and the King's full brother and Minister of Defense Sultan (b. 1924) were old men, and the fact that King Fahd suffered a stroke in 1996, further indicated their eroding ability to rule. Moreover, these leaders were divided into family factions who made it clear that problems of royal succession also affected their conduct. There were King Fahd and his six full brothers, all of them in senior positions, including Minister of Defense Sultan and Minister of Interior Naif. Crown Prince Abdullah led a counter-faction.[12]

In a series of petitions, notably in May 1991 and September 1992, yet another factor accounting for the reawakening of violent Islam was expressed. This concerned criticism of the regime and demands for improvement. The petitions called, among other things, for the creation of an independent consultative council which would provide advice to the ruler on various issues. They also called for fair sharing of the oil income, for restrictions on corrupt officials and for ceasing appointments in the public administration of Royal Family cronies. There was also a call to re-establish the judiciary as an independent institution.[13] While these demands reflected a deep sense of dissatisfaction with the pillars of "Faysal's Order" in particular, and with the Saudi regime in general, the criticism that had the most impact on the emergence of a new, violent opposition concerned King Fahd's decision to invite Western, US-led forces to base themselves in the Gulf area within Saudi Arabian territory in 1990. Further, these US forces were going to fight Iraq in order to liberate Kuwait from Iraqi occupation, which meant that US forces based in Saudi Arabia would be fighting against what most Saudis considered to be a fellow Muslim state. Most ordinary Saudis accepted the US–Saudi alliance as a strategic necessity, but the petitioners were critical of Saudi reliance on Western forces for the Kingdom's defense, and of US forces fighting Iraq.

Moreover, in the mid-1990s, the Saudi alliance with the United States was regarded in religious terms as a symbol of wrongdoing on the part of the Kingdom's leaders. In the eyes of Saudi "Afghanis" and disciples of Saudi preachers, this was deemed as succumbing to an incursion by foreign Crusaders. They viewed this as a bond with an infidel power; that its forces were being stationed on Saudi land defiled the sanctity of Saudi Arabia as the home of the two Holy Places. Criticism was voiced by groups of active Islamists who claimed that the Saudi king, as a Muslim leader, was forbidden to align Saudi Arabia with an infidel force to fight another Muslim state. The king, they claimed, could only embark on war in favor of Muslim interests. The large distance between the Gulf region, where the Western forces were stationed, and the Hijaz, where the Holy Places were located, was disregarded by these Islamists. They also ignored the fact that the Saudi government avoided signing an official military pact with the United States, and settled for an unofficial arrangement. Furthermore, the fact that the United States did not terminate its stand-off with Iraq's Saddam, and actually allowed him to continue his rule, especially after Iraq's military defeat in 1991, was regarded by some as a Washington-designed "conspiracy" to entrench its military presence throughout the Gulf and capture its oil. This conspiracy was referred to as "an attack against Islam" with universal applications. Accordingly, following the dissolution of the Soviet Union, the United States was planning to subjugate Islamic states in order to control the world[14] – a startling reverse version of Samuel Huntington's "Clash of Civilizations." To amplify their criticism, the Islamist critics focused not just on the royal leaders, but on the established clerics (*'ulama'*), members of the Supreme Council of *'ulama'*, who had justified the King's policies and provided a religious ruling (*fatwa*) to this end. The established clerics were condemned for condoning the government's corruption and misconduct, notably the Saudi alliance with the US, thus failing to conform to true Islam. The Islamists claimed that the established clerics were betraying their mission and turning into part of the establishment. The fact that the main Saudi cleric 'Abd al-'Aziz Bin Baz probably co-signed the first petition (but his name did not appear on subsequent petitions) did not change the tone or target of the critics. They tried to delegitimize the moral and religious foundation of the royal leaders as a means to delegitimize the latters' policies.[15]

Crystallizing trends of militant Islamic opposition

In the early 1990s, three main trends resulted from the above-mentioned motives. One consisted of clerics, which scholars and journalists called the Islamic awakening (*Sahwa*), who were considered by the government as "peripheral" in political terms. They were younger than the leading and known *'ulama'* of the establishment, and were not schooled solely in the Wahhabi doctrine. Their sermons espoused a blend of common Wahhabi and Muslim Brotherhood contemporary political ideas. The most salient among them were Safar al-Hawali, who had been Dean of the Islamic Studies Faculty in the Umm al-Qura University in Mecca; Salman al-'Awda, a native of the pious Wahhabi town Burayda in the al-Qasim area who taught at the Imam Muhammad University in Riyadh; and 'Aid al-Qarni of Abha in the 'Asir area. They voiced fierce criticism against the established *'ulama'*, who followed the policies of the Royal Family. They depicted the enemy as "the West" and "the secularists" who favored Western ways (*'ilmaniyyin*) as its servants. The war with Iraq in 1991 was a wanton ambush by the West on a fellow Islamic state. They demanded an effective advisory role to the rulers for Islamic clergymen, but only for "worthy" Islamicists of the new, independent type, rather than the existing supreme but too established ones. The government must follow (as raised in the 1992 petition) Islamic interests, carried out by an Islamic party. Thus, the legitimacy of the Saudi government and of its supporting clergy was doubted: Shari'a Islamic values must supersede them. These clerics gained popular support by spreading their sermons through the media of cassettes and writings. A popular protest gathered in favor of al-Hawali, and al-Awdah's arrest by the government in 1994 attracted several thousand supporters.[16]

A by-product of the *Sahwa* clerics' activities was the establishment of an Islamist opposition organization in May 1993, the Committee for the Defense of Legitimate Rights (CDLR, Lajnat al-Difa' 'an al-Huquq al-Shar'iyya). This group also openly defied the policies of the government. Its leader Muhammad al-Mas'ari, a Professor of Physics and an amateur Islamist, was exiled by the government in 1995. His activities then continued from London, where he and his second-in-command Sa'd al-Faqih (who thereon split from Mas'ari and established the Movement for Islamic Reform – MIRA) launched what Ma'moun Fandy called a "cyber opposition" campaign against the Saudi government.[17]

A second trend was manifested in several flare-ups in the provinces. Saudi society consisted of tribal, regional groupings that had never formed a unified nation. Instead, Saudi groupings continued to exhibit regional-tribal characteristics that influenced their cultural and political conduct. Thus, one active religious opposition emerged in 'Asir. This drew on the unemployed elements of the local Ghamid tribe, and on the massive number (*c*.2,000) of 'Asiris who had fought in Afghanistan and developed a "*jihadi*" animus against the superpowers and their local supporters. Interestingly, the 'Asiris, who had an ethnic bond with Yemenis, became close with the Yemeni *jihadists* in Afghanistan. Through these contacts they were exposed to Egyptian Muslim Brotherhood ideologies via a Yemeni-fundamentalist clergyman 'Abd al-Majid al-Zindani, who had been in Afghanistan and acquainted himself with the 'Asiris. Zindani's ideas drew on those of Sayyid Qutb, which propagated the view that the West and its "subservient" Arab allies were nothing but a new idolatry, and that these regimes should be destroyed as the Prophet Muhammad had destroyed the pre-Islamic idol-worshipers.[18]

Zindani himself had known Osama bin Laden in Afghanistan, and had influenced his thought. A group of Zindani's followers in Yemen were behind the attack on the US warship *Cole* in October 2000 in Aden – an act that considerably inspired the 'Asiris. Several 'Asiris were among the 15 Saudi citizens who took part in the attacks of 11 September 2001. The town of Abha, the capital of 'Asir, which is also the seat of a college for Shari'a studies, became the center of an insurgent religious movement, which produced members of al Qaeda and many of its supporters. Thus, the ideas of the Muslim Brotherhood, channeled through Yemen, penetrated Saudi Arabia and gathered momentum in 'Asir.[19]

A different flare-up of opposition evolved in the northern region of al-Jawf which borders Jordan and Iraq. There, in response to the outbreak of the Palestinian Intifada, and to what appeared to be passive and limited assistance provided to the Intifada by the Arab states, some 4,000 inhabitants of al-Jawf, notably from its main town al-Sakaka, initiated a continuous series of pro-Palestinian demonstrations that often turned into riots. In 2002 to 2003, their slogans were critical of the Saudi Royal Family, and their frustration reflected both the spread of unemployment and radical Islamic preaching typical of this region. Political violence continued into 2004, when unofficial news spread of the assassinations of the region's deputy governor and the police chief of the region's top Shari'a court.[20] As in 'Asir, the Muslim Brotherhood opposition elements were often influenced by fundamentalist principles stemming from the Jordanian–Palestinian Hizb al-Tahrir party, which rejected any regime not fully based on Shari'a principles.

Likewise, certain bastions of opposition emerged in places such as the southern part of the Gulf, where the Dawasir tribe roamed. That area, as well as the cities of al-Qasim, north of Riyadh, produced a number of Wahhabi radicals. In the Hijazi cities, activities of anti-Saudi groups were also reported. In these two areas, as in 'Asir and al-Jawf, opposition feelings were kindled by local, tribal and regional loyalties that originated from pre-Saudi occupation in the 1920s. Such feelings rose again as the luster of the Saudi Royal House period began to fade. Moreover, these feelings were also influenced by the non-Wahhabi Islamic denominations that had governed these regions before the Saudi occupation. Although Wahhabi norms became the prescribed legal denomination of the Saudi State, Shafi'i principles, which had been the erstwhile religious denomination[21] of the majority in the Hijaz and 'Asir, had not completely disappeared.

A third Islamic opposition trend was manifested in the underground formation of al Qaeda cells, consisting mainly of returned *mujahidin* from Afghanistan, who aligned with provincial opposition activists. Osama bin Laden presumably came from a Shafi'i family, true of many inhabitants of Hawdramat (South Yemen) where his family had originated. However, it seems that bin Laden used this position not to reject Wahhabism, but, in fact, to approach it from the viewpoint of an "outsider" who was interested in minimizing the differences between the Shafi'i and the dominant Wahhabi denominations. Thus, he tried to bring various denominations as well as Muslim Brotherhood principles together and to bridge the differences among them. Likewise, he sought to unify Muslims of different nations: Yemeni, Saudi, Palestinians, Egyptians, Afghanis and Pakistanis. This was manifested in the actual formation of al Qaeda during the early 1980s in Afghanistan, where fighters from those countries were operating together under the joint religious leadership of clergymen such as Zindani of Yemen, Zawahiri of Egypt, the Palestinian Azzam and others.[22] In addition to the above-mentioned 'Asiris, there were probably hundreds of Saudis from the Hijaz, al-Qasim and Najd who had gone to Afghanistan in the 1980s and returned to Saudi Arabia in the 1990s with experiences of fighting and expelling a superpower from a Muslim territory.

The common denominator of these al Qaeda elements was an ideological principal, over-simplified but widely supported: to create Shari'a rule, fight Western "occupying forces" (i.e., those stationed in Muslim states), and to weaken the local regimes that support them.[23] Bin Laden led the Saudi opposition up the ladder of extremism to levels higher than any of his predecessors. First, because he accused King Fahd personally of *shirk* for serving an infidel power, the United States, and for acting as a legislator over the Saudi state, which is a role reserved for God. Second, because he advocated that *jihad* should spread to all the "occupied" Muslim communities, beginning with Saudi Arabia which had become "a colony of the US." Accordingly, *jihad* must even reach the heart of the United States. Echoing the killer of President Sadat, he declared that George W. Bush was the "Pharaoh" of these times who must be destroyed.[24]

After leaving the Kingdom in 1994 for Sudan, bin Laden re-established al Qaeda along the lines of a universal body capable of attacking targets all over the globe.[25] The Saudi authorities viewed him as a dissident and stripped him of his Saudi citizenship in 1994, preferring to keep him away from the Kingdom. The authorities ignored his activities, which included channeling money to terrorist causes, on the condition that he would not return to act in the Kingdom itself. A tacit agreement might have been concluded between bin Laden and the Saudi Secret Services to this effect. One Saudi official may have alluded to such an understanding when he said, "Isn't it better to go off and fight a foreign *jihad* rather than hang around the [Saudi] mosques without a job and cause trouble in Saudi Arabia?"[26] However, the tacit cooperation with bin Laden lasted only until May 2003, when his followers started terrorizing the Kingdom.

In conclusion, it seems that three strands were at work in the Saudi opposition. The first was the "wild" stream of mainly Wahhabis, consisting of people who were critical of the Saudi leadership and its cooperation with the West, in particular. They rejected the authority of the established *'ulama'* and preached for *jihad* and *tafkir*. Most of them were clergymen supported by their followers, continuing the roles of Hawali and 'Awdah. The second consisted of provincial anti-government groups motivated by socio-economic, tribal and religious causes. They were of mixed denominations, some of them former Shafi'is, but who were, however, cooperating with, and open to, the radical Wahhabis. A third strand drew on al Qaeda activists, consisting mainly of former "Afghani" fighters, and advocating bin Laden's extremist ideology.

The *Sahwa* advocated a religion-dominated lifestyle and its members were very critical of the establishment. Three main clergymen are worth mentioning. Muhammad bin 'Uqla al-Shu'aybi was active in Buraydah in the region of al-Qasim, and justified the September 11 attacks against the United States. He issued a religious ruling that anybody who supported an infidel during a war with a Muslim party would also be regarded as an infidel. This wording seemed to be a call against Saudi leaders. Shu'aybi justified actions against the US as a "*jihad* against the US and its following countries." He hailed and identified with al Qaeda, but did not join its ranks.[27] In Riyadh, Ali al-Khudayr issued religious rulings against moderate clerics, journalists and thinkers who called for co-existence with the West. In the words of a critic of al-Khudayr, his rulings manifested "exclusion, monopoly over truth … [and] the criminalization of opponents."[28] Nasr al-Fahd of Riyadh stood out as another clergyman, and a member of a relatively well-to-do family, who propagated views similar to those of Ali al-Khudayr.

Khudayr, Fahd and another cleric, Ahmad Khalidi, published a ruling in May 2003 following the initial terrorist activities of al Qaeda in the Kingdom, stating that the present *jihad* was an act of defense for the existence of Islam (*Jihad al-Daf'*) and was therefore fully justified. Moreover, under these circumstances, the collateral killing of Muslims in such an action was also justified. These three clerics also forbade the Saudis from surrendering to the authorities 19 wanted Islamic activists who were suspected of participating in the terrorist actions of May 2003. Their surrender and detention would be tantamount to helping "the Crusaders."[29]

These clergymen were not participants in terrorist groups. Rather, they voiced their arguments through the Internet and/or by preaching in mosques, and their messages were sometimes propagated by means of audio and video cassettes.[30] Their influence was in their ability to introduce an opposition agenda that most Saudis had to either agree with or reject. They were able to place a question mark on the Kingdom's cooperation with the West; cooperation that had hitherto prevailed. Moreover, they addressed the issue of political violence as a legitimate tool to be used in Saudi relations with the West, vis-à-vis lenient Saudis who were willing to compromise their religion by justifying the price of innocent Muslims, even Saudis, being killed as collateral damage.[31] However, they did not call for direct revolutionary action against their leaders or for a complete downfall of the Saudi regime. They did not cross this barrier.

The second group embarked on terrorist activities. Sporadic activities had occurred in earlier years, but a full campaign of terrorism commenced on 12 May 2003. This was in response to the American occupation of Iraq, which was tacitly and covertly supported by the Saudi government and, to some degree, received overt Saudi assistance, notably in servicing US air strikes. The terrorist activity was also a pre-emptive action against the Saudi government which was planning to arrest many of al Qaeda's activists. Bin Laden himself and Saudi al Qaeda leaders were presumably those who decided to depart from the cease-fire that had prevailed between al Qaeda and the Saudi authorities. To be sure, the turning of al Qaeda to carry out terrorism against the Kingdom was secondary to al Qaeda's insurgency in Iraq: the US occupation made Iraq arenas conducive to guerrilla attacks against the US forces. The attacks in Saudi Arabia only derived from this main goal.[32] The attacks in Saudi Arabia were not a full-fledged *jihad*, but only a sideshow of it. Al Qaeda leaders activated what had probably been dormant cells of members residing in the Kingdom.

The al Qaeda organization in the Arabian Peninsula under bin Laden focused on attenuating Western, notably the US's standing in the Kingdom, ultimately seeking its elimination and overthrowing the Saudi monarchy. The initial regional organization of al Qaeda was led by Yusuf al-ʿAyiri, of Yemeni origin, who reported directly to bin Laden. ʿAyiri and his lieutenants were responsible for setting up five autonomous cells which would be exclusively focused on operations in Saudi Arabia. ʿAyiri was killed by Saudi forces in an operation on 31 May 2003. His organization, however, was able to establish an entire infrastructure of safe houses, ammunition depots and a support network.[33] This impression is also evident from the words of another al Qaeda commander, ʿAbd al-ʿAziz al-Muqrin, who addressed his people in what he called "bastions and regiments" in the "mountains, cities and among the sympathizers." While al-Muqrin's words may not be completely reliable, it is clear that terrorist groups rooted themselves in major cities, in the Gulf and Najd, and in rural areas, such as al-Jawf and ʿAsir. The discovery of stashes of arms and ammunition in such places, arrests of terrorists, as well as their actual activities, demonstrate that they were indeed able to spread out.[34]

Following the study by Anthony Cordesman and Nawaf Obaid, the five cells established by ʿAyiri were the centers from which all terrorist activity directed against the Saudi state originated. The first cell was the largest and the strongest, and was directly responsible for the May 2003 attacks headed by Turki al-Dandani, and was the first group to demonstrate that al Qaeda had become a major threat within the Arabian Peninsula. The second cell, headed by ʿAli ʿAbd-al Rahman al-Fuqasi al-Ghamdi, carried out the May 12 attacks in Riyadh. The third cell was led by a Yemeni national, Khalid al-Hajj, who was thought by some to be the actual, "real head" of the al Qaeda network in Saudi Arabia. Al-Muqrin was the leader of the fourth cell, which was largely responsible for the November 2003 bombings. He then became leader of the entire organization in

Saudi Arabia, and was subsequently killed in a clash with government forces in June 2004. However, it was the fifth cell that proved to be the most important, for this was where the other cell members took refuge after their own strong-holds had been destroyed by the government's counter-terrorist activities. The fifth cell became the most prolific in Saudi Arabia. This cell was also respons-ible for generating the heaviest impact, such as the December 29 bombings of the Interior Ministry and the Security Recruitment Office, as well as other major attacks in 2004. During the fighting, 'Ayiri and other commanders were killed and replaced by lower-ranking activists.[35]

In terms of their geo-socio background, two main points can be concluded. First, examining the background of the list of the 26 "most-wanted" al Qaeda activists, as publicized by the Saudi authorities (23 of them were Saudi citizens), no special pattern can yet be detected. Ten of them came from tribal origins, from nine tribal groups which have been identified as Bedouin, spread all over the various provinces in the Kingdom. The other 13 came from four urban regions: Najd, al-Qasim, Mecca and al-Jizan (in 'Asir). Al Qaeda definitely found recruits in a variety of regions.[36]

There were protracted disagreements among the leaders with regard to the timing and potential targets of attack. 'Ayiri was often very vocal with his con-cerns regarding the poor preparation among his fellow members, as well as the lack of time, shortage of resources and insufficiency of supply routes from Yemen. In addition, with recruitment not being as high as expected, there were various issues which concerned 'Ayiri enough to postpone the missions, despite other al Qaeda members wanting to forge ahead. For example, Ayman al-Zawahiri, an Egyptian surgeon who became theological adviser to bin Laden, disagreed with 'Ayiri and felt that rather than continued preparation, operations should begin immediately.[37] Despite the traditional al Qaeda approach of extreme patience and a slow and steady development of support networks capable of inflicting a major attack, Zawahiri's suggestion of attacking soft targets repeatedly, such as Americans inside of Saudi Arabia as a way of para-lyzing the Saudi government, was the actual approach taken. However, with time this method proved to be a miscalculation, and was later overruled by bin Laden because it compromised popular support and, thereby, the future strength of al Qaeda.

However, the second point concerns the impression or perception among al Qaeda members that "95 percent of the al Qaeda activists were Yemenis." This impression voiced by bin Laden's former bodyguard Nasir al-Bahri attests to the fact that Yemenis, either from 'Asir or Yemen itself, were bin Laden's ethnic compatriots, presumably of the Shafi'i denomination, and most receptive to his call.[38] The few details known about Salih al-'Awfi, who had become al Qaeda's leader in Saudi Arabia after Muqrin's death until he was captured by the Saudi authorities in December 2004, exemplifies this pattern. A native of 'Asir, 'Awfi served in the Saudi army for four years as a military jailer but was dismissed in 1992. Bitter at the Saudi authorities, he spent several years in Afghanistan. He returned for healthcare and tried to open a car dealership business in Riyadh.

He then visited Germany several times, where he met members of al Qaeda cells. He was then assigned by bin Laden to help establish the Saudi network of al Qaeda in the Kingdom.[39] Thus, 'Awfi represents a relatively uneducated person who lost even a menial job in the Saudi army. He was then driven by economic and ideological reasons to join al Qaeda. The number of activists like 'Awfi is not clear, but there were thousands of sympathizers mostly among students, lower-class blue-collar professionals, leavers of the army and National Guard (a tribal-based army unit). Ideologically, the *jihadi* activists in Saudi Arabia were adamant in pursuing an extremist line. Their ideas became known in the Saudi press as "extremist thought" (*tatarruf fikri*). Unlike some of the *Sahwa* clerics, who recanted their previous support for indiscriminate killing, al Qaeda activists stressed that it was justified to kill Saudi citizens, together with Westerners, due to the Saudi leaders' persecution of al Qaeda activists after the 11 September 2001 events and after they had strayed from the appropriate Islamic path. As such, Saudi officials and administrators, let alone members of the armed forces, were considered legitimate targets for killing, a mode which Saudi extremists did not condone.[40] Suleiman al-Dawasri, a *"jihad* fighter," depicted *jihad* as an absolute duty aimed to liberate the oppressed, all of them true Muslims, from those who turned their backs on true Islam and allowed the Land of the two Holy Places to be occupied by "American women soldiers." Thus, the license to fight the Saudi government was unquestionable.[41] Al Qaeda's members boast about their eagerness and readiness to fight and slay their enemies and, if necessary, to die. This zeal for the cause was manifested in al Qaeda's electronic paper *Sawt al-Jihad*, which continuously published "heroisms."[42]

In terms of its development, Saudi terrorism can be divided into three main stages. (1) From May to August 2003, when the attacks were directed against Westerners, notably Americans, residing in Saudi Arabia, mainly in residential and military compounds. (2) Between August and November 2003, when the attacks were directed against Saudi security forces and offices. Saudi civilians, in cars or as bystanders, were also targeted. As a consequence, the perpetrators came under mounting criticism for the bloodshed, even from sympathetic clergymen, such as Khudayr and al-Fahd. As a result, the terrorists began to choose their targets more carefully. (3) Between November 2003 and throughout 2004, they turned mainly to abductions and killing Western residents and visitors who had been working for the Saudi security bodies. These were more limited operations which nevertheless caused a continuous backlash in Saudi cities.

The terrorists did not attack main oil installations or major government ministries, or perhaps failed in their attempts to do so. Nevertheless, the terrorists had achieved one main goal in their struggle: they were able to pose a strategic "image threat" to the Kingdom. The possibility of attacks on oil installations caused Saudi leaders to press other oil-exporting states to lower prices and increase their own production and sales, so as to maintain a high level of supply and keep the price around $50 per barrel. The Saudis did not want the terrorist attacks to affect the price of oil, which, in turn, could hurt Western economies. The Saudi leaders, however, feared anti-Western public opinion and therefore also did not want to appear to be too cooperative with the West. However, their fear of losing credit in Western markets was a real threat, which the Saudi leaders had to avert. Moreover, a mark of uncertainty concerning the Kingdom's internal dismantling spread in the West, which cast a doubt on the image of stability attributed to Saudi Arabia.[43]

Al Qaeda's shortcomings and Saudi responses

Saudi intelligence had been receiving information throughout the 1990s regarding the planning and interworkings of al Qaeda but did not embark on an actual response until 2003. Following the 12 May 2003 attacks in Riyadh, a list of senior operatives connected to 'Ayiri was drawn up and the first al Qaeda cell was infiltrated by the Saudi government.[44] As a result of this raid, al-Ghamdi surrendered and al-Dandani was killed, and the rest of the remaining members fled, later reconnecting with various other nascent cells. This dispersion caused problems for other cells, which, from thereon, were forced to share their resources, thus lowering their own supplies. The influx of new members also undermined their autonomy, making it easier for the Saudi government to infiltrate the remaining cells.

Rebuilding the network was difficult. The leaders appointed after Ghamdi were not successful in creating their own cells. In addition, 'Ayiri was killed in a shoot-out with Saudi security forces at a road-block in late May 2003. Later, in March 2004, Khalid Ali Hajj was ambushed and killed by Saudi security forces in Riyadh, and was succeeded by Muqrin until his death in June 2004.[45] Once this top tier of leadership was destroyed, less experienced militants took charge, which also served to weaken the power of each individual cell and the network as a whole. Moreover, a major weakness of the al Qaeda organization has been its poor recruitment effort and turnout. Although bin Laden expected a much larger turnout of recruits and volunteers to replace those who had been lost, this was not actually the case. The heavy blows that the Saudi government forces had dealt to the top ranks of the organization severely depleted the quality of the leadership and members, and even forced al Qaeda to begin recruiting young and very inexperienced men to their call for *jihad*.[46] Due to these shortcomings, the al Qaeda network in Saudi Arabia did not evolve into a full-fledged guerrilla organization, neither deeply spread out nor widely supported by society. Al Qaeda had many sympathizers, but the structure remained that of a small, limited underground.

The Saudi response to the new crop of militants was able to severely affect the capability of al Qaeda by mid-2004. Due to lack of manpower and infrastructure, the militants were often forced to carry out missions hastily and without proper planning. However, despite the problems facing al Qaeda, it still remained a serious threat to the safety of Saudi civilians and the foreign population living on Saudi soil. Al Qaeda remains committed to funding, training and encouraging future operations on Saudi territory, as well as in other countries (such as Iraq and Chechnya), as does Saudi Arabia to deterring it.

The events of 11 September 2001 brought a considerable amount of attention to Saudi Arabia and its efforts in combating militarism. As a result, a few weeks after the attacks, Saudi Arabia agreed that it would allow US planes and troops stationed in that country to participate in military action against bin Laden in the war in Afghanistan.[47] On 20 September 2001, the Kingdom also announced that it would sever ties with the Taliban on the grounds that the Taliban government "continues to use lands to harbor, arm, and encourage those criminals [al Qaeda] in carrying out terrorist atrocities which horrify those who believe in peace and the innocent and spread terror and destruction in the world."[48]

Additional security actions were also taken in Saudi Arabia. After 11 September 2001, over 600 individuals were detained, and nearly 2,000 were questioned about suspected ties to terrorism. Since the period following May 2003, other than the direct penetration of al Qaeda cells, the security arrangements in many locations throughout Saudi Arabia have improved, especially at public buildings and residential facilities. Through its cooperation with notably Western countries, Saudi Arabia learned of new techniques and programs and is now better able to organize the Ministry of the Interior, the National Guard and the regular military forces. Al Qaeda's campaign therefore had a drastic but limited effect.

Despite allegations which appeared in some Western media publications that the Kingdom had participated and furnished material in order to support al Qaeda, specifically in the September 11 attacks, the US "9/11 Commission" found that no such evidence existed.[49] The Commission's report also denied that Saudi nationals were inappropriately allowed to leave the United States in the days following the attacks. Although this report clearly absolves Saudi Arabia from any direct financial connection with al Qaeda, the Commission did acknowledge the failure of the government to properly supervise Islamic charities within the Kingdom.[50]

The Saudi government was ambivalent towards the radical developments evolving in their Kingdom. On one hand, they sought to suppress radicalism which could endanger their regime. On the other hand, the authorities could not turn their backs on Wahhabi Islam, which was the legitimizing cornerstone of their regime. Therefore, they denounced the radicals, but continued to nurture Islam. In the same vein, the Saudi authorities were directing radicals to advance Islamic causes in other states: they allowed private funds to be channeled through charity foundations to support mosques and Islamic community activists in Africa, Central Asia, Europe and the United States. In fact, these funds were often channeled for terrorist activities. For example, the al-Haramayn Foundation was used to facilitate *jihadi* groups in Chechnya and the Balkans. Saudi funds were passed on to Hamas fighters and also to families of Palestinians who had been killed in the Al-Aqsa Intifada. The Saudi Minister of the Interior Na'if ibn ʿAbd al-ʿAziz headed a foundation for the compensation of participants in the Intifada.[51]

Likewise, the Saudi authorities did not stop the radicals' preaching, but rather in 1997 established a new supreme council of the *'ulama'*, the main aim of which was to overrule the religious opinions of the radicals on their "home ground," i.e., in Islamic terms, through religious rulings. Thus, in recent years, members of the supreme council have been arguing two main points. The first, that the radicals' activities, notably those of the terrorists, precipitate internal struggle and chaos (*fitna*) among believers which is counter-productive and forbidden by the Shari'a. The second is that the king, who is also the leader (*imam*) of the Wahhabi community, has the right to make supreme policy decisions. This right was reinforced in the Basic Law that the Saudi government legislated in 1992, to offset any attempt to shatter the fabric of the Saudi regime. Hence, by using precedents from the Prophet Muhammad's conduct, they argue that the king alone possesses the right to declare *jihad* and/or to cooperate with foreign, even "infidel," forces. This demonstrates that the authorities do not wish merely to use force to suppress the terrorist opposition, but also to win the public debate concerning the king's authority to align Saudi Arabia with the US for defense purposes. Other tactics were also used. One was to "bring back" the exaggerating elements that had gone "too far" in their religious interpretation. In a comment made by Crown Prince 'Abdullah in late May 2004 (after the government had used force to eliminate four main terrorists), he called upon those who "went astray" to return to the "right path." In so doing, the government sought to avoid a major internal conflict and to depict the terrorists as a marginal and containable problem. Moreover, 'Abdullah's declaration, made at the same time, that the "Zionists" had loomed behind many of the Saudi terrorist incidents was designed to cause a similar effect: to direct the accusation of terrorism towards common, foreign enemies of Islam, as Zionists were considered to be, rather than towards indigenous Saudis.[52]

Another main Saudi effort to ease the government's tension with the extremists (the *'ulama'* as well as with al Qaeda members) was the initiative to embark on a "national dialogue" (*al-Hiwar al-Watani*), which Crown Prince 'Abdullah initiated in November 2002. Overtly, the meeting's goal was to create cooperation among groups distant from the center: Shi'a, youth, women and clergymen of various denominations. However, a more covert, political and immediate aim of this initiative was to present to the public the religious opinions of relatively moderate clergymen, who would counteract and discredit the arguments of the radicals. The parties embarked on a duel of rulings and more opinions entered the dialogue, turning it into a broad discourse. The highlights of this discourse were demands made by "liberal" elements to allow a greater measure of freedom of the press and to implement a promise, already made by the government in 1992, to hold elections for provincial councils. These signs of "democratization" and "reform" were appreciated in the United States. The Minister of the Interior, Prince Naif, made it clear, however, that Western hopes to turn the Kingdom into a "Constitutional Monarchy" were premature. For example, Prince Naif stated in April 2003 that election results can be fixed in advance, or, to put it simply, that democratization was not an immediate option. In June 2003, a journalist, Jamal Hashoogy, the former editor of the daily *al-Watan*, entered this discourse by stating that the Saudis should learn not only from the writings of Ibn-Taymiyya – one of the most radical Islamist thinkers who inspired the ideas of *takfir* – but those of other, more moderate thinkers as well. Hashoogy lost his job as editor, but his statement, accompanied by others espousing a similar message, indicated that various opinions were vying for dominance, and that the *jihadist* position had not won over the public.[53]

In a broader context, the national dialogue could be viewed as an attempt to create a new ideological solidarity, or a new consensus among the different religious trends. As such, it had a healing, state-building function: to rebuild stability in Saudi society and to do so through open discourse. In such a discourse, the voices of religious radicals would be diluted and mixed with more moderate preachings, so as to blunt the edge of the radicals' works and depict terrorism as a marginal issue. The rise of more moderate, yet active and vocal clerics in the public sphere manifests that this policy had some relative success.[54] Moreover, a successful initiative in this regard was the government's ability to persuade some of the *Sahwa* clerics to take back their earlier support of the "*jihadists.*" Following several months' detention in a Saudi prison, Ali al-Khudayr and Nasr al-Fahd, as well as Salman al-ʿAwda, stated publicly that indiscriminate killing of Muslims and defiance of the Saudi leader were forbidden and would lead to internal unrest (*fitna*).[55] This caused controversy between the *Sahwa* and the *jihadists*, embarrassing the latter and which weakened their arguments.

The government probably did not believe in its ability to overpower terrorism by means of public discourse; therefore, it did not shy away from using force. Since May 2003, about 1,000 suspects have been detained, and about 2,000 clergymen have been questioned. Security forces cracked down on several terrorist cells, discovering and destroying tons of explosives and arms. Several "charity foundations" that had been channeling money for the funding of terrorism, notably the al-Haramayn fund, were shut down. Shoot-outs with terrorists occurred daily. The series of blows peaked in June 2004 when some of the leading terrorists were killed, leading to a lull in the terrorist activity. However, the infrastructure of many young Saudi cells still exists and can be reset into an operational mode.

In summary, the radical potential in the Wahhabi upbringing of Saudi extremists and the globalized connection with radical Muslims in other states and centers still exists. The readiness of bin Laden to start another campaign is also in no doubt. The possibility of a new extremist, or terrorist, wave in Saudi Arabia is most tangible.

Notes

1 R. Bayly Winder, *Saudi Arabia in the 19th Century*, London: Macmillan, 1965; J. Kostiner, *The Making of Saudi Arabia, from Chieftaincy to Monarchical State, 1916–1936*, New York: Oxford University Press, 1993.

2 A. al-Yasini, *Religion and State in the Kingdom of Saudi Arabia*, Boulder, CO: West-view Press, 1985, pp. 68–70.

3 J. Kostiner, "On Instruments and Their Designers: The Ikhwan of Najd and the Formation of the Saudi State," *Middle Eastern Studies*, 1985, vol. 21, pp. 298–323.

4 Al-Yasini, op. cit., pp. 41–103.

5 D. Champion, *The Paradoxical Kingdom*, New York: Columbia University Press, 2003, pp. 8–11, 63–109.

6 J. Buchan, "The Return of the Ikhwan, 1979," in D. Holden and R. Johns, *The House of Saud*, New York: Holt, Rinehart & Winston, 1982, pp. 511–526.

7 M. Collins Dunn, "Is the Sky Falling?," *The Middle East*, July–August, 1994; *Middle East Economic Digest*, 9 August 1996; O. Winckler, *Arab Political Demography*, vol. I, Brighton: Sussex Academic Press, 2005, pp. 16–18, 43, 78–84, 96–100, 140.

8 A. Cordesman, "Saudi Arabia Enters the 21st Century," *Opposition and Islamic Extremism*, Washington DC: Center for Strategic and International Studies, December 31 2002, pp. 12–15. Available online at www.csis.org/burke/saudi21/521–04.pdf (accessed 11 September 2000).

9 J. Teitelbaum, *Holier Than Thou: Saudi Arabia's Islamic Opposition*, Washington DC: The Washington Institute for Near East Policy, 2000, pp. 1–17; U. Shavit, "Islamist Ideology, Al-Qaeda's Saudi Origins," *Middle East Quarterly*, vol. 13, 2006, pp. 3–14; A. Atwan, *The Secret History of Al-Qa'ida*, London: Saqi, 2006, pp. 150–167; S. al-Nabulsi, "Ayhuma Afraja al-Akhbar, al-Suʿudiyya Ama al-'Usuliyya Dawr al-Ikhwan al-Muslimin fi al-Usuliyya al-Irhabiyya al-Suʿudiyya" [Who Grew the Other Saudism or Fundamentalism? The Role of Muslim Brotherhood in the Saudi Fundamentalist Terrorism], 17 August 2003. Available online at www.amcoptic.com/shaker.htm (accessed 28 April 2005).

10 Teitelbaum, op. cit., p. 101; Shavit, op. cit.; H.R. Dekmejian, "The Rise of Political Islamism in Saudi Arabia," *The Middle East Journal*, 1994, vol. 48, pp. 630–636.

11 International Crisis Group, "Saudi Arabia Backgrounder: Who are the Islamists," *Middle East Report*, 21 September 2004, no. 31 (Henceforth: ICG Backgrounder); Atif So'adawa, *Mustaqbal al-Afghan al-'Arab*, The Future of the Afghani 'Arabs, Cairo: al-Dimuqratiyya, 2002, pp. 203–212.

12 S. Henderson, *After King Fahd: Succession in Saudi Arabia*, Washington DC: The Washington Institute for Near East Policy, 1995, pp. 25–37; Champion, op. cit., pp. 71–75.

13 Teitelbaum, op. cit., pp. 17–25; Dekmejian, op. cit.

14 See e.g. A. al-Shayeji, "Dangerous Perceptions: Gulf Views of the U.S. Role in the Region," *The Middle East Policy Council Journal*, October 1997, vol. 5, no. 3. pp. 1–13.

15 Teitelbaum, op. cit., pp. 115–123; G. Okrulik, "Understanding Political Dissent in Saudi Arabia," *Middle East Report Online*, 24 October 2001. Available online at www.merip.org/mero/mero102401.html (accessed 15 March 2007).

16 Teitelbaum, op. cit., pp. 28–43; M. Fandy, *Saudi Arabia and the Politics of Dissent*, New York: St. Martin's Press, 1999, pp. 61–114; T. Craig Jones, "The Clerics, the Salwa, and the Saudi State," *Strategic Insight*, 2006, vol. 4, no. 3. Available online at www.ccc.nps.navy.mil/si/2005/mar/jonesMar05.asp (accessed 3 August 2007).

17 Fandy, op. cit., pp. 115–176, 229–248.

18 Jason Burke, *Al-Qa'ida, the True Story of Radical Islam*, London: I.B. Tauris, 2004; International Crisis Group, "Saudi Arabia Backgrounder: Who Are the Islamists?," *Middle East Report*, 21 September 2004, no. 31.

19 *Majallat al-Sunna*, November 2001, no. 110.

20 M.S. Doran, "Somebody Else's Civil War," *Financial Times*, 5 October 2001; M.S.

Doran, "Palestine, Iraq and American Strategy," *Foreign Affairs*, 2003, vol. 82, pp. 26–28.

21 There are four legal-theological denominations, or schools, in Sunni Islam: Hanbali, Hanifi, Maliki and Shafi'i. Wahhabism is a puritanical derivative of the Hanbali legal school.

22 *Al-Quds, al-'Arabi*, London, 23 February 1998.

23 M. Steinberg, "The Theology and Strategy of al-Qa'ida and the Global Jihad" (in Hebrew), *Qeshet Hahadasha*, 2005, nos 12, 13, 14.

24 A. Pfarfrey (ed.), *Extreme Islam: Anti-American Propaganda of Muslim Fundamentalism*, Los Angeles; Feral House, 2001, pp. 290–292; Interview with Osama bin Laden by ABC reporter Jon Miller, May 1998. Available online at www.pbs.org/wgbh/pages/frontline/shows/binladen/who/ (accessed 15 March 2007).

25 Jon Miller, op. cit.

26 D. Jehl, "A Nation Challenged: Saudi Arabia, Holy War, Lured Saudis as Rulers Looked Away," *New York Times*, 27 December 2001.

27 *Washington Post*, 15 December 2001.

28 *Al-Watan* (Riyadh) in *Mideast Mirror*, 24 November 2003.

29 *Al-Sharq al-Awsat*, 11, 18, 30 November, 2003; Steinberg, op. cit.

30 Jones, op. cit.

31 Steinberg, op. cit.

32 See E. Karmon, "Al Qaeda and the War on Terror After the War in Iraq," *Middle East Review of International Affairs*, 2006, vol. 10, pp. 1–22; *Middle East Media Research Institute* (MEMRI), Special Dispatch Series no. 1003, 12 October 2005.

33 A. Cordesman and N. Obaid, "Al Qaeda in Saudi Arabia: Asymmetric Threats and Islamist Extremists," *Center for Strategic and International Studies*, 26 January 2005, p. 4; see also International Crisis Group, no. 31, op. cit.

34 Interview with Muqrin, *Sawt al-Jihad*, reported by MEMRI, 16 August 2004.

35 Cordesman and Obaid, op. cit., p. 4; T. Craig Jones, "Violence and the Illusion of Reform in Saudi Arabia," *Middle East Report*, 13 November 2003; *Gulf States Newsletter*, 11 June 2004, vol. 28, issue 736; On 'Ayiri, see R. Meijer, "Rereading al-Qaeda, Writings of Yusuf al-'Ayiri," *ISIM Review*, 2006, vol. 18, pp. 16–17.

36 *Al-Sharq al-Awsut*, 26 April 2005.

37 Cordesman and Obaid, op. cit., p. 5.

38 *al-Quds al-'Arabi*, 3 August 2004.

39 *Al-Watan* (Riyadh), 8 December 2003; *al-Sharq al-Awsat*, 7 December 2004.

40 *Al-Watan* (Riyadh), 31 December 2004.

41 S. Stalinsky, "The 'Islamic Affairs Department' of the Saudi Embassy in Washington, DC," *MEMRI*, 26 November 2003, Special Report no. 23.

42 See, for instance, *MEMRI*, 16 August 2004, no. 18, quoting the activist Fawwaz al-Nashmi.

43 D. Gold, *Hatred's Kingdom: How Saudi Arabia Supports the New Global Terrorism Network*, Washington DC: Regnery, 2003; International Crisis Group, "Saudi Arabia Backgrounder," op. cit.

44 A. Cordesman and N. Obaid, "Saudi Counter Terrorism Efforts: The Changing Paramilitary and Domestic Security Apparatus," *Center for Strategic and International Studies*, 2 February 2005, pp. 4–5.

45 Ibid.

46 Ibid.

47 Ibid., p. 11.

48 "U.S. Consulate Attackers are Vilified." Available online at www.news.scotsman.com.

49 Cordesman and Obaid, "Saudi Counter Terrorism Efforts," op. cit., p. 19.

50 Ibid, pp. 11–19.

51 Gold, op. cit.; see also G. Baghat, "Saudi Arabia and the War on Terrorism," *Arab Studies Quarterly*, 2004, vol. 26, pp. 51–63.
52 "Saudi Officials Reinforce Crown Prince Abdallah's Accusation that Zionists Are Behind Terror Attacks in Saudi Arabia," *MEMRI*, Special Dispatch Series, no. 726, 3 June 2004.
53 N. Raphaeli, "Demands for Reform in Saudi Arabia," *Middle Eastern Studies*, 2005, vol. 41.
54 See S. Lacroix, "Between Islamists and Liberals: Saudi Arabia's New Islam-Liberal Reformists," *Middle East Journal*, 2004, vol. 58, pp. 345–364.
55 *Al-Sharq al-Awsat*, 18 and 30 November 2003.

5   Islamic radicalism and terrorism in the European Union

The Maghrebi factor

Michael M. Laskier

The European Union (EU) hosts a variety of Islamist radicals, originating from different parts of the Muslim world. In order to better understand the Muslims in Western Europe, this chapter focuses on the status, role, and evolution of North African (Maghrebi) Islamists. The countries that receive the greatest attention here are France, Spain, Italy, The Netherlands and Belgium.

Europe rarely offers census information based on ethnic and religious groups. Despite the lack of data indicating the precise number of Maghrebis in the EU, partial findings corroborate that they are a sizeable force. For example, the majority of Belgium's Muslims are Moroccans. In Denmark, of the 270,000 Muslims, the majority originate from Morocco. Of France's six million Muslims, 70 percent are from Algeria, Morocco and Tunisia. Italy hosts 825,000 Muslims, with the majority originating from Morocco, and smaller groups coming from Tunisia and Algeria. In The Netherlands, of the nearly one million Muslims, the largest group is the Moroccans. Spain's Muslims, numbering almost a million, are predominantly Maghrebi (the great majority Moroccans). EU states such as Sweden, Switzerland, the UK, and Germany also have Muslim communities of which only a tiny percentage are Maghrebi.

There are deep feelings of frustration among European Muslims from the Maghreb. These feelings do not apply to first-generation Muslim immigrants who are in their sixties, but to the second and third generations, mostly European-born Muslims, and to younger immigrants. The second-generation Muslims fall into the age range of 30 to 50, while the third generation consists of those under the age of 30 who are the children of the second generation.

Undeniably, the Maghrebi Muslims, especially in France, have encountered diverse forms of racism and exclusion at different periods over the past several decades. The decrease in dependence on unskilled workers coupled with the decline of heavy industry since the 1970s and 1980s exacerbated unemployment rates. These realities angered Muslim youth and discouraged them from integrating into Europe and embracing humanist and liberal values.[1] They oppose assimilation into European society and turn to the different strands of Islamism.

This assessment is elaborated upon by Jonathan Laurence and Justin Vaisse, who argue that since 2000, the French tightened policies vis-à-vis Muslims in their neighborhoods, harassed youths, and performed arbitrary arrests. The end

result produced strained relations with disgruntled teenagers. An equally aggravating factor was the continued de facto ghettoization and slum culture. There
were "tough" neighborhoods in other parts of the EU, but not quite as bleak as
the French slums. These neighborhoods encouraged self-destructive behavior.[2]
The unglamorous concrete-slab *cités* in which Muslims dwelt were abandoned
over the years by those who could afford to leave: first, by the French blue-
collar workers and later by more successful immigrants. The population that
remained consisted of the Muslim underclass that wallowed in unimaginable
misery: school underperformance, unemployment, and drug-trafficking. With
high unemployment, the slums also became milieus of profound boredom. When
local associations and community programs were severely underfunded, the
communities became stagnant, without activities for residents.

These were not the only motives for the radicalization among Maghrebi and
other Muslims. Ideological reasons rooted in internal and external religious and
political influences, and pressures of global Islamism were added determinants
that outweighed socioeconomics. This study addresses the pivotal issues of (1)
immigration, communal leadership, and organizations versus the proliferation of
radical Islamist groups; (2) the return to "glorious Islam" and the factors contributing to Islamist revivalism; (3) Islamist radical propaganda and its potential
threats, the ways in which Maghrebi Muslims are recruited and mobilized into
extremist organizations, and how the funding of terror is conducted; and (4)
noted Islamist movements/cells and their *modus operandi* on the European
continent.

Four central theses permeate this study. First, growing numbers of young
Maghrebi Muslim immigrants as well as second- and third-generation Maghrebi
Europeans are a potential threat to the continent's internal security, in addition
to becoming increasingly burdensome to Europe's social welfare system.
Second, it is misleading and invalid to claim that Islamists who oppose European values and reject their Western surroundings are a negligible force. Third,
the dream of transforming the EU into an Islamic bastion or annexing it to the
Maghreb or to a greater Islamist state may be far-fetched, but it is adhered to by
a variety of Islamist groups. Fourth, Maghrebi Islamist organizations are franchised in several key member-states of the EU. This has been achieved through
immigration, the presence of foreign students, prisoners in European jails, and
second- and third-generation European Muslims. This chapter addresses the
ways and means to cope with these challenges on a continent that is undergoing
demographic, religious, and cultural changes.

Immigration, leadership and organizations, and the motives
for Islamist radicalization in the EU

Mass immigration of Muslims into Western Europe gained momentum immedi-
ately after World War II. Large groups of immigrants migrated from the former
French colonial Maghreb (Algeria, Morocco, and Tunisia). The majority of
Maghrebis initially immigrated to France, but subsequent migrant waves

reached other European states. The 1960s saw a steady influx of more than 100,000 workers a year, whereas a decade later as many as three million foreign workers lived throughout the continent. Without this cheap source of labor, a nation like France could not have modernized its economy. Today, however, as France transitions from an industrial economy to a service economy, into which an increasing number of non-Muslims are entering, unskilled or semi-skilled foreign laborers are no longer necessary.[3]

After benefiting from family reunification programs and acquiring citizenship, the Maghrebi immigrants in Europe became permanent residents. Successive immigration waves were reinforced by a significant number of descendants. Over the past three decades the Maghrebi and other Muslims – Arabs, Berbers, and other non-Arabs – comprised the majority of immigrants throughout Europe. It is estimated that close to 15 million Muslims, approximately 4–5 percent of its total population, lived in Europe at the onset of the third millennium. As the current immigration level and fertility rates far exceed those of the indigenous population, Europe's Muslim population promises to double in less than two decades.[4]

The current fertility rate among Muslims is estimated at three children per woman, compared to 1.38 among indigenous European women. This reality and both large-scale legal and illegal immigration enabled the European Muslim community to grow at 50 percent per decade. Native populations, on the other hand, are shrinking and rapidly aging. Relying on the predictions of French demographer Jean-Claude Chesnais, in 2010, people aged 65 and over in France will outnumber those aged 0 to 14 among the indigenous French. Muslim youths in the *banlieues* (suburban areas populated by Maghrebis and Africans) could then become the majority of all French citizens under age 20.[5]

Given the large size of the Maghrebi Sunni Muslim community in EU states such as France, Spain, Italy, and The Netherlands, an elaborate and complex communal organizational apparatus has emerged over the past several decades. A noteworthy example of this phenomenon is best illustrated in French society. Its oldest Muslim institution founded in the 1920s is the Grande Mosquée de Paris (GMP), a moderate federation headed by Imam Dr. Dalil Boubakeur. The mosque is partially financed by the Algerian government, but favors interfaith dialogue with Jews and close cooperation with the French government in order to acquire greater legitimacy in French society. The same applies to the Islamic institutions in Marseilles, dominated by Maghrebis and headed by Saudi-born former mufti Souheib Bencheikh, one of Boubakeur's allies.

The Union des Organisations Islamistes de France (UOIF), which functions as a loose federation of Muslim associations, was founded in 1983 and gradually emerged as a branch of the Egyptian Muslim Brotherhood, despite the fact that the majority of its leaders are Moroccans. It seeks to win *hallal* (the Islamic equivalent of kosher) in school and factory cafeterias for wide segments of Muslim society and to institutionalize the teaching of Arabic in certain schools. Some claim it is a moderate organization despite its Muslim Brotherhood orientation. Others believe the UOIF is concealing its extremist positions about

European values, the US, and Jews. The truth lies somewhere in the middle; the UOIF is probably concealing extremist ideologies regarding European values.

Lhaj Thami Brèze, a political scientist of Moroccan origins and president of the organization, acknowledges that the UOIF is partially funded by "benevolent associations" in Saudi Arabia and the Persian Gulf states. He insists that the UOIF imams embrace a "moderate reading" of the Qur'ān and are faithful to the principles of the French Republic. "We're the new generation of French Islam," he declares, "Boubakeur doesn't defend Islam here; we do."[6] Since the 1980s, the UOIF controls 30 cultural centers throughout France, supervises two major mosques, humanitarian organizations, women's groups, and the Comité de Biefaisance et de Soutien à la Palestine. It boasts of affiliation with 250 other associations as well as youth and student sections.[7]

A third major institution is the Fédération Nationale des Musulmans de France (FNMF), headed by Muhammad Bechari. The Kingdom of Morocco funded the organization in order to wield influence over the many Moroccan members and affiliates. Both UOIF and FNMP rival the Mosquée de Paris over religious and political issues affecting the political climate and relations between Rabat and Algiers. Although the FNMP is intimately tied to the Moroccan government and Palace, it also receives funds from the Saudi Islamic World League. All of these organizations engage in interminable conflicts and bickering, and fail to function as an effective umbrella apparatus.

The Union des Jeunes Musulmans (UJM) was first founded in 1987 as an affiliate of UOIF, and has since become a movement for young Moroccan Muslims born in France. The Lyon-based organization prodded Maghrebi Muslims to become involved in communal politics. The UJM came under the influence of Tariq Ramadan, the charismatic Swiss-born grandson of Egyptian Shaykh Hassan al-Banna, founder of the Muslim Brotherhood in the late 1920s. For some time, Ramadan was *persona non grata* in France before being allowed to set his French operations in the heavily populated Muslim Saint-Denis area in Paris. Ramadan's supporters portray him as a proponent of a "silent revolution" in Islam, a reformer (*islahi*) who speaks favorably of Muslim integration into Europe and opposes violence and terrorism. However, critics of radical Islamic ideologies argue that he is a wolf in sheep's clothing, discreetly spreading the notion of anti-Western violence espoused by the late fanatic *salafi* leaders of the Egyptian Muslim Brotherhood – al-Banna and Sayyid Qutb – throughout the EU.[8]

The UJM program is not devoid of militancy. For example, it seceded from UOIF and defends the values of Arabism and Islamic culture while only passively respecting the values of the Fifth Republic. UJM members are well educated and, like other community organizations, they have failed to link effectively with the young masses from the poverty-stricken *banlieues*.[9]

In 2003, the three major organizations of French Islam, the GMP, the FNMP, and the UOIF, collaborated with the French authorities to found the Conseil Français du Culte Musulman (CFCM), conceived by Interior Minister Nicolas Sarkozy. The idea behind the CFCM was to achieve greater integration of

Muslims and Islam into French society while maintaining some Muslim identity, similar to the French-Jewish consistories. Yet the CFCM was soon overcome by internecine rivalries. The president, Dr. Boubakeur, was criticized by young Muslims for being erudite *à la française* and therefore unaware of their socioe-conomic difficulties and cultural needs. The more militant elements accused Dr. Boubakeur of being subservient to the military-backed regime in Algiers. The UOIF was equally under criticism by militants for representing the middle classes and neglecting poor neighborhoods.[10]

Towards the late 1990s, the aforementioned organizations lost most of their clout in the EU to the less-established militants and Islamists. In France, Spain, Belgium, and The Netherlands, Islamic radicals were divided into four major sects. The first is the non-violent Jama'at al-Tabligh (Society for the Spread of Islam) whose activists are the equivalent of Christianity's Jehovah's Witnesses. They are not linked to al Qaeda or other global Islamist strands, but al Qaeda occasionally penetrated their ranks in France under the guise of *tablighi*s. The *tablighi* school of thought stems from the Indian subcontinent, though the move-ment is mainly financed by Saudi Arabia and Kuwait petrodollars.[11] Overtly anti-Western and anti-Semitic, and opposed to the Western way of life, assimila-tion and the division between religion and state, these proselytizers have nonetheless operated legally since the 1970s to win over disillusioned young Muslims to pietistic Islam.

The second stream is the non-violent *salafi*, professing anti-Western ideas but functioning with the tacit approval of the authorities. The *salafi* signifies the notion of "pious predecessors," those who were the Prophet's early disciples. It became a school of thought at the end of the nineteenth century for leading Islamic reformers seeking reconciliation between Islam and modernity. In fact, however, *salafi* trends were translated throughout the twentieth century into arch-conservative ideologies which sought to purge Islam of any orientation emanating from the West. *Salafi* followers extol the Qur'ān, Sunna, and Shari'a, and challenge the validity of European secular constitutions. Whereas the *tab-lighi* strand is an Indian subcontinent phenomenon, the *salafi* currents are pro-moted by Saudi and Egyptian Islamist thinkers. The *salafi* advocates won adherents among second-generation Muslims (known in France as *beurs*) in the early 1990s through the initiative of political exiles who escaped the repression of the Algerian regime. Their main base of operation at the time was in Mar-seilles. The *salafi* garnered support for their vision in the mosques through the dissemination of written literature and video cassettes. They competed fiercely with the *tabligh*.[12]

The third sect is the pro-violent *jihadi-salafi*. Their activists vow to carry out violent acts against the West in general, and Americans in particular, and have been banned by the authorities. Although they tend to replace the word "*jihad*" with the word "combat," their goal is *jihadist*.[13] They draw inspiration from extremist ideologies attributed to Sayyid Qutb and Saudi imams who advocate Wahhabi ideas. Their creed denigrates women and non-Muslims, dehumanizes those who are not adherents, and forms the ideological groundwork for Osama bin Laden's endeavors. The pro-violent *salafi* cells are encouraged by local and international clerics and propagandists. Local imams preach in unofficial makeshift "cellar" and "garage" mosques that are distinguished from official mosques.

The fourth stream of Islamic radicalism is linked to the highly secretive Takfir wa al-Hijra. Deeply and covertly implanted in Morocco, Algeria, and Egypt, this ideology views all non-Muslims, Shi'a Muslims, and Sunni Muslims who deviate from the "straight path" as Godless heretics (*kuffar*). The sect believes a violent struggle must be waged against the apostates. *Takfir* extremists, who gained experience fighting in Bosnia and Chechnya during the 1990s, prefer to separate themselves from society and dwell in isolation. Maghrebi and Algerian exiles and immigrants cultivated home-grown *takfir* cells in France, Spain, and The Netherlands. They avoided existing mosques, making their exposure and arrest difficult.

Several years ago the French authorities uncovered a *takfir* cell (regarded as violent as the *jihadi-salafi*) operating west of Paris.[14] In recent years, part of this group, the *neo-takfir*, emerged as the dominant element among *takfiri*s. They opposed Western society without separating from their surroundings, making them almost indistinguishable from the violent *salafi*. By infiltrating "infidel society," *neo-takfiris* are the logistical backbone and manpower source of *jihad* groups in Spain, France, The Netherlands, and Belgium.[15]

Before 2000, Muslim-run political parties did not exist in Europe. Subsequently, a change took place in France and Belgium. The Parti des Musulmans de France (PMF) was founded in 1997 in Strasbourg by the Algerian Muhammad Ennacer Latrèche. The PMF has participated in all local elections, but has never obtained more than 0.67 percent of the vote. The group received attention for its fanatically anti-Semitic and Holocaust-denying ideology.[16] In contrast, the Belgian-based Muslim Parti de la Citoyenneté et Prosperité (PCP), composed mostly of Moroccans advocating radical Islamist ideas, won more than 8,000 votes in Brussels in 2003. Approximately 4 percent of the Muslims living in Brussels voted for the party. Although both parties are still embryonic and not represented in Parliament, in their objective to gain legitimacy for Muslims through the political process, they are adopting Islamic radical notions.[17]

In order to solidify the institutional legitimacy of established Muslim organizations, European governments have made efforts to accommodate what they regard as more moderate leadership. The French government did this in 2003 by aiding Boubakeur's Mosquée de Paris, the UOIF, and the FNMP by forming the umbrella organization CFCM. Interior Minister Sarkozy hoped that under the aegis of a religious umbrella association, intercommunal conflicts between the organizations would cease, thus weakening the influence of the Wahhabi creed, the Muslim Brotherhood, and the *Tabligh* among young Muslims.[18] Thereafter, the CFCM and the three federations came under close governmental scrutiny. Taking precautions, the government sent the established institutions the same warning it had directed at the *salafi* and *takfiri* streams: avoid incitements and the promotion of causes that run contrary to French interests.

To clarify his position, Sarkozy addressed more than 10,000 Muslims at the UOIF convention in April 2003. He insisted that Muslim women remove their veils for the photographs on their French identity cards. He reaped jeers and whistles. While it is likely that Sarkozy's statement put him in poor standing with Muslims, it sent a reassuring signal to the rest of France that he vigilantly defended a secular Republic.[19]

The return to "glorious Islam"

The previously discussed socioeconomic factors are by no means a single explanation for the appearance of Islamic extremism in Europe. For example, France's foreign policy, especially its relations with North African states, is heightening tensions in the Muslim world. Over the past few years, Algerian Islamists have accused France of supporting the military-led regime in Algiers. Consequently, the Algerian Groupe Islamique Armé carried out a number of attacks on French nationals in Algeria. The wave of terrorism in Algeria extended into France, taking a heavy toll on human lives and property. The French government responded by banning five Islamic periodicals and withdrawing financial assistance to the Mosquée de Paris.[20] Similarly, France's support of the Moroccan monarchy under King Hasan II and his successor Muhammad VI was not necessary favored by the French Moroccans.

The rise of Islamism in the French case is due to three additional factors. The first factor, globalization, offers Muslims direct access to information. "Global imams" and transnational religious figures – not only local clerics – preach and condone violence throughout Europe. They make extensive use of the tools and techniques of modern globalization to impart their ideas, such as Radio Orient, satellite television, and the Internet. Satellite television has been crucial in the cultivation of this new radicalism, as global imams counsel belligerence and inveigh against assimilation.[21] This is how the austere visions of Wahhabi and Muslim Brotherhood clerics such as Hasan Ya'aqubi, Shaykh Yussuf al-Qaradawi, Moroccan and Saudi-educated Omar al-Qazabri, and Shaykh Abd al-Rahman al-Sudais are popularized. The Egyptian-born al-Qaradawi is president of the International Association of Muslim Scholars and the spiritual guide of many Islamist organizations; he resides in Qatar. An avid follower of the late Hassan al-Banna, al-Qaradawi condones Palestinian suicide bombings. He speaks of the Islamic conquest of Europe simply by encouraging demographics and Muslim conversions to take their course.[22] Several of these global imams adhere to the slogan: "A Muslim has no nationality except his belief," attributed to the late Sayyid Qutb. Muslims in Europe are encouraged to declare: "We may carry their nationalities, but we belong to our own religion." In other words, Muslims should not play by Western society's rules but only by the path of Islam, and, if possible, impose this way of life on the host society.[23] As Fouad Ajami observes:

What is *laicité* (secularism) to the Muslims in France and their militant leaders? It is but the code of a debauched society that wishes to impose on

Islam's children ... the ways of an infidel culture. What loyalty in any rate is owed France? The wrath of France's Muslim youths in the *banlieues* is seen as revenge on France for its colonial wars. France colonized Algeria in the 1830s; Algerians, along with the Tunisians and Moroccans, return the favor in our own time.[24]

Moreover, events in Bosnia, Somalia, Chechnya, and Israel–Palestine led some young French and other EU-based Muslims to detach themselves further from their milieu by developing empathy with all the "Muslim victims in the world."[25]

The second central factor in French radicalization is the problem of local imams. Most imams, radical and non-radical, arrive from abroad and are often trained in Saudi Arabia or by Saudi clerics. They have no real understanding of the societies in which their followers live and often lack familiarity with local languages. They are hardly in a position to ease ethnic and religious tensions or aid Muslim integration.

Moreover, an increasing number of Muslims turn to rogue mosques because they regard official mosques as centers of Islam "for the rich." In the various makeshift mosques – located in cellars and garages – self-proclaimed imams impart their knowledge of new brands of Islam. Fanatical imams seize upon the Muslims' frustrations over socioeconomic issues to downgrade Western values. They indoctrinate Muslims to strongly oppose the US and EU international policies, describing these as "anti-Muslim," "pro-Zionist," or "pro-Jewish." The fanatical clerics of the rogue mosques have been reinforced – in high schools and universities – by Islamist refugees who fled their native societies. In the universities there existed, and probably still exists, sleeper cells of pro-violent Islamist movements associated with the Muslim Brotherhood, Hizballah, and the Maghreb.[26]

An estimated 90 percent of imams in France are foreign citizens, mostly from the Maghreb. Despite the identification of the UOIF with streams within the Muslim Brotherhood, its leader, Lhaj Thami Brèze, called for moderation and claimed in 2003 that some clerics adapt to French societal rules, but admitted that many do not. To avert a crisis between the French-Muslim communities and the authorities, he declared: "Our preachers must speak French; they must have been here for many years if they are not French citizens and their sermons must strengthen peace."[27]

Dr. Boubakeur is harsher in his criticism of the imams, noting that only 500 of the 1,500 places of Islamic worship in France have proper imams, while the others have "clowns."[28] Brèze would like to entrust the government-supervised CFCM with the task of drawing up a list of approved imams. Boubakeur, who is also president of the CFCM, broached this matter during a meeting with the then prime minister Jean Pierre Raffarin. Nevertheless, as late as 2006, three years since its inception, the CFCM as a religious umbrella apparatus has yet to free itself from the internal divisions that overwhelm the different streams of Sunni Islam, and attend to the task of challenging the radical imams. Numerous Muslims oppose government interference via the Council.[29] Over the past decade, Muslim unhappiness toward the authorities' interference in religious practices has increased.

The third main factor in the radicalization of Muslims is the prison experience. In European prisons in general and France in particular, the majority of prisoners are frequently Muslims.[30] This will be discussed below.

The Islamization process, imbued with the verbal violence of intolerance, oriented young Muslims to incite violence. This included attacks against politicians, opinion-makers, members of academia, women's liberation activists, Jews, and homosexuals. Muslims who in the eyes of the extremists "insulted" Islam, including Sunnis who practiced Sufism, were also not spared.[31]

In response to these "insults," Islamists have launched large-scale protest demonstrations that deteriorated into violence. The first major protest that sent ripples across France occurred on 22 October 1989, when thousands of Muslims staged demonstrations in Paris to reinstate Muslim girls expelled from the Gabriel-Havez Secondary School for wearing the *hijab* (headscarf). The then French Education Minister François Bayrou had introduced a regulation banning the wearing of "ostentatious religious insignia" in French schools. The headscarf controversy ignited violent demonstrations, hunger strikes, and lawsuits. Interior Minister Pasqua had said that the French government would fight the Islamic activists in its schools and would not tolerate attempts to obstruct the integration of Muslim immigrants into French life. French Muslims took up the matter and tried to promote the idea of government-funded Qur'ānic schools with a religious syllabus. The demand was deemed unacceptable by the French government. Simultaneously, due to the gradual increase of the Maghrebi population in France and the opening of new mosques and Islamic centers throughout the country, an elaborate chain of private Islamic schools developed over the years. Muslim activists claimed that since the French government provided funds to the private Catholic Mission schools, they should receive similar assistance for Islamic schools.[32]

A second major protest was the outbreak of full-scale riots by young Muslims in Paris on 27 October 2005, which spilled into other areas of France and neighboring countries. On the surface, the trigger for the riots was the accidental death of Ziad Benna and Bouna Traore, two Muslim teens of Tunisian and Malian origin, who were electrocuted while hiding from police in an electrical power substation in a Parisian suburb. Within days, riot police and firefighters were battling scores of young Muslims, some armed with weapons and Molotov cocktails. The authorities feared that the events would lead to a "mini-civil war"; therefore, they imposed a curfew and a state-of-emergency rule.[33] On the first day of the emergency rule the mayor of the Paris suburb of Noisy-le-Grand appealed to the army to intervene and end the lawlessness in his town. Muslims in this suburb dragged European women out of their cars by the hair, stoned them, and set vehicles on fire; others fire-bombed a local psychiatric hospital.[34]

The riots claimed one death and caused €200 million in damaged property. Some argued that religion was absent from the riots, and that socioeconomic malaise, lack of upward mobility, and French racism were responsible for the events. The young Arab *beurs* and French Africans from the slums, they said, reported countless cases of discrimination, such as being refused entrance to nightclubs and police brutality. The reaction in the French media was that the rioters who temporarily took control of the streets were "youths." The riots, however, were the result of poverty and a lack of social services, not of Islam. Despite this, French Muslim leaders of formal institutions were privately concerned that the riots were the result of continuous incitement against French society by radical global and local imams through the Internet and satellite television. The UOIF issued a *fatwa* (Islamic legal opinion) condemning the riots as un-Islamic, but demonstrated a total lack of influence over the situation; Muslim teenagers did not cease rioting and burning cars just because of an order from the formal and established leadership.[35]

For his part, Interior Minister Sarkozy regarded the situation with the utmost gravity, issuing a statement that the government "must not let the rule of the gangs and the rule of the bearded ones prevail," referring to radical imams.[36]

Other assessments dismissed the socioeconomic exploitation arguments, contending that the violence was the predictable denouement of the gradual transformation over two decades of Muslim enclaves into crime-ridden, self-isolated, anti-societies that de facto seceded from French society in virtually every aspect, except for economic dependence on the welfare state. With 70,000 cases of vandalism and arson, 29,000 cars burned, pervasive drug trafficking and an epidemic of gang rapes in the course of 2005 alone, these ghettos were an explosion waiting to happen. It was suggested that secession from French society by a growing number of second- and third-generation Muslims had been voluntary on their part:

> Misguided government policies in the socioeconomic and immigration spheres have certainly contributed in a major way by creating a climate of hopelessness and extreme alienation in which the siren call of Islamism has flourished. But it is difficult to envisage the kind of radicalization that has taken root without three decades of organized subversion and infiltration of French Islam by the fascist-like Wahhabi-*salafi* ideology.[37]

Those sharing this outlook predicted that the outcome of the riots may encourage Muslim youths to upgrade the unrest to more serious proportions. In addition to terrorism in France, these will include volunteering in greater numbers to fight in such places as Iraq's insurgent stronghold of Fallujah. According to Olivier Roy:

> [T]he police estimate there were about 20,000 participants across France in the riots, so if you have 1 percent of the 20,000 who become radicalized that is 200. In sociological terms it is negligible, but in terms of impact – 200 *jihadists*, yes, that counts.[38]

Pierre de Bousquet, France's counter-terrorism chief, also warned: "Among the fiercest youths some may find for their disquiet, their frustration, their violence an outlet in international *jihad*."[39]

Islamist religious radicalism, propaganda, and terrorism: financing, recruitment, and potential threat

Islamic radicals in the EU fall into three categories: foreign residents, second-generation immigrants (most often native-born), and converts. The first category is that of young Middle Easterners and Maghrebis who come to European universities as students, speak Arabic, and are from middle-class backgrounds. They become born-again Muslims in the continent before joining a radical group. The 9/11 World Trade Center pilots are excellent examples of this first category. The second category consists of second- and perhaps third-generation European Muslims. Some are university-educated and upwardly mobile, forming the leadership elite, but the majority are school drop-outs who usually come from destitute neighborhoods constituting the plebeian stratum of activists who provide "the muscle." They speak European languages as their mother tongue and are European citizens. The third category, the smallest in number but not necessarily in importance, is composed of converts, many of whom became Muslims while serving time in prison.[40]

In France, where Muslims represent 10 percent of the French population, unofficial estimates indicate that more than 60 percent of prison inmates are Muslim. Many of these inmates are recent converts, yet the authorities continually monitor the activities of Islamic radicals among the prison population. In Spain, one in ten inmates is of Moroccan or Algerian descent. In October 2004, the Spanish authorities dismantled a cell that had been planning bloody attacks inside the country. Most of the men, calling themselves "The Martyrs of Morocco," had been recruited in prison and had no prior involvement with Islamic radicalism. The members were a mélange of converts and those born into the faith.[41]

Members of all three categories join mosques as born-again Muslims or converts and many leave to fight abroad. Before 9/11, the destination was Afghanistan. Since spring 2003, many travel to Iraq to fight the Americans. Among the newly converted terrorists, almost all sever family connections. They usually become urban nomads, frequently moving nationally and internationally.[42] Another category is the recent immigrants and political exiles that were previously an integral part of the radical Islamist leadership core.

Maghrebi Islamists in Europe used crime to finance their terror operations. In addition to receiving funds from affluent Islamic "donors," means of financing included robberies, forging documents, money laundering, fraud, and the sale of counterfeit goods. Whereas terrorists in Algeria supported themselves by robbing banks, razing villages, and "taxing" inhabitants of lands they controlled, in France, home-grown Algerian franchise terrorist cells were funded by monies provided by Algerians living in the West, and funds raised in Sudan and Iran.[43]

More ominous is the fact that Maghrebi groups built strong operational alliances with drug lords and criminal mafia networks operating in the EU and the Maghreb. The encroachment of radical Islamists into the world of drug trafficking is extremely worrisome to European authorities, who estimate that terrorist organizations have infiltrated approximately two-thirds of the $12.5 billion-a-year Moroccan hashish trade. Evidence from recent terrorist activities confirms that profits from drug sales have directly financed terrorist attacks. According to the Spanish authorities, Jamal Ahmidan, a drug dealer of Moroccan descent and an operational mastermind of the 2004 Madrid bombings, obtained 220 pounds of dynamite for the attacks in exchange for 66 pounds of hashish. Moroccan groups also used profits from drug sales to finance the abortive attacks on NATO ships in Gibraltar (2002) and the Casablanca bombings of May 2003.[44]

Terrorist activities do not require large sums of money. The 9/11 terror attacks cost al Qaeda only $500,000. The cost of the London bombings of 7 July 2005 did not exceed €27,000. While counterfeit goods and currency are sources for financing acts, they are also means of sabotaging and destabilizing local economies.

Terrorist operations require manpower, and recruitment is a major activity for terrorist groups. Since the 1990s, Algerian, Moroccan, and Tunisian organizations and operatives in the EU emerged as major sources of enlisting new activists for their own aims as well as for al Qaeda's worldwide operations. The disaffected Maghrebi Muslim population in Europe has been and will remain vulnerable to recruitment by extremists. In both Algeria and Europe, Algerian terrorists recruited men from modest socioeconomic backgrounds, as well as the unemployed, and from ideologically oriented Islamists originating from well-to-do families.[45] Even if Europeans are sometimes at fault for their biases vis-à-vis non-Western European communities, one cannot ignore the Islamist ideological inspiration behind the estrangement of segments of Muslims from society at large. Therefore, Muslims are recruited not only due to social disaffection, but also because they are ideologically motivated, irrespective of their socioeconomic background.[46]

In discussing the enlistment of new activists, Robert S. Leiken, based on his own study, discloses that out of 373 terrorists, some 25 percent were EU citizens.[47] Similarly, Mathew Levitt, director of Terrorism Studies at the Washington Institute for Near East Policy, asserts that "Europe has served as a launching pad for terrorists plotting attacks elsewhere."[48] Given the number of EU terrorists, the French domestic intelligence service, Les Renseignements Généraux, has tried to establish a formula to calculate the number of radical Islamists in a given Muslim population. They calculate that there is an average of 5 percent Islamists, 3 percent of whom can be classified as dangerous. In applying this formula to France with a Muslim population of six million people, there are 300,000 potential terrorists. The most vulnerable states are France, Belgium, The Netherlands, Italy, Spain, Britain, and Germany.[49]

However, the threat of terrorism is not uniform throughout the EU. Germany hosts the second largest Muslim community in Europe (mostly Turks), who are more secular and Western than the French Maghrebis. They are probably better integrated into German society. Yet Germany is hardly indifferent to the threat. As in France, the government is increasingly tougher on Islamists, even as it fosters integration. This double strategy underpins Germany's new immigration law: it facilitates the expulsion of Islamic radicals, but also makes language classes mandatory for immigrants.[50]

Conversely, liberal policies towards immigrants and clear-cut integration laws do not provide ironclad guarantees for the reduction or prevention of terrorism and other forms of violence. Despite efforts to place one million Muslims on equal footing with the indigenous Dutch population of 15 million, problems with Maghrebi and other Islamist radicals in The Netherlands have recently increased due to growing religious ideological devotion. Local police uncovered several dangerous plots by Dutch Moroccans, including a plan to blow up a nuclear power station. The Dutch security forces (AIVD) estimated that there were hundreds of terrorists in the country.[51]

Based on one survey reporting on the challenges Europe faces regarding Maghrebi immigration, a major problem is the loss of loyalty to the host country. Whereas in 1993, 71 percent of Muslim youths of Maghrebi origin felt some affinity towards French culture, less than 45 percent of them felt the same way in 2003.[52] In suburban public schools with large Muslim populations, central aspects of teachings are virtually banned resulting from this radicalization process. An official French Ministry of Education study of the ongoing Islamization of French schools in the suburbs, Rapport Obin, paints a disturbing picture of a school system that is descending into Islamist obscurantism. It documents the ways in which Islamist extremists forced students to refuse to study the Holocaust, the evolution of species, and European philosophers as well as "unacceptable" writers. Girls were subject to a strict dress code – no skirts, dresses, or make-up – and barred from attending physical education classes. A de facto sexual segregation existed in the classrooms. The study warned that the violent anti-Semitism and widespread Osama bin Laden hero-worship was turning public schools in the *banlieues* into religious counter-societies, with "norms on a collision course with those of modern, democratic society."[53]

Islamist movements and cells

Types of movements and the al Qaeda connection: emphasis on the GIA, GSPC, and GICM

The predominantly Algerian and Moroccan Islamist radical movements in most EU member-states that advocate terrorism and violence often carry the names of similar movements in North Africa. The presence of al Qaeda-affiliated and unaffiliated groups in Europe caught the attention of the EU authorities following a series of arrests between 2003 and 2005, and subsequent to investigations in Germany, France, Britain, Italy, Spain, and The Netherlands. There were as many as 21 networks active in Europe in 2005, some of which had ties with over 60 groups in the Maghreb. These groups were home-grown and operated by Muslims living in the EU who knew the country. Because numerous Muslims possessed European passports they moved more easily across Europe and the Middle East.[54]

Although inspired by the base movements in Morocco and Algeria, the European home-grown Maghrebi counterparts are not entirely subservient to the base organizations in North Africa, nor do they coordinate their activities with them regularly. At the same time, many movements and cells of EU-based Maghrebi movements constitute "franchise organizations" of sorts, affiliated with the North African base movements.

Other groups receive financial support from various sources. Some extremist cells have al Qaeda connections. Others appear to enjoy considerable autonomy and collaborate with a variety of clandestine cells linked to non-Maghrebi causes. Abu Mus'ab al-Zarqawi, al Qaeda chief operative in Iraq killed by US forces in 2006, maintained contacts with Maghrebi Islamists in Europe, while Maghrebis in the continent had links with Iraqi, Chechen, and Pakistani elements.

One of the leading Algerian groups in Europe of the 1990s was the Groupe Islamique Armé (GIA). After Algeria plunged into civil war in 1992, the GIA extended its networks into Algeria and Europe. The GIA grew out of the now outlawed Algerian Front Islamique du Salut (FIS), a political party that won mass electoral votes in the June 1990 Algerian municipal elections and continued to win the first round of parliamentary elections in 1991 before being suppressed by the military. In Algeria, the GIA aspired to overthrow the secular Algerian regime and replace it with an Islamic state. Its Islamist-inspired franchise in Europe was cultivated by Algerian political exiles who fled their country and consisted of new immigrants and recruits among European Muslims. From the onset, it planned to sabotage US interests and carry out terrorist acts against Europeans. The GIA harbored strong disdain towards France, which had colonized Algeria for 132 years, and had supported the Algerian military-backed regime.

The GIA in Algeria and Europe was overshadowed by a more dangerous rival Algerian Islamist group: the Groupe Salafiste pour la Prédiction et le Combat (GSPC in Arabic: Jama'a Salafiyya lil Da'wa wa al-jihad). Initially, the GSPC was founded in 1996 as an offshoot of the GIA, but it soon aspired to become the torch-bearer of the anti-government struggle in Algeria. The GSPC dedicated itself to toppling the Algerian government and replacing it with an Islamic caliphate, as well as conducting terrorist operations against Western targets in Europe and the Maghreb. Like the GIA, GSPC's leaders emerged from the armed wing of the FIS, the Armée Islamique du Salut (ALN). The GSPC Algerian-based leaders included Nabil Saharaoui, who was killed by the Algerian army in June 2004, Yahya Jawadi and Abu-Ammar. Its Algerian and European networks nurtured close ties with al Qaeda. With the support of Osama bin Laden, GSPC distanced itself completely from the GIA in 1998 and became the largest terrorist group in Algeria. Together, the GIA and GSPC were responsible for the deaths of 100,000 Algerians.[55]

By 2000, GSPC had taken command of GIA's network of operatives and funding across Europe and the Maghreb. Haydar Abu Doha, a London-based Algerian known as "the Doctor," played a predominant role in GSPC's transformation from a local armed group into an international terrorist organization. He moved to Britain in 1999 after serving as a senior official in al Qaeda's Afghan terrorist operations. A German-based Algerian, Muhammad Bensakhria, and an Italian-based Tunisian, Tariq Ma'aroufi, helped Doha to establish GSPC cells across Europe and recruit activists. They expanded the Algerian base of recruits by incorporating militants who had left behind dormant conflicts in Bosnia, Chechnya, and Afghanistan. Bensakhria and Ma'aroufi also created a vast support network that provided newcomers with counterfeit documents, lodging, and spending money.[56] The GIA survived after 2001 as a marginal force.

The depth of the GSPC network in Europe was apparent when Italian police arrested some of its operatives in Milan in April 2000, while French police carried out similar arrests several months later. In June 2002, Muhammad Bensakhria was arrested in Spain; Haydar Abu Doha was apprehended shortly thereafter. Tariq Ma'aroufi is still wanted in Italy but remains free because of his Belgian citizenship, which prevents his extradition.[57] AIVD disclosed in 2004 that GSPC recruited young Muslim immigrants at mosques in The Netherlands.[58] In December 2002, French officials arrested two Algerians and two Moroccans linked to the GSPC in Frankfurt who were in possession of chemicals.[59] The US State Department also targeted the GSPC for its al Qaeda affiliation, designating it a foreign terrorist organization. The arrest of its operatives in recent years caused setbacks for the GSPC in Europe and Algeria, but it is anything but vanquished. New leaders emerged to replace those arrested or on the run. The estimates of GSPC terrorists after 2004 range from 300 to 700 in Algeria and Europe.[60] Since the latter half of 2006, the GSPC became an official arm of al Qaeda with its new name, "Al Qaeda in the Islamic Maghreb."

The GSPC is but one of the franchised networks of Maghrebi cells operating in Europe. Moroccan Muslims are a major part of the Islamist market on the continent. This is well illustrated in Spain, where Moroccan groups won some dominance at the expense of their Algerian counterparts. In the 1990s, Algerians dominated the scene given the absence of Islamist heterogeneity in the area of recruitment, terrorism, and propaganda. The *salafi* Moroccans in Spain were then integrated into the Syrian-led Abu Dahdah network.[61] According to a senior Spanish police official, cooperation between Algerians and Moroccans had not developed because many Algerians considered Moroccans to be untrustworthy. Conversely, the Moroccans viewed the Algerians as excessively violent. In Spain and other parts of the EU, these differences were cast aside after 2000 in favor of a multinational approach due to the increase of Moroccan immigration into Spain.[62]

The dissolution of the Abu Dahdah network at the end of 2001 resulted in the elevation of Moroccan organizations into positions of prominence. The organization that stepped in to fill the vacuum was the Moroccan-based *salafi* Groupe Islamique Combattant Marocain (GICM; in Arabic: Jama'a al-Islamiyya al-Muqabila bi'l Maghreb).[63] Founded in Morocco during the 1990s, its leaders were influenced by a mélange of Wahhabi-*salafi* and even *takfir* principles.[64] The group's original spiritual leader, pro-Wahhabi Muhammad Fizazi, advocated anti-Western messages in his home town of Tangier before receiving a 30-year prison sentence for justifying violence against the political order.[65]

Similar to the Algerian GSPC, the Moroccan-based GICM established cells throughout Europe and achieved al Qaeda affiliation. Older GICM Moroccans probably attended al Qaeda terrorist training camps in Afghanistan and fought in the battlefields of Chechnya and Dagestan.[66] It is not entirely clear, however, how many second-generation European Muslims received training in Afghanistan up until 2001. Membership of the Moroccan-based organization is at least several hundred strong; no data is available about the size of the European GICM franchises.

Until recently, the Moroccan-based GICM was led by Chief of Operations Abd al-Karim Mejjati, an alumnus of the prestigious Casablanca-based Lycée Lyautey. Mejjati resided in an affluent suburb of the city. After completing his medical studies in France he returned home in the latter half of the 1990s and turned to Islamism and terrorism, undergoing training in Afghanistan and fighting in Chechnya. While serving as an al Qaeda operative, Mejjati became an explosives expert. He has been on the run since late 2003. Since September 2003 the State Department has regarded him as "a menace to the US," whereas the Saudis are pursuing him for involvement in the Riyad bombings that same year. Mejjati also masterminded the suicide attacks in Casablanca on 16 May 2003.[67] Organized by the GICM as coordinated suicide bombings on multiple targets in Casablanca, the attack targeted an old Jewish cemetery, the Farah luxury hotel, the Belgian consulate, a Jewish-owned Italian restaurant, and a luxurious Spanish social club called the Casa de Espana. Twenty-nine Moroccans and European nationals were killed, not including a dozen Islamist terrorists, and 100 were injured. The Moroccan government regarded the events as its own "9/11."

Information communicated by the Moroccan government revealed that the terrorists belonged to an offshoot faction of GICM called Sirat al-Mustaqim (The Righteous Path). In addition to Mejjati, a major architect of the Casablanca attacks was Pierre Robert of Tangier who converted to Islam in 1990 and maintained close ties with al Qaeda. Robert is alleged to have planned terrorist attacks in Europe, including an attack on a French nuclear power plant. He was arrested and is serving a prison sentence in Morocco. The Europeans and the FBI dispatched terrorist experts to Morocco to assist with the interrogation process in the hopes of learning more about the dangers affecting both Morocco and the West. It is important to understand the origins of the Casablanca attacks because the same groups later carried out the Madrid attacks.

Of all European countries, Spain was the most concerned with the consequences of Moroccan terrorism because its proximity to the country allows for illegal immigration. Spain was a target for Moroccan and other Maghrebi terrorists – European-born and newcomers – because of the ease with which they were able to infiltrate the country. Second, four of those killed in Casablanca were Spaniards. Third, the fact that the Casa de Espana in Casablanca was a terrorist target raised speculation that Spain could be victimized by suicide bombers because of the support the Spanish government lent to the Iraqi war effort.[68] Finally, the Spaniards were informed by the Moroccan authorities that the funds for the bombings came from GICM Moroccan cells operating between Spain, France, Italy, and Belgium.[69] Indeed, there existed by then a strong European connection between the franchised groups and the base movement in Morocco. The Casablanca suicide bombings would serve as a prelude for the Madrid train bombings ten months later.

Lorenzo Vidino concluded in April 2005 that "It is not far-fetched to speak of Europe as 'a new Afghanistan,' a place that pro-al Qaeda groups have chosen as its main arena to direct operations worldwide." He meant to say that al Qaeda of the post-Taliban regime had no real options except for Europe.[70] Al Qaeda did establish a foothold in Europe, yet it is not all-embracing and all-empowering, as had been the case in pre-2001 Afghanistan.

Other intelligence experts, among them Claude Moniquet, argue that it would be erroneous to link each and every terrorist plot to al Qaeda, although they have played an "historical role" in weaving an international terrorist coalition uniting dozens of organizations. Now that this has been achieved, an "International Islamist Terror" exists. Information, arms, and funds are exchanged among Moroccan, Algerian, Chechen, Pakistani, Saudi, Iraqi, and other organizations. These organizations often collaborate in sophisticated ways. The main role of al Qaeda revolves around setting the general framework of the *jihad*, at times also designating targets and giving lawful authorization (*fatwa*) to act.[71]

Newly conceived cells like the Maghrebi-dominated Hofstad Group in The Netherlands – a force that severed its links with GICM and embraced both *salafi* and *takfiri* ideologies – is probably not linked to al Qaeda. Further, as noted earlier, in recent times some newly formed *jihadi* cells also tended to limit their dependence on the Moroccan and Algerian base or "mother organizations." In fact, the same appears to be the case in recent years with new home-grown cells that did not become franchise groups of North African central base movements in the first place. Violent acts by these organizations are of a purely local nature. The younger the cells and the age group of activists, and the fact that they were not trained outside Western Europe, the less a possibility of their connection to an external network. Yet all in all, the variety of violent *jihadi-salaf-takfiri* as well as the non-violent *salafi* groups must be considered dangerous. As Moniquet warned in April 2005:

> The most well-established Islamist organization in Europe, and the most dangerous, is at present the GICM. The group suffered losses in Europe and in Morocco, but the battle is far from being over in [Morocco] where ... reforms are still needed [by King Muhammad VI] to fight terrorism. Developments ... in years to come will have a major influence on the situation in Europe. If terrorism is not eradicated, if it remains vigorous, the

consequences will be seen in the old continent, and it would be because of the importance of Moroccan communities established there, within which terrorists can recruit new sympathizers.[72]

The modus operandi of terrorist activities in Europe

Terrorism in Europe gained momentum towards the end of 1994, when four French Algerian Islamists (it is unclear whether they were recent immigrants or second-generation Muslim Europeans) hijacked an Air France plane. The hijacking incident ended after several days when French commandos stormed the hijacked jet in Marseilles, killing the four Islamists. In reprisal, the GIA engaged in a sequence of violent acts inside France in 1995. On 26 August 1995, Khaled Kelkal, a French Muslim and GIA member, attempted to derail one of France's high-speed trains. Other bombs went off in September and October: two in double-decker metro rail cars in suburban Paris, and one in a provincial Jewish school. In total, there were at least six attacks in three months, killing ten people and wounding 114.[73] The number of terrorist incidents in France dropped off in 1996.[74]

In the subsequent decade, terrorist actions in Europe in which Maghrebi immigrants, exiles, or European Maghrebis were the main actors abounded. On 4 April 2001, the Italian security forces apprehended four members of an al Qaeda-affiliated European ring known as Varese led by a Tunisian immigrant Sami bin Khemais Essid. This group operated out of Milan, a city with some 100,000 Muslim immigrants, the majority of them Maghrebis. Most of Varese's operatives were Moroccans. An offshoot of the GSPC, Varese prepared attacks on US installations. One year later, on 26 February 2002, Varese placed a bomb near the Interior Ministry in downtown Rome, but the attack was detected and prevented. Only days earlier the police uncovered a tunnel that suspected Muslim terrorists were digging in the vicinity of the US embassy in Rome, apparently intending to carry out an attack. The authorities caught four Moroccans in possession of maps showing the city water supply grid. They were sentenced to five years in prison.[75]

The terrorists in Italy were neither socioeconomically homogeneous nor were they deeply religious. This also applies to the Muslims throughout the rest of Europe. Terrorists sprouted from the lower classes of immigrants or Maghrebi Europeans, while others were relatively well-off. Most joined the ranks of the Islamists as born-again Muslims. While no data are available as to Sami bin Khemais Essid's socioeconomic background, radical religious notions affected him in the 1990s. Until bin Khemais arrived in Italy in 1994 as an illegal immigrant from Tunisia, he neither frequented a mosque nor observed Muslim rituals. In 1997, he rediscovered his religion at the Islamic Cultural Center in Milan and then joined the GSPC, which was co-opted by al Qaeda.[76]

As part of Italian officials' probing into Islamists, it was reported that the Islamic Cultural Center in Milan and the Varese were virtually one and the same, serving as one of al Qaeda's principal logistics bases in Europe. The

Digos (Italian anti-terrorism police) disclosed that before the Varese was disrupted, it recruited terrorists and dispatched them to Afghanistan for training when the Taliban were in control.[77]

Islamists operations in Italy did not cease at this point. In 2003, the Italian police and Special Operations Forces uncovered a link between GSPC operatives in Milan and their extremist associates in a number of European countries, primarily Germany, Spain, and The Netherlands. That same year, the Italian authorities disrupted an apparent plot by Maghrebis to attack the NATO base in Verona. The primary focus of the Islamists' activities in Italy, however, appears to have been that of a staging ground for recruiting suicide bombers to conduct attacks against US-led forces in Iraq. The Milan probe revealed that young North Africans were "trawled for" in the European mosques, given money, and supplied with visas to travel to Iraq to conduct suicide operations.[78]

Shortly thereafter, special operations agents from Genoa and Florence arrested an Algerian imam, Rashid Maamiri from the Sorgane mosque in Florence, and four Tunisians – all of whom admitted to being involved in a European cell linked to the Iraqi Ansar al-Islam, the pro-al Qaeda Islamist movement in Iraq led by Mus'ab al-Zarqawi. Those arrested had taken part in recruiting suicide bombers from Italy to fight in Iraq. At least five suicide bombers of Maghrebi origin traveled from Italy to Iraq in the spring of 2003. It was also disclosed that the Italians identified other cells recruiting fighters from all parts of Italy to travel to Iraq.[79]

In 2006, three Algerian men were arrested because of their suspected association with GSPC. Investigators said these men were in Italy to provide logistical support but concurrently acted as "potential operatives" who "were ready to attack." They were identified as Yamine Bouhrama, Khalied Serai, and Muahmmad Larbi, and detained on "suspicion of association with the aim of international terrorism," a charge introduced in Italy following 9/11. Based on the findings of the Italian intelligence service SISMI, Bouhrama received training at Chechen and Georgian terror camps and learned to assemble explosive belts for suicide bombers.[80]

It was noted earlier that Spain's anxieties over Islamist terrorism had its merits. In 2004, more than one-third of the 55 mosques in Madrid had some connection with radical Islamist groups, or the presence of Maghrebi extremists had been detected in them.[81] Equally important are the activities conducted in the autonomous Spanish enclaves Ceuta and Melilla of the Mediterranean area, formerly Moroccan territories conquered in the sixteenth century. These enclaves emerged as dangerous breeding grounds for terrorists seeking to liberate these areas from Christian Spain. Other such breeding grounds were the Canary Islands and the Sahara Desert.

There is ample evidence to conclude that Islamist groups, which set the goal of undermining the legitimacy of the Moroccan political order in parts of northern Morocco, and wreaking havoc in Spain, joined forces with the Moroccan mafias and drug barons. The latter smuggled hashish via Tangier into Spain and other parts of the EU; they relied on the services of the Islamists. The mafias were equally bent on challenging the authority of the Moroccan government and monarchy leading to a marriage of convenience between the two forces.[82] This joint activity angered Spain and its neighboring European countries, notably Italy and France, and resulted in the delay of including Morocco in the projected Euro-Mediterranean Free Trade Zone.[83]

In retrospect, the Casablanca attacks of May 2003 set the stage for the far more lethal terrorist act in Spain: the 11 March 2004 (hereafter 3/11) train bombings in Madrid. Until the London bombings on 7 July 2005, the 3/11 attack was considered the worst terrorist attack in Europe. As many as 191 people lost their lives and 1,900 were wounded. Once again, Spain's Moroccan and Algerian Islamists were responsible. Sixteen of those arrested in Spain during investigations were said to be members of al-Usud al-Khalidiyyin (The Eternal Lions), an affiliate of the *salafi* GICM. The evidence showed that Algerians could be members of a Moroccan-led cell.[84]

Jamal Zougam, his half-brother Muhammad Chaoui, and Muhammad Bekkali masterminded 3/11. They were arrested in Madrid three days later. All three had prior dealings with al Qaeda and shared almost identical experiences with other leading veteran Islamist terrorists – fighting in the battlefields of Afghanistan, Bosnia, Chechnya, and Dagestan. The capture of Zougam (originally from Tangier) led to the exposure of the long list of Islamists with whom he kept contact. Zougam is known to have visited Norway to meet with an exiled leader of the Iraqi Ansar al-Islam, the group responsible for countless suicide attacks on US forces in Iraq.[85]

Zougham frequently stayed in his native city of Tangier with the Benyaiche brothers, members of the Moroccan-based GICM, according to Owen Bowcott. The history of the Benyaiche brothers is well documented. One brother, Abdallah, died when the Americans bombed the Tora Bora cave complex in Afghanistan. The second brother, ʿAbd al-ʿAziz, was arrested in Spain for alleged membership in an al Qaeda cell. The third, Salah al-Din, served a long prison sentence in Morocco for the Casablanca bombings. When Spanish police, acting at the request of a French judge, raided the Zougam family apartment in Madrid in 2001, they found videos of the Benyaiche brothers fighting as *mujahidin* in Dagestan. Another of Zougham's associates was reported to be the previously mentioned Robert Pierre, a Frenchman who was serving a life sentence for the Casablanca bombings.[86]

It would be folly to assume that the terrorist attacks were largely conducted to protest Europe's military intervention in Iraq, similar to the claim that 9/11 was in protest at unwavering US support of Israel. After all, France, which consistently opposed the US invasion of Iraq and has maintained a pro-Palestinian foreign policy since 1967 to assuage the Arab world, became victimized by terrorism in the 1990s. Yet logic hardly figured in the plans of the terrorists.[87] In December 2002, a series of arrests in France uncovered a plot by Maghrebi extremists to bomb the Russian embassy in Paris on behalf of Chechen Islamist radicals. Later, on 15 June 2004, twelve Maghrebis were arrested in Paris for planning to bomb the subway system.[88] Less than a year later, France's Sarkozy disclosed information about a Chechen cell in Lyon with active Maghrebi members, and the Groupe Farid Benyettou in the nineteenth arrondissement of Paris consisting of French Algerians about to leave for Iraq. In September 2005, a GSPC cell was disrupted near Paris, led by Safé Bourrada, a French Algerian who recruited French Muslims to fight in Iraq.[89]

Belgium, too, was vehement in condemning American intervention in Iraq from its inception, yet Islamist attacks were nevertheless planned there. In April 2004 Belgian federal police pre-empted two attacks: one against a Jewish school in Antwerp, the other against an inauguration ceremony open to the public of a major tunnel in the same city.[90]

The Islamists hardly made distinctions among Europeans in *bilad al-kufr* ("land of the Infidels"); Europe is host to a war between order and its enemies.[91] The Islamists who targeted Madrid on 3/11 were already planning the attack in 2001, long before the start of the Iraq war, and obviously without the knowledge that Spanish troops would be in Iraq.[92]

Despite the withdrawal of the 1,500 Spanish troops from Iraq after 3/11 by the new government of President Jose Luis Rodriguez Zapatero, the threats hardly diminished. A plan to blast the National Audience, Spain's highest court handling high cases of corruption and terrorism, was foiled by *Operaction Nova*. The main target was Judge Baltazar Garzon, a powerful figure charged with prosecuting ETA Basque activists and pro-al Qaeda terrorists. Interestingly, the architects of the attack were a group that called themselves "Martyrs for Morocco" espousing the causes of the GIA. It was made up of militants from Algeria, Morocco, Mauritania and Afghanistan.[93] Indeed, two years after 3/11, new cells routinely continued to be disrupted in Spain. In 2004 alone, Spanish police detained 100 Islamists. The trend continued in 2005, with more than 80 militants apprehended. On 10 January 2006, Spanish police caught 20 suspected Islamists alleged to have recruited sympathizers to join the Iraqi insurgency. They were detained during pre-dawn raids in Madrid, Barcelona, and the Basque town of Tolosa.[94]

The Netherlands emerged as another arena of Maghrebi Islamist terrorism. Local radical networks consist mainly of young Dutch Muslims with Moroccan backgrounds in search of their identity and status in Dutch society. Among the second generation of other immigrant communities, such as the Turkish, Bosnians, and Pakistanis, a similar process exists, but on a much smaller scale than in the Moroccan community.[95] In September 2002, the Dutch authorities arrested 12 Maghrebis who recruited young Moroccans and provided them with stolen or forged passports to fight in other countries. One of the central locally based Islamist networks, the Hofstad Group, failed to assassinate Somali-born Member of Parliament Ayaan Hirshi Ali. In addition, they failed to booby-trap vehicles that were to explode outside Parliament, security service headquarters, and Schiphol Airport.[96]

Terrorist efforts in The Netherlands climaxed on 2 November 2004. On that day, Theo Van Gogh, a controversial film director, who had produced a brief 11-minute documentary on the abuse of Muslim women by Muslim men in Europe

(*Submission*), had been murdered on the streets of Amsterdam in broad daylight. The documentary irked the Islamists and served as the prime motive for the murder. Van Gogh's assailant was Muhammad Bouyeri, a son of Moroccan immigrants. Bouyeri shot Van Gogh at least six times and slit his throat with a butcher's knife. The terrorist's final act was to impale a five-page letter attacking the enemies of Islam on the chest of his victim. He surrendered to police after a short manhunt.[97]

The murder of Van Gogh and the acts of violence perpetrated by Hofstad were local initiatives without operational control or guidance from international networks. Rather than exhibiting disgust at the murder, young Dutch Muslims became more attracted to radical Islam. Bouyeri emerged as a hero, a model to be emulated by others.[98]

This brutal act was one of the three successful operations of Islamist terrorism, the other two being Madrid 3/11 and the London bombings. Van Gogh's death came in the aftermath of innumerable failed actions throughout the EU. The Hofstad Group was behind the murder. Whereas at least 12 Hofstad radicals conspired to eliminate Van Gogh, the task was finally entrusted to 27-year-old Bouyeri who typified a European-born terrorist. Bouyeri was a well-integrated Muslim until he drifted into the world of Islamist extremism. His parents arrived in Amsterdam in the 1960s and he was born soon thereafter. He held Dutch and Moroccan citizenship, completed high school and went on to study computer science at a Dutch university. In 2000, Bouyeri became a born-again Muslim, adding verses from the Qur'ān into articles he wrote for a community newspaper, and exchanging his jeans for a floor-length robe. He quit his job, collected welfare checks, and spent time at the Tawhid Mosque, whose activities had been observed by Dutch intelligence. Bouyeri's apartment in Amsterdam became Hofstad's meeting place to hear the sermons of a Syrian *salafi* imam known as Abu Khatib who incited young Muslims of Maghrebi origin against Western civilization.[99]

Concluding remarks: confronting Islamism in Europe

The anger of prominent Europeans becomes apparent in light of Islamic hostility towards the West. For example, On 24 September 2006, former Spanish prime minister José-Maria Ansar balked at the demand by Muslims that Pope Benedict XVI apologize for criticizing the Prophet Muhammad. Asnar complained that he had never heard Muslims apologizing for occupying Spain for 800 years. "The West," he said, "always must offer apologies, but they, the Muslims, for some reason never reciprocate. The West is now engaged in a war for survival with Islam. It is a war of 'either them or us'." Bernard Lewis claims that by the end of the twenty-first century, Europe will be "part of the Arab west, the Maghreb." Samuel P. Huntington, cautioned in 1993 about the looming "clash of civilizations" that will take place between the West and Islam. Observers of Islamism, among them Fouad Ajami and Mark Silverberg, sound the bells of alarm, pointing to Muslim dreams of reconquering parts of the West, especially Spain.[100]

Our study reinforces some of these concerns. Islamism – both non-violent as well as malignant *jihadi/takfiri* trends – does pose dangerous challenges to European security, including Europe's Jewish communities. Young, angry Muslims are a burden on the social and political fabric of the continent. They are an ever-growing force, hardly marginal, and the proliferation of heterogeneous cells and movements is becoming a stark reality. Some Europeans downplay the calls for alarm; how could 15 million Muslims, in a continent with 450 million people, achieve such feats? How can the divided Muslim world and the largely impoverished Maghreb overcome the EU? Others embrace Lewis, arguing that by the end of the century the high birth rate among Muslims and the aging of old Europe will ensure a Muslim majority, or near majority, in major European cities. At best, Islamism, which is becoming increasingly attractive to young Muslims, shall lead to destabilization and even chaos.

Europe's annexation to a Maghrebi or other Muslim entity is not likely in the near future. Yet Muslim extremists dream of such an occurrence. Huntington's pessimism that the cultural, religious, and political clashes are imminent should not, however, be ruled out or underestimated. Islamism is a virus that affects Islam and is a destabilizing phenomenon. Moreover, tensions in Europe are microcosmic as they exist throughout the world where modern transnational globalization and global Islam are at odds.

What should be done to curb these developments? The following are six main recommendations.

1   Major EU countries with large Maghrebi and other Arab-Muslim populations, such as France, Spain, Sweden, and Belgium, should coordinate actions and intelligence exchanges among themselves and with Israel and the US to fight Islamist radicalism. The escape by Europe into anti-Israeli behavior and anti-Americanism has been a futile effort to bond with the peoples of Islam.

2   Together with the US, other members of the G-8, and moderate Arab states, Europeans should work towards breaking the financial back of the Islamists. This includes freezing and/or sequestering bank accounts and immovable assets, and imposing in Europe stiff penalties on credit card fraud, money laundering, counterfeit documents, and drug trafficking as if these were the very physical violent terrorist crimes themselves. With Arab states, such as Morocco, Europe must demand that Morocco fight the drug lords, halt drug trafficking and stop the application of drug money for the use of terrorism. If these steps are not followed, sanctions should then be imposed, such as the cancellation of trade agreements and other EU–Moroccan economic arrangements.

3   The EU should reduce the flow of legal and illegal immigration. Several EU states are taking initial steps to reduce immigration and deport extremists. Radical imams have been expelled from France in recent years. The French are bent on investing government funds and collaborating with the CFCM to train local imams who are versed in the culture and language of the

country. Other EU member-states ought to emulate this model to reduce the fanaticism of the Algerian, Moroccan, and Syrian foreign clerics. As for the illegal immigration per se, besides mobilizing sufficient manpower, Spain must seal its borders using the most sophisticated electronic and computer techniques. The Netherlands has pioneered the "get-tough" policy with legal and illegal immigrants by declaring at the end of 2004 a four-year moratorium on any new immigration of "asylum seekers." The Dutch Parliament also voted recently to expel 26,000 such individuals. It is considering a new anti-terrorism law modeled on the USA's "Patriot Act," which following 9/11 permits the authorities to carefully monitor and investigate every US or non-US citizen suspected of being a security risk. In countries where wire-tapping and other listening devices to monitor local as well as long-distance telephone calls exist, these measures ought to be fortified; in places where they are lacking these policies need to be implemented. In light of the terrorist threats, and despite the partial infringement on the freedom of movement, the policy seems unavoidable. The Dutch have recently undertaken a major step to examine persons who enter and wish to remain in The Netherlands, but more work still needs to be done throughout Europe. Another way of possibly curbing large-scale immigration is the intensification of EU assistance to the Maghreb and to other Muslim states by improving the standards of living via the growing Euro–Mediterranean partnership program (EMP) in Morocco, Tunisia, and Algeria. It has been argued by European policy-makers that the better the lives of people in their countries of origin, the lesser the immigration flow into Europe.

4   In line with stern policies on immigration, political exiles, and rogue imams, the legal systems in the EU must be amended to facilitate the adoption of new provisions enabling the authorities to take pre-emptive measures against Islamism.[101] The European legal system can no longer remain lax. Furthermore, as Leiken notes, a terrorist can still enter Europe undetected. If noticed, he can easily change his name or glide across borders, relying on a cumbersome bureaucracy that fails to take action. Since 3/11, the Spanish Interior Ministry finally tripled its full-time anti-terrorism agents. Spanish law enforcement established a task force combining police and intelligence specialists to keep tabs on Muslim neighborhoods, prisons, mosques, Islamic bookshops, and *halal* butchers and restaurants.[102] These measures should be adopted and intensified by other EU states.

5   EU member-states must counter Islamist propaganda with government-sponsored programs for young Muslims. These could include extensive programs for youths to integrate them into society, reduce potential terrorism by engendering fruitful activities in the Muslim milieu, and fostering relations between Muslims and European secularism. In addition to community programming, the government must also counter Islamist propaganda through the media with aggressive European cultural programs over satellite television and via the Internet.

6   Europe cannot ignore the Muslim underclass. Much has to be invested in

dismantling the ghettos and diffusing tensions, and grappling with unemployment. This may or may not eliminate the threat of terrorism, for, after all, Islamism – both non-violent and violent – is based on religious ideologies, and the eradication of poverty does not necessarily signify the commencement of harmony and coexistence among people. Yet in any modern society, immigrants and their descendants can, and should, have better standards of living.

The threat of Islamism in Europe is real, and greater than any other domestic problem. Should large segments of European Muslims and new immigrants fail to accept the values of the host societies, Europe and the Muslims will find themselves on a collision course. There can be no doubt that in the past decade as well as at the present time, an increasing number of radical Islamists and their followers are bent on challenging European society – culturally and/or by means of terrorism.

Notes

1 "The Radicalization of Muslim Youth in Europe: The Reality and the Scale of the Threat," Testimony of Claude Moniquet, Director-General, European Strategic Intelligence and Security Center, 27 April 2005, at the Committee of International Relations Subcommittee on Europe and Emerging Threats, US House of Representatives.
2 J. Laurence and J. Vaisse (December 2005) "Understanding Urban Riots in France," *New Europe Review*. Available online at www.neweuropereview.com/English/French-Riots-English.cfm.
3 R. Tlemcani (March 1997) "Islam in France," *Middle East Quarterly*, vol. 4, no. 1. Available online at www.meforum.org/pf.php?id=338.
4 R. S. Leiken, "Europe's Angry Muslims," *Foreign Affairs*, July–August 2005, vol. 84, no. 4, pp. 120–35.
5 A. Alexiev, Vice-President for Research, Center for Security Policy in Washington, DC, "France at the Brink," *Center for Security Policy*. Available online at www.centerforsecuritypolicy.org/Franceatthebrink.pdf.
6 J. Graff (27 April 2003), "One Faith Divided," *Time*. Available online at www.time.com/time/magazine/article/0,9171,901030505–447184,00.html (accessed 17 May 2003); see also Y. Camus (10 May 2004), "Islam in France," *Institute for Counter-Terrorism*. Available online at www.ict.org.il/articledet.cfm?articleid=514.
7 "La France face à ses Musulmans: émeutes, jihadisme et dépolitisation: rapport No. 172," *International Crisis Group: Working to Prevent Conflict World Wide*, 9 March 2006, pp. 1–37.
8 C. Fourest, *Frère Tariq*, Paris: Grasset, 2004, p. 425; A. Dankowitz (17 February 2006), "Tariq Ramadan – Reformist of Islamist?," *The Middle East Research Institute* (MEMRI), No. 266. Available online at www.memri.org/bin/opener_latest.cgi?ID=IA26606.
9 "La France face à ses Musulmans: émeutes, jihadisme et dépolitisation: rapport No. 172," op. cit.
10 Ibid.
11 Ibid.
12 Ibid.
13 J. J. Stemann, "Middle East Salafism's Influence and Radicalization of Muslim

Communities in Europe," *Middle East Review of International Affairs*, 7 September 2006, vol. 10, no. 3.

14 "The Hydra of Jihad," *The Century Foundation*, 2004. Available online at www.tcf.org/Publications/HomelandSecurity/clarke/3_hydra.pdf.

15 H. Mili, "Jihad without Rules: The Evolution of al-Takfir wa al-Hijra," *Terrorism Monitor*, 29 June 2006, vol. 13, no. 4.

16 Camus, op. cit.

17 "The Radicalization of Muslim Youth in Europe: The Reality and the Scale of the Threat," op. cit.

18 Alexiev, op. cit.

19 Graff, op. cit.; see also Camus, op. cit.

20 A. Seljuq (July 1997), "Cultural Conflicts: North African Immigrants in France," *The International Journal of Peace Studies*. Available online at www.gmu. edu/academic/ijps/vol2_2/seljuq.htm.

21 "The Radicalization of Muslim Youth in Europe: The Reality and the Scale of the Threat," op. cit.

22 M. Silverberg (June 2006), "The Coming of Eurabia," *Jewish Federation of Northeast Pennsylvania*. Available online at www.jfednepa.org/silverberg/eurabia.html.

23 "The Radicalization of Muslim Youth in Europe: The Reality and the Scale of the Threat," op. cit.

24 F. Ajami, "The Moor's Last Laugh: Radical Islam Finds a Haven in Europe," *Wall Street Journal*, 28 March 2004.

25 "The Radicalization of Muslim Youth in Europe: The Reality and the Scale of the Threat," op. cit.

26 Ibid.

27 Leiken, op. cit.

28 Ibid.

29 Ibid.

30 "The Radicalization of Muslim Youth in Europe: The Reality and the Scale of the Threat," op. cit.

31 E. Bakker, "Radical Islam in the Netherlands," *Terrorism Monitor*, 13 January 2005, vol. 3, no. 1.

32 Silverberg, op. cit.; Seljuq, op. cit.

33 J. Dougherty (5 November 2005), "Radical Islam Blamed for French Rioting," *WorldNetDaily*. Available online at www.wnd.com/news/printer-friendly.asp? ARTICLE_ID=47236.

34 Alexiev, op. cit.

35 Dougherty, op. cit.

36 J. Sakurai (25 February 2006), "Riots Have Created Fertile Ground for Islamic Militancy," *NCTimes*. Available online at www.nctimes.com/articles/2005/11/19/news/nation.

37 Alexiev, op. cit.

38 Sakurai, op. cit.

39 Ibid.

40 O. Roy (2007), "The Challenge of Euro-Islam," *Hoover Institution*, Stanford, CA: Hoover Publishers. Available online at www.hoover.org/publications/books/fulltext/practical/77.pdf; see also Leiken, op. cit.

41 I. Kfir (26 July 2005), "Islamic Extremism on the Rise in Europe," *Institute for Counter-Terrorism*. Available online at www.ict.org.il/articles/articledet.cfm? articleid=541; Testimony of Lorenzo Vidino of the Investigative Project, Washington, DC, before the House Committee on International Relations – Subcommittee on Europe and Emerging Threats, 27 April 2005.

42 Roy, op. cit.; Leiken, op. cit.

43 "Armed Islamic Group" (14 November 2005), *Council on Foreign Relations*. Avail-

able online at www.cfr.org/publication/9154/armed_islamic_group_algeria_islamists. html l (accessed 20 March 2007).
44 Kfir, op. cit.; Testimony of Lorenzo Vidino, op. cit.; J. Katterer, "Networks of Discontent in Northern Morocco: Drugs, Opposition and Urban Unrest," *Middle East Report*, 2001, vol. 218, p. 2.
45 "Armed Islamic Group," op. cit.
46 "The Hydra of Jihad," op. cit.
47 Kfir, op. cit.
48 Ibid.
49 "The Radicalization of Muslim Youth in Europe: The Reality and the Scale of the Threat," op. cit.
50 Kfir, op. cit.; "After van Gogh," *Economic Community*, 11 November 2004.
51 Kfir, op. cit.
52 E. Conan and C. Makarian, "Enquete sur la montée de l'Islam en Europe," *L'Express*, 26 January 2006.
53 Alexiev, op. cit.
54 K. Ridolfo (7 July 2005), "Europe Proving to be a Growing Base for Al-Qaeda," *Radio Free Europe/Radio Liberty*. Available online at www.rferl/feature articleprint/2005/07/63294.html.
55 "The Hydra of Jihad," op. cit.
56 Keats (14 January 2003), "The Salafist Group for Call and Combat (GSPC)," *CDI Terrorist Project*. Available online at www.cdi.org/terrorism/gspc.
57 "The Hydra of Jihad," op. cit.; K. Haahr-Escolano (24 February 2005), "Italy: Europe's Emerging Platform for Islamic Extremism," *Terrorism Monitor*, vol. 3, no. 4. Available online at www.jamestown.org/terrorism/news/article.php?issue_id=3242 (accessed 20 March 2007).
58 "The Hydra of Jihad," op. cit.
59 Keats, op. cit.
60 "The Hydra of Jihad," op. cit.
61 J. Jordan and R. Wesley, "The Evolution of Jihadist Networks in Spain," *Terrorism Monitor*, 12 January 2006, vol. 4, no. 1.
62 Ibid.
63 Ibid.
64 M. Laskier, "A Difficult Inheritance: Moroccan Society under King Muhammad VI," *Middle East Review of International Affairs*, September 2003, pp. 1–20.
65 Jordan and Wesley, op. cit.
66 Ibid.
67 "The Hydra of Jihad," op. cit.
68 "Terrorism in Morocco: A Security Concern for Spain" (6 April 2004), *Real Instituto Elcano*. Available online at www.domingodelpino.com/pluma/rielcano/terrorism.html.
69 "The Hydra of Jihad," op. cit.
70 Kfir, op. cit.; Testimony of Lorenzo Vidino, op. cit.
71 "The Radicalization of Muslim Youth in Europe: The Reality and the Scale of the Threat," op. cit.
72 Ibid.
73 R. M. Gerecht (April 2004), "Holy War in Europe," *American Enterprise Institute for Public Policy Research*. Available online at www.aei.org/include/pub_print.asp?pubID=20248.
74 Tlemcani, op. cit.
75 S. Trifolvic, "Islamic Terrorism in Europe: Shape of Things to Come," Special Report dated April 2002, The Rockford Institute: Center for International Affairs, pp. 1–4.
76 Ibid.
77 Ibid.

78 K. Haahr-Escolano, op. cit.

79 Ibid.

80 "The European Terrorist Union: Three Terrorists Arrested in Italy Ready to Strike" (17 November 2005), *MilitantIslamMonitor.org*. Available online at www.militantislammonitor.org/article/id/1282.

81 Haahr-Escolano, op. cit.

82 Ibid.

83 "Terrorism in Morocco: A Security Concern for Spain," op. cit.; Katterer, op. cit.; M. M. Laskier, "The Processes of Democratization, Reformism, and Islamist Protest in Morocco of the Last Decade," *Hamizrah he-Hadash*, vol. XLVI, 2006, p. 151.

84 "The Hydra of Jihad," op. cit.

85 C. E. Jesus (23 April 2003), "The Fight against Islamist Terrorism after the 3/11 Attacks," *Real Instituto Elcano de Estudios Internacionales y Estratégicos*. Available online at www.realinstitutoelcano.org/analisis/486.asp.

86 O. Bowcott (20 March 2004), "In Morocco's Gateway to Europe, Disbelief Greets Arrests over Madrid Bombings," *Guardian Digital Edition*. Available online at www.guardian.co.uk/print/0,3858,4884348–111026,00.html.

87 Ajami, op. cit.

88 "The Radicalization of Muslim Youth in Europe: The Reality and the Scale of the Threat," op. cit.

89 "La France face à ses Musulmans: émeutes, jihadisme et dépolitisation: rapport No. 172," *International Group: Working to Prevent Conflict World Wide*, 9 March 2006, pp. 1–37.

90 "The Radicalization of Muslim Youth in Europe: The Reality and the Scale of the Threat," op. cit.

91 Ajami, op. cit.

92 Jordan and Wesley, op. cit.

93 Haahr-Escolano, op. cit.

94 "The Radicalization of Muslim Youth in Europe: The Reality and the Scale of the Threat," op. cit.

95 "Violent Jihad in the Netherlands: Current Trends in the Islamist Terrorist Threat" (March 2006), *Ministry of the Interior and Kingdom Relations*. Available online at www.aivd.nl/contents/pages/65582/jihad2006en.pdf.

96 "The Radicalization of Muslim Youth in Europe: The Reality and the Scale of the Threat," op. cit.

97 Silverberg, op. cit.

98 "Violent Jihad in The Netherlands: Current Trends in the Islamist Terrorist Threat," op. cit.

99 A. Ulrich, H. Stark, C. Meyer, and D. Cziesche, "How Widespread is Terrorism in Europe?," *Der Spiegel*, 11 July 2005.

100 Silverberg, op. cit.; Ajami, op. cit.

101 Kfir, op. cit.; Testimony of Lorenzo Vidino, op. cit.

102 Leiken, "Europe's Angry Muslims," op. cit.

6 Explaining the causes of radical Islam in Europe

Jonathan S. Paris

Bernard Lewis has taught us about the civil war within Islam and the encounter of that civil war with the West.[1] The Muslim encounter with Western modernity and globalization has given rise to a nativist reaction. Nowhere is the encounter between Muslims and the West sharper than in Western Europe, which has experienced significant immigration of Muslims from the Middle East, South Asia, and elsewhere.

This chapter examines identity issues among Muslims in Europe and the new sense of global solidarity shared by European Muslims with other Muslims throughout the world. Two factors are radicalizing European Muslims today: identity issues, and a growing global Muslim connectedness and pride. Although the focus of this chapter is on the UK and France where most of my interviews took place, I address a phenomenon that is occurring broadly throughout Western Europe.

Muslims in European society struggle with dissatisfaction with traditional and modern forms of identity. The grandson of an Egyptian who is born in France feels neither Egyptian nor French. A new identity eludes him, and extremist imams, together with messages from internet websites and Arab satellite media, fill the identity vacuum and persuade him to believe in a radical view of Islam. His allegiance to the European country where he now lives, and to the culture of his immigrant parents and grandparents, has been weakened in favor of a new Muslim identity.

One consequence of the re-identification of the offspring of immigrants as "born-again" Muslims is their increasing separation from European cultural values rather than integration into their host countries in Europe. This chapter presents five important factors in the rise of radical Islam in Europe and then describes four inadequate government responses that are noticeably failing to stem Muslim radicalization.

Factors that radicalize the Muslim population in Europe

Decline in nationalism

Europe is experiencing a decline in nationalism just as transnational Islam is rising. The twentieth century was tough on Europe: two world wars, a holocaust, the abrupt end of colonialism, the loss of relative power status compared to America and Russia, and the attempt to create a new EU identity are some of the myriad factors that make nationalism passé.[2] Many native French have trouble embracing French patriotism, given the twentieth-century legacy of collaboration under the Vichy in World War II and colonial rule in North Africa.[3] The British elites are bending over backwards to provide cultural autonomy to their immigrant communities without quite spelling out what it means to be British (which is, itself, a mix of English and other national identities). Can the Polish worker who comes to Germany, let alone third-generation Turks living in Cologne, expect to become German? In Holland and Scandinavia, there does not seem to be a host national identity to offer.

The best defense against political Islam may be nationalism which, like religion, draws on primordial bonds dating back generations. If Kuwaitis think like Kuwaitis, not like Muslims, they can be weaned away from global extremist influences such as al Qaeda.[4] This strategy may work in America, where Jacksonian nationalism remains strong, but the erosion of nationalism in Europe makes it difficult to persuade French or Dutch Muslims to enthusiastically identify themselves as French or Dutch citizens. What may work in America, Russia or even in the Middle East, where relatively young states seek national legitimacy, may not work in today's Europe.

The European Muslim feels only a vague national identity with his host country. Given the confusion over the definition of a Frenchman or a European, what European values should Muslim immigrants absorb? The second and third generations of Muslims in Europe have largely rejected the traditional ethnic roots of their parents, but have failed to become wholly accepted by the majorities in European states despite their linguistic and cultural education in their host countries. Unmoored from the past and the present, they become easy prey to those who promise a future with power and respect derived from a politicized version of Muslim identity – hence, the allure of the born-again Muslim.[5]

Negative demographic trends

Demographic trends reinforce the challenges of integrating Muslims into European society. A high Muslim birth rate in Europe and an alarmingly low birth rate among indigenous Europeans, combined with the tendency for Muslims to live in urban areas, suggest that many European cities will have Muslim majorities by 2020 or 2025, even with immigration restrictions on Muslims into Europe.

In many Western European cities, the Muslim population exceeds 10 percent. Such a high number complicates assimilation. In a few cities, the population of Muslims is approaching the 50 percent tipping point, or will do so in the coming decades given current demographic trends of a declining European native birth rate, a higher Muslim birth rate, and continuing immigration.

In Bradford, UK, one of the early destinations of Pakistani immigrants after the Second World War, the 1991 census recorded 64,000 Muslims representing

13 percent of the population. By 2001 there were 94,000 Muslims, a 50 percent increase from 1991. In 2001, Muslims represented 19 percent of the overall population but over 30 percent of students and 50 percent of toddlers. By 2011, Muslims will represent close to 30 percent of the population in Bradford and over 50 percent of its students.[6] The high growth rates and youth bubble create a burgeoning pool of young Muslim males, the key source of recruitment for Islamists.

By 2025 to 2030, there will be Muslim majorities in the under-twenties urban cohort throughout Europe. Even in the absence of the virulent Islamist ideologies swirling around Europe today, it is difficult to imagine the smooth assimilation of Muslim immigrants into European society, given their exuberant demography coupled with downward population trends among native Europeans. These demographic movements may be the gravest challenge to European stability and prosperity in the coming decades.

Muslim "preceptoralism"

European-born children and grandchildren of immigrants of Muslim faith are increasingly being politicized as Muslims with separate identities from their host European societies by persuasive messages from both local and global "preceptors." By preceptors, I mean a range of figures and phenomena including imams in London, Birmingham, and Lyon, local Muslim leaders and spokespersons, international Islamic icons like Osama bin Laden, Ayman al Zawahiri, Mahmoud Ahmadinejad, and Hassan Nasrallah in Afghanistan, Iran, and Lebanon, *jihadi* internet websites and 24/7 Arab satellite media.

"Preceptoralism" is a term coined by the Yale social scientist Charles E. Lindblom in the 1975 classic *Politics and Markets*, to describe intense ideological indoctrination using persuasive messages to mobilize cadres of true believers. Preceptors tend to be charismatic orators who rely on persuasion to gain the voluntary enthusiasm of their disciples rather than on fear and command used by the average dictator in the command system, or on appeals to individual self-interest based on material and economic incentives in the capitalist-oriented exchange system.[7] Preceptoral leaders are mobilizers of the street who prey on lost souls and transform them into true believers through indoctrination.[8]

More attention needs to be given to the role of persuasion from imams in mosques than to the narratives conveyed on the *jihadi* internet and in bookshops. Organized radical groups like Hizb-ut-Tahrir, based in the UK, are brainwashing new generations of British Muslims by indoctrinating them with homophobic, anti-Semitic, chauvinistic, anti-women rhetoric calling for the return of the Caliphate. Yet British Home Office authorities refuse to ban them because these groups have not broken the law.[9]

The techniques used by imams in their recruitment and mobilization of Muslims in Europe are similar to those used in Maoist China, where small groups would meet to engage in self-criticism and introspection to learn the ideological elements of the Red Book. Omar Bakri Mohammed, a Syrian-born imam and founder of one UK group, Al-Muhajiroun, articulates the process of persuading a new recruit. Activist members:

> are careful to let the individual come to his or her own conclusion about the issue through conversation and dialogue ... [L]et himself tell me the problem. You don't figure it out for him. You want him to figure out the problem [and take the decision to look deeper into Islam]. *Unless he himself determines the problem, he will never have conviction.* That is the fundamental condition of conviction – self-determination. [Emphasis added][10]

Once the individual is in the fold, the successful imam no longer needs to give specific orders to his followers.

The final stage of indoctrination is the critical point on the conveyor belt to militancy where identity issues crystallize into an ideological dynamic. The convert is given a Muslim name, replacing his secular one, and becomes part of a much larger and more powerful group than his host country or his parents' country of origin. The imams nurture this feeling that they owe their primary loyalty not to their nation of residence or to their race or ethnicity but to Islam. The young Muslim male from Leeds now identifies with Muslim victims all over the world – from Chechnya, Bosnia, and the Palestinian territories to Iraq. He also has an explanation for his grievances against his host country: *Islamophobia*. He now thinks that they discriminate against him not, as in the case of other non-Muslim minorities, because of his dark skin color, but because he is Muslim.

Timothy Garton Ash links up the various psychological and social mechanisms discussed above in explaining the pathology of the offspring of immigrants, which he calls the "Inbetween People." Discussing the Dutch-Moroccan murderer of Theo Van Gogh in Holland, he writes:

> Bouyeri's story has striking similarities with those of some of the London and Madrid bombers, and members of the Hamburg cell of al Qaeda who were central to the 11 September 2001 attacks on New York. There's the same initial embrace and then angry rejection of modern European secular culture, whether in its Dutch, German, Spanish, or British variant, with its common temptations of sexual license, drugs, drink, and racy entertainment; the pain of being torn between two home countries, neither of which is fully home; the influence of a radical imam, and of Islamist material from the Internet, audiotapes, or videocassettes and DVDs; a sense of global Muslim victimhood, exacerbated by horror stories from Bosnia, Chechnya, Palestine, Afghanistan, and Iraq; the groupthink of a small circle of friends, stiffening one's resolve; and the tranquil confidence with which many of these young men seem to have approached martyrdom. Such suicide killers are obviously not representative of the great majority of Muslims living peacefully in Europe; but they are, without question, extreme and excep-

tional symptoms of a much broader alienation of the children of Muslim immigrants to Europe. Their sickness of mind and heart reveals, in an extreme form, the pathology of the Inbetween People.[11]

The impact of Arab satellite media exposure of Israeli-Palestinian and Iraqi violence

One senior Foreign Office official told me that in focus groups among British Muslims during the height of the second Intifada in early 2003, the salience of Palestinian issues was higher than Kashmiri issues despite the fact that the vast majority of the interviewees were descended from Kashmir and other parts of South Asia.[12] This vicarious identification suggests the cumulative impact of Arab satellite media exposure of Israeli-Palestinian violence, and offers a partial explanation of the context in which two educated British Muslims of Pakistani descent went to Tel Aviv to blow themselves up at a popular bar filled with teenagers in the spring of 2003. The perceived denial of dignity and recognition on the part of the Palestinians is transmitted to the European Muslim with a desire to act and to "impose oneself on the West through an act of terror."[13]

This *identity of vicarious grievances* that European Muslims feel for their brethren in Palestine, Iraq, Chechnya, and Kashmir arises out of the focused persuasive messages from Islamist imams and leaders, internet sites and media outlets.[14] Alienated from the country in which they reside, European Muslims have developed an empathy with Muslim victims throughout the world, and convince themselves that their own exclusion and the persecution of their brothers have the same roots: rejection of Islam by the West.[15] The result of this saturation of preceptoral messages and vicarious identity is the development of a renewed global Islamic solidarity. It is interesting that the Ottoman Empire and its German advisers in the First World War tried and failed to use an appeal to Islamic solidarity to mobilize Muslims from British and Russian-controlled parts of the Middle East and South Asia to revolt against their non-Muslim overlords. The *jihad* of the twenty-first century is much more ideologically based, media-oriented, "virtual," and effective than the German-concocted Ottoman *jihad* a century ago.

The Muslim world's reaction to the Danish cartoon drawings of the Prophet Mohammed and to Pope Benedict's speech in 2006 citing a medieval Byzantine ruler's unflattering comments about Islam are examples of a renewed global Islamic solidarity that results from preceptoral messages emanating from Islamist imams, leaders, internet and Arab satellite media. The collective Muslim "we" was offended and signaled in its strong response to the Danish magazine's cartoons and the Pope's speech in Regensburg, Germany, that "when you say something or do something you are not just talking to the Egyptians or to the Syrians or to the Saudis, but you are talking to the entire Muslim world."[16]

The cartoon controversy silenced most European moderate Muslims who were privately aghast at the demonstrations, embassy burnings, and killing of hundreds of people over the publication of cartoons. So strong is the collective Muslim identity that the individual finds himself unable to speak out. The ambivalent moderate Muslim cannot bring himself to support the infidel against a violent or extremist fellow Muslim.[17] Identifying moderates and preventing them from being pilloried as traitors within their own community are two important challenges.

The role of Muslim leadership

One would have thought that following the 7/7 London bombing, the Muslim community and national leaders would have addressed the serious *reputation* damage wreaked by terrorists on the Muslim community by confronting radical and separatist trends. Instead, they too often promoted the grievance politics of Islamophobia and mobilized otherwise apolitical Muslims to blame government policies on the Middle East.

The British Muslim leaders request that the government moderate its policies in Iraq and Israel-Palestine in order to prevent their constituencies in Leicester from radicalizing. To illustrate this point, the Muslim Council of Britain, the country's leading Muslim organization, issued a press release in response to the Home Secretary's call for British Muslim parents to be vigilant of their children's slide towards extremism.

> **Press Release**
> **Government Has a Duty Also to Help Prevent Spread of Extremist Ideas**
> In response to the speech earlier today from the Home Secretary, John Reid, the Muslim Council of Britain firmly believes that all parents, both Muslims and non-Muslims, have an important responsibility in being vigilant and ensuring that their children are not misled by criminal and extremist elements in society. However, the MCB notes that the government needs to also recognize the impact of some of its own policies, domestic and foreign, in contributing to the spread of extremist-ideas.
>
> "It is as though in response to the threat of Global Warming and the threat of rising water levels, the government were to ask all of us merely to place sandbags outside our homes to prevent flooding. Surely, the more sensible way forward would be to tackle the causes of Global Warming. Similarly, in continuing to ignore the damage that some of our foreign policies, particularly in the Middle East, have done to our national security, the government is not facing up to a major contributory factor behind the rise of extremism," said Dr Muhammad 'Abdul Bari, Secretary-General of the Muslim Council of Britain.[18]

Rather than focus attention on the "bad apples" that are sullying the UK Muslim community's reputation, the British Muslim leadership tends to divert attention to unpopular foreign policies. This amounts to political blackmail. British policy towards Iraq and Israel-Palestine should be governed by the local adversaries' actions (i.e., whether or not terrorists are launching suicide bombings or rocket attacks), rather than the vicarious echo effect transmitted by Arab satellite media on the Muslim community living in Bradford, UK.

Some might argue that one solution is to change Western foreign policy: asking for even-handedness on Israel-Palestine and withdrawal from Iraq. However, the problem is that Islamist-inspired terrorism occurs also in places with persistent anti-American and anti-Israeli policies like France and Belgium.

When President Jacques Chirac voiced opposition to the Iraq war in 2003, Muslim taxi drivers in Paris called him Muhammad Chirac.[19] Yet the Islamists target European countries that oppose the war as much as those that support the war. The ire of the Islamists appears to be Western democratic values, not the politics or foreign policy of individual countries. The Islamist political agenda is to contest Western humanist values: sexual equality and freedom of religion and speech. They want religious-based political parties and the creation of Shari'a tribunals for civil and domestic matters. Even if they cannot achieve these precise goals, they hope to deepen the divide between Muslims and non-Muslims and thereby radicalize Muslim communities.[20]

Inadequate government responses

Government disregard of fence-sitters

A major factor that handicaps efforts to stem radicalization of European Muslims is the tendency of governments to ignore "fence-sitters," the large group of ambivalent Muslims who prefer the benefits of modern European life and economic opportunity but also sympathize with the political aims of terrorists such as the 7/7 London bombers. They are called fence-sitters because they sit on the border of radicalization. They could go either way.

To demonstrate just how important fence-sitters are to fighting domestic terrorism, European governments do not have the resources to monitor effectively the 1 percent hardcore Islamists in their countries when another 10 percent of the Muslim populations are providing tacit support to the hardcore. In Ireland, the IRA was not defeated until the fence-sitters ceased to provide tacit support to IRA activists.[21]

British authorities cannot easily root out home-grown Islamic terrorists as long as large numbers of British Muslims look the other way. According to a poll commissioned for a British television program aired in August 2006, 23 percent of British Muslims felt the 7/7 London bombers were justified due to British support for the US War on Terror. Elements within the larger Muslim community sometimes shield local *jihadis* from authorities as they conspire to make future attacks or link up with other *jihadis* in Iraq and elsewhere. British authorities must convince fence-sitters that their tacit support of terror activities damages the reputation of the Muslim community. These fence-sitters must be shown the benefits of their cooperation in informing authorities of extremist activities.

The importance of fence-sitters to law enforcement officials is reinforced by the increasing indigenization of radicals. Until the Bouyeri assassination of Dutch filmmaker Theo Van Gogh, the Dutch government emulated other European countries' counter-terrorism practices by monitoring foreigners, such as veteran Afghan and Bosnian *salafi-jihadis*, whose distinctive dress made them easy to spot. The foreign *jihadis* do not pose the same security challenge for authorities as does the monitoring of the "New *Jihadis*," home-grown, third-generation Moroccan Dutch radicals, often teenagers, who are incubating in their local Moroccan communities in The Netherlands and elsewhere.[22] It will be difficult for authorities to persuade the fence-sitters in these communities to turn in their neighbors and kinsmen.

A broader political problem faced by the West is that many fence-sitters among the silent majority of Muslims who live peacefully in Europe will join the extremists if they perceive that Muslims have prospects of achieving "victory" in Europe.[23] Fence-sitters tend to go with the winning side. Both European governments and Muslim leaders need to persuade the broader Muslim community that siding with radical Islam is a lost cause.

European governments' disproportionate emphasis on criminalizing terrorism

Some European government responses are so inadequate that they represent additional causes of radicalization. The defect in British and other European government approaches to the radicalization of Islam is their refusal to grapple with the ideology of Islamist movements, the mobilizing factor of young Muslims in Europe. One side is fighting a war under the banner of Islam, while the other side, comprising European states and society, is treating the war as a social or criminal problem to be rectified through improved social engineering and court hearings.

The problem with the European approach is that criminalizing terrorism ignores the radicalizing effect of the imam-preceptors, who do not actually commit a criminal act. If persuasion is the critical enabler of radicalization, then criminal law-enforcement approaches to the War on Terror that focus on the operational but not on the motivational side may not be sufficient to deal with the terrorist threat. Emphasis must be placed on influential figures such as Abu Hamza al Masri, the imam who preached to such congregants as Richard Reid, the Shoe Bomber, and Zacarias Moussaoui, the twentieth 9/11 hijacker. By understanding and responding to imams like Abu Hamza, who make deep impressions on their followers, such as Muslim Brotherhood leader Yusuf Qaradawi, whose internet-issued *fatwas* justify suicide bombings in Iraq and Israel, governments can begin to mitigate the threat of terror in Europe. For every charismatic imam, there are possibly 20 more young men converted to the cause of killing themselves in carrying out missions against non-believers in the name of Islam.

Inadequate military response

By the same logic, the US tendency to emphasize military solutions to this ideological war is similarly flawed. Military attacks, like court proceedings, tend to target the end-user, the terrorist, rather than those who inspire the attacks. The hypothetical aforementioned 1:20 ratio of imam to operatives provides a context for understanding former US Defense Secretary Rumsfeld's memorable 16 October 2003 query: "Is our current situation such that 'the harder we work, the behinder we get?'" In other words, is the pool of extremists from whom terrorists are drawn growing faster than known terrorists can be captured or killed? From mosques and schools to one-on-one mentoring to "virtual *jihad*" over the internet, the multiplier effect of recruitment by radical preceptors becomes apparent.

Misguided policy focus

Government attempts to co-opt political Islamists from the Muslim Brotherhood and elsewhere in order to isolate radicals are misguided. Many Muslim leaders in Europe present themselves to governments as moderates who can rein in extremists. The agenda of the Muslim Brotherhood, for instance, is not a violent one, but a political one: to politicize the Muslims in Europe into voting blocs that advocate Muslim agendas on domestic issues such as the role of Shariʻa law, and on international issues such as the illegitimacy of the State of Israel. This strategy takes advantage of the desperation of government elites and their unwillingness to confront political Islam, despite the undermining effect of political Islamists on European values such as free speech and gender equality. The longer term problem is not *jihadis* but the non-violent political Islamists who are mobilizing the heretofore politically apathetic majority of European Muslims into an advocacy group on foreign policy and veiling. The enfranchisement of young Muslims may allow political Islamists to take advantage of their exuberant demography to affect European policies in profound ways, posing a long-term danger.

France, in particular, is at a critical moment with respect to the teeming underclass living in social ghettos outside its main cities, especially Paris. If the harsh tactics of the police that in part provoked the autumn 2005 riots are replaced by engagement and dialogue between the preponderantly Muslim teenagers and young men and the community outreach groups, then the Islamists may be unable to prevail. Absent the ability of the post-Chirac leadership to generate reform and jobs in the *banlieues*, however, the Islamists will provide an alternative for those unemployed lost souls who now either join a nihilistic gang or try to assimilate and suffer the associated social stigma of going straight from their cohorts in the ghettos. Political Islam will always offer empowerment in the face of social rejection by French society.

A crucial question is: What happens if those rioters in the *banlieues* start voting? Enfranchisement is a good thing.[24] However, some officials in the

French Interior Ministry worry privately that enfranchising angry young males may not reduce radicalism. While French Muslims have hitherto not voted as a bloc,[25] this may be attributable to the low voting rate among young Muslim males. Not unlike the Hamas surge in the January 2006 elections, future French elections could see angry Muslim males mobilizing behind populist politicians either from the Islamist camp or their leftist allies in the anti-American and anti-globalist camp. If Muslim political activists are able to forge a coalition of Muslim identity voters and non-Muslim leftists, anti-globalists, and anti-American voters, they could exert a preponderant influence on the domestic and foreign policies of their governments. It is hard to imagine how contrary voices calling for closer European–American collaboration will prevail in the face of the growing empowerment of political Muslims in Europe.

Conclusion

It is difficult to pinpoint the myriad factors that give rise to Muslim identity issues. Important background issues include unemployment, social exclusion, disappointment in expectations relative to their parents' generation and their non-Muslim peers, erosion of traditional authority, erosion of national identity and decline in support for European liberal democratic values, and the failure of a pan-European identity to replace eroding national identities. Add to this mix European hyper-secularism and hostility to faith, and one finds fertile grounds for radicalization.

The decline of ethnic attachment, cultural mores, parental authority, and traditional family values combined with identity shopping of many young Euro-peans in a region with amorphous identities leaves a vacuum for Islamist imams to sell a Muslim identity that is attractive to many young European Muslims. Islamism offers an elixir of power to compensate for feeling powerless in the face of Western and especially American power. On a more local level, one French writer describes the difficulty for the young French Muslim male, who despairs of ever leaving his ghetto and becoming part of French society, to resist the attraction of power offered by Islamists. By choosing the Islamist route, he avoids both the stigma of being labeled a delinquent gang-member in the *ban-lieue*, and the "Uncle Tom" label from his peers as a traitor who attempts to embrace French norms. The best way to overcome his feeling of powerlessness is to become a born-again Muslim.[26]

Discrimination and socio-economic deprivation alone do not account for radicalization. The fallacy of highlighting socio-economic deprivation as the root cause of radicalism is demonstrated by the fact that poverty, exclusion, and racism experienced by European Muslims are also experienced by other groups *that are not Muslim* in Europe, including sub-Saharan African and Caribbean immigrants and their offspring. These groups have not become radicalized.[27] The catalyst for the radicalization of European Muslims that is absent among their non-Muslim cohorts is *the pull of Muslim solidarity*. European Muslims are part of a gigantic wave of Islamism sweeping the globe post-9/11.

By understanding the indoctrination of European Muslims as the source of radicalization and separation from mainstream European values, governments can begin to craft appropriate policies to counter radicalization. The essential point is to counter the political agendas of Islamists. The radicalization of European Muslims is not just a terrorist problem, or primarily a terrorist problem. It is a political problem in that the mobilizing of European Muslims to advocate political goals such as the imposition of Shariʿa law, the banning of homosexuality, a differentiation of rights between genders, the delegitimization of Israel, the pursuit of anti-American policies, and the support of radical *jihadis* and Islamists abroad are as much the goals of non-violent political Islamists as they are of radical Islamists.

An artificial dichotomy between radical and political Islamists leads European governments to mistakenly empower political Islamists as "moderates" in order to isolate radical *salafi* Islamists under the theory that the main imperative is to prevent alienated Muslims from launching another London or Madrid bombing. Both types of Islamists advocate an intolerant, separationist value system antithetical to the Western value system that undergirds European democracies. The real split is between secular Muslims who want to climb the economic ladder and who identify themselves primarily as doctors, teachers, engineers or students, and only as Muslims in terms of their faith; and Islamists (both political and radical) who assert a world view based not on religious piety but on a global political movement.

The growth of Muslim true believers in Europe is a cause for great concern to European society and governments. Countering increasing radicalization is not an easy task.[28] It may require a forthright assertion of European values, and a recalibration of European laws in order to isolate the imam preceptors and prevent them from spewing their hatred in a way that attracts young Muslim followers.

Notes

1 See B. Lewis, *Islam and the West*, Oxford: Oxford University Press, 1994, and, more recently, *The Crisis of Islam: Holy War and Unholy Terror*, New York: Random House Trade Publishers, 2004.
2 See also T. Judt, *Post-war; A History of Europe since 1945*, Harmondsworth: Penguin, 2006.
3 Conversation with the French philosopher, Alain Finkelkraut, in Paris, 3 November 2005.
4 O. Bakri Mohammed, head of Al-Muhajiroun and the imam-preceptor-mentor of the Mike's Place bombers in Tel Aviv, 2003, said after the Tel Aviv attack that "he was very proud of the fact that the Muslims grow closer every day, that the Muslim land is one land and *there is no more nationalism or Arabism*" (emphasis added). See Q. Wiktorowicz, *Radical Islam Rising: Muslim Extremism in the West*, New York: Rowman & Littlefield 2005, pp. 6–7. I develop this theme more fully in my article, "When to Worry in the Middle East," *Orbis*, fall 1993, vol. 37, no. 4, pp. 553–565.
5 The attraction of the contemporary "virtual *umma*" is a core theme of Olivier Roy in *Globalized Islam*, New York: Columbia University Press, 2004.
6 A. R. Alexiev, presenter at Conference, "Les Democraties face au defi Islamiste,"

Institut pour la Defense de la Democratie and Center for Security Policy, Paris, 13 March 2006.

7 See C. E. Lindblom, *Politics and Markets*, New York: Basic Books, 1975, ch. 4.

8 Shmuel Bar, an Israeli expert on Islamist ideologies, used the term "lost souls" in an interview on 25 January 2006. See also Eric Hoffer's classic book on mass movements, *The True Believer*, New York: Harper & Row, 1951.

9 Conversation with Home Office official at a RUSI conference in London, autumn 2006. His argument was that banning HT would force them underground and make them more difficult to monitor. William Sieghart, Chairman of Forward Thinking, a UK NGO, made the same point to me following his dialogue with HT representatives (conversation in Berlin, 11 March 2007).

10 Q. Wiktorowicz, *Radical Islam Rising: Muslim Extremism in the West*, New York: Rowman & Littlefield, 2005, p. 97.

11 T. Garton Ash, "Islam in Europe," *New York Review of Books*, 5 October 2006, vol. 53, no. 15.

12 Conversation with Mr. Fox, FCO Near East, 7 May 2003, Sussex, UK.

13 Farhad Khoshrovar, in "Currents and Crosscurrents of Radical Islamism," CSIS Transatlantic Dialogue on Terrorism Report, April 2006, p. 12.

14 This term was coined by the French-Iranian sociologist, Farhad Khoshrovar. Conversation with Khoshrovar in Paris, 16 February 2006.

15 Claude Moniquet testimony at house committee, April 2005. Available online at www.esisc.org.

16 *International Herald Tribune*, 8 February 2006, p. 8, col. 5. The collective identity pre-dates 2006. One young Moroccan-Dutch woman said that before the 9/11 attacks on New York, "I was just Nora. Then, all of a sudden, I was a Muslim." Ash, op. cit.

17 B. Bawer, *While Europe Slept: How Radical Islam is Destroying Europe from Within*, New York: Doubleday, 2006, p. 229. There are exceptions, such as the two courageous North American Muslim women, Irshad Manji from Toronto and the Syrian-born Californian, Wafa Sultan.

18 MCB Press Release, 20 September 2006. Abdel Bari was also quoted as saying that the British government should not be surprised if it finds itself deluged by two million terrorists, over 700,000 in London alone (two million happens to be the approximate Muslim population of the UK) if the government does not change its Islamophobic ways. *Daily Telegraph*, 10 September 2006, p. 1.

19 Interview with Hervé de Carmoy, Paris, 16 February 2006.

20 Claude Moniquet, House testimony, infra. Available online. at www.esisc.org, p. 4.

21 Shamit Saggar, University of Sussex lecture, 16 March 2006. Professor of Political Science at the University of Sussex and former adviser on minority affairs to the British Prime Minister's Office, Saggar is an example of the hugely successful integration of Indian Ismaili immigrants expelled suddenly from Idi Amin's Uganda in 1972. In addition to his focus on fence-sitters as the key to prevailing over radical elements in the British Muslim community, Saggar also propounds an integration formula based on bonding and bridging. There is nothing wrong with bonding elements in a minority community (for example, Orthodox Jewish schools) provided that there is also a tendency within the minority community to bridge into the larger society, such as in the case of the Eastern European Jewish immigrants in the first half of the twentieth century and the Indian immigrants from East Africa in the 1970s. Pietism among the Pakistani and Bangladeshi Muslim communities is a form of bonding that poses few problems in itself. The problem is the lack of bridging into the majority community, the absence of contact between the Pakistani and Bangladeshi communities, and the growing politicization of youth in these communities.

22 Moniquet, op. cit.

23 This has implications for US policy towards Iran. If President Ahmadinejad appears to win the showdown with the West over the nuclear issue, many fence-sitters in

Europe and around the world will conclude that radical Islam led by people like Ahmadinejad is winning, that Allah is winning and the West is in retreat. If such a perception takes hold among Muslim populations, pro-American moderate regimes in the region, along with more tolerant Muslim figures in Europe, will lose ground.

24 See the International Crisis Group report issued following the riots in early 2006, which calls for enfranchisement of underprivileged young French adults in these ghettos as an important step forward. See also Jonathan Laurence and Justin Vaisse, *Integrating Islam, Political and Religious Challenges in Contemporary France*, New York: Brookings Institution Press, 2006.

25 See S. Giry, "France and Its Muslims," *Foreign Affairs*, July/August 2006, vol. 85, no. 5, pp. 87–104.

26 C. Beyler, "The Jihadist Threat in France," *Current Trends in Islamist Ideology*, Hudson Institute, vol. 3, p. 92.

27 British and French Muslim immigration to Europe is relatively recent, dating from the late 1940s in the UK and the 1960s and 1970s in France. In order to fill acute labor needs, temporary workers were brought over – sometimes the males of entire villages in Pakistan to the UK and in Algeria to France – with the idea that they would return. Instead, they stayed and their families joined them. While *bonding* within these first-time immigrant communities remained strong, evidenced by the retention of strong ethnic ties to their countries of origin, *bridging* into the wider society was weak. They have lagged behind socio-economically. Some of the reasons why bridging is stronger among America Muslims is that they are far fewer in number than in Europe, they are more educated as they come from more advantaged communities in the Middle East and South Asia, and, finally, Muslim Americans are just another hyphenated American group more easily integrated into a society of immigrants. See "Currents and Crosscurrents of Radical Islamism," CSIS Transatlantic Dialogue on Terrorism Report, April 2006, p. 7. The unskilled working-class origins of European Muslim immigrants, as compared to the more highly educated, often professional background of American Muslim immigrants, explain some, but not all, of the socio-economic lag of the former. The Indian community emigrated *en masse* from Uganda to the UK in the 1960s with little economic wherewithal, and were expected to encounter similar difficulties in integrating. Yet, within a generation, many offspring of Ugandan Asians are successful professionals, engineers and so on.

28 The arrest of two dozen people in London and other British cities in August 2006 for plotting to blow up planes *en route* from London to the United States is a chilling reminder of how deep the problem of radical Islam in the United Kingdom has become. Nearly all the suspects are British-born Muslims of Pakistani descent. While there appear to be connections with Pakistani extremist groups, possibly even al Qaeda, the inescapable conclusion of this plot is that many British-born Muslims hate their country and America enough to blow themselves up in airplanes carrying innocent passengers. See J. S. Paris, "Radical Islam a Worrisome, Deep Problem in Britain," *Baltimore Sun*, 13 August 2006.

7 The evolution of Iranian interventionism

Support for radical Islam in Turkey, 1982–2003

Patrick James and Yasemin Akbaba

Overview

With the horrific events of September 11 2001, religion is back in the forefront of International Relations (IR). In spite of incidents in the real world of politics, religion failed to take a prominent role in scientific research in the modern era. Religion is sometimes referred to as the "overlooked dimension,"[1] while Andreas Hasenclever and Volker Rittberger point to "little systematic research on the impact of religious faith on the course of conflicts,"[2] and Pavlos Hatzopoulos and Fabio Petito observe that a rejection of religion "seems to be inscribed in the genetic code of the discipline of IR."[3] However, religion today is in return from "exile"[4] and represents a thriving area of research in IR. Studies are proliferating quickly in the new millennium; approaches run the gamut from theoretical essays through case studies to aggregate data analysis.[5] Religion is once again understood to be important to the study of IR, and one scholar even calls for an "international political theology."[6]

This study focuses on Iranian support for radical Islam in Turkey following the transition from the 1979 Revolution through 2003. Iran is a unique and interesting case to pursue in the study of religion and IR for several reasons: its theocracy, its possession of vast quantities of strategically important commodities, and its inclusion in the "Axis of Evil" designated by President George W. Bush at a defining moment in the War on Terror. Iran's relationship with Turkey becomes an especially intriguing aspect of its foreign policy due to the latter's secular tradition and geographic proximity. In other words, in spite of their geographic proximity, Iran and Turkey form an interesting dyad due to their contrasting ideologies. Self-identification by each country is opposite to the other. While Turkey disregards the role of religion in its state identity, Iran designates Islam as its reason for existence. Therefore, their interaction with each other at the international level is quite important for both actors. Henri Barkley summarizes this argument:

> Iran and Turkey, brought together by geography and separated by ideology and regime interests, have had a long history of conflict and cooperation. ...

[E]ach regime, because of its fundamental ideology and identity, represents an existential threat of sorts to the other. The Turkish–Iranian divide goes back to the end of the fifteenth century when the Sunni–Shi'a division was the single most important ideological fault line. Today, the respective regimes interpret the secular–religious divide in very much the same way.[7]

Analysis of Iranian interventionism vis-à-vis Turkey will be guided by a framework developed by Carment, James and Taydas.[8] Their model of intervention in ethnic conflict can be extended easily to the ethnoreligious domain of the present study. The framework from Carment *et al.* focuses on ethnic composition and related factors, along with the degree to which institutional constraints are present, to explain a state's propensity for interventionism. A framework that considers domestic determinants such as ethnic composition and institutional constraints is ideal for Iran–Turkey relations, since Iran's willingness to export Islam is expressed not only through international rhetoric, but also through domestic policies.

This study starts by introducing the framework from Carment *et al.* in further detail and identifying Iran's place within it. The chapter continues with a narrative history of Iran's support for radical Islam in Turkey from 1982 to 2003. This is followed by an assessment of the case history in the context of the framework. The next section explores alternative avenues of analysis to explain changes in Iranian intervention in Turkey. The final section offers general conclusions and ideas for future research.

Third-party intervention and expectations about Iran

Carment *et al.* have put forward a model of ethnoreligious intervention that focuses on the presumed effects of institutional constraints in combination with ethnic composition.[9] For present purposes, the key expectations concern states categorized as ethnically diverse and (un)constrained in institutional terms. Iran, as will become apparent later on, is considered ethnically diverse over the full period of study but switches from low to mixed with respect to institutional constraints.

The Carment *et al.* model conveys expectations about potential intervening states that vary on the basis of diverse or dominant ethnic composition and high or low institutional constraints. This creates a typology with four ideal types, two of which are relevant here.[10] For the low-constraint, diverse state, the expectation is "passive lobbying." Leaders of such states are deemed unlikely to pander directly to the interests of any one ethnic group. Potential ramifications for domestic politics account for the anticipated relatively restrained approach towards intervention. Making ethnicity a salient aspect of foreign policy is inherently risky for a diverse state because it could trigger infighting between groups or even incite potential internal enemies to seek support from neighboring states. Large-scale military intervention, for example, would be out of the question aside from the most extraordinary circumstances. Normally, elites in low-constraint, diverse states will express a moderate preference for involvement. Intervention is anticipated to take a relatively "safe" form – limited and even covert support for an ethnoreligious minority located elsewhere – should be the norm to the extent that it is observed. In sum, passive lobbying rather than intense public pressure or military intervention is deemed most likely in this context.

Diverse, high-constraint states face a double-edged sword with regard to possible intervention. In addition to caution brought about by diversity, a relatively high level of institutional constraint should create a *realpolitik* disposition. Intervention is held back by institutions and the risk of a "boomerang" effect at home as a result of ethnic diversity. Thus the likelihood of intervention is at a minimum among these states because a successful policy would need to pass both domestic and foreign tests regarding its value. This does not mean, of course, that intervention will always be ruled out as a policy. *Realpolitik* disposition in the Carment *et al.* model refers to a minimal "win-set" for the decision makers as referred to by Robert Putnam,[11] i.e. minimal available choices that will be considered acceptable to the mass public. When the model's expectation is *realpolitik*, this means a state's cost–benefit calculations will be influenced by strictly practical notions. In other words, the state is expected to follow pragmatic policies. Most of the time, for an ethnically diverse state with high institutional constraints, this means less intervention. However, intervention remains an option if it might serve some pragmatic purpose. For example, the elite may be subjected to pressure from ethnic "outbidding." Followers may demand action to reinforce the regime's legitimacy in their eyes as a standard bearer for some ethnoreligious grouping. Leaders may have to bid for support by intervening in some form abroad. Interventions can be expected to occur only when there is a minimal risk of costly domestic side-effects coupled with the expectation of real gain in foreign policy, and can also be expected to increase power if such actions are anticipated. This adds up to a realist approach that reflects the perceived national interest.

For a diverse, low-constraint state, passive lobbying in practice would include "cheap talk." While ethnic affinity might encourage more action, prudence would dictate very limited support. Material support for a minority abroad, to the extent that it occurs, could be expected to take a minimal and covert form. The reasons behind these expectations go back to reverberations anticipated with a diverse audience at home that may react badly to support abroad for members of one particular group as opposed to another. With respect to a diverse, high-constraint state, a realist policy based on the national interest may show more variation. Support for a minority abroad at times might look like passive support, but at others could be more open and substantive if outbidding takes place. A regime might need to establish credibility along some dimension to placate its most intense supporters. Even more variation can be expected from a hybrid regime that is moving from low to high institutional constraint. Policies there might become turbulent in reflection of the changes taking place inside the potential intervening state itself.

Carment *et al.* also refer to two "enabling conditions" with regard to intervention.[12] These conditions can come into play for any type of potential intervening state and impact upon its disposition to act. One condition is transnational ethnic affinity, in which members of a group identify with each other across national borders. This linkage is affective rather than instrumental and normally connects a majority in one state with a minority in another. Prominent examples include the Tamils of South India, the Chinese of Southeast Asia and others. With such affinities, which can focus on religion as easily as ethnicity, intervention becomes more feasible. Conditions for the minority are likely to be monitored closely, with a high sensitivity as to how it is being treated. The other enabling condition is ethnic cleavage. This refers to the degree of division in a society that is present as a result of high ethnoreligious consciousness, which in turn reflects regime repression, civil unrest and loss of civil liberties. All things being equal, high affinities and cleavage increase the likelihood of intervention.

How, then, does Iran fit into the presented framework between the years of 1982 and 2003? This period begins after the Iranian Revolution and ends with the terminal point for data needed to provide rigorous assessment of institutional constraints. Polity IV data are the most authoritative available on political institutions. The Polity data establish that Iran moved from being categorized as a transitional state (1979–1981) to an autocracy (1982–1996) and then exhibited a mixture of autocratic and democratic traits, leaning towards the latter (1997–2003).[13]

Iran is ethnically diverse. The *CIA World Factbook* records Iran's Persian population as 51 percent. The second largest group, the Azeris, come in at 24 percent, with seven other designations making up the rest of the population.[14] Reinforcing this sense of diversity is the presence of eight groups classified as Minorities at Risk (MAR) by the project of the same name.[15] The MARs in Iran include Arabs, Azerbaijanis, Baha'is, Bakhtiari, Baluchis, Christians, Kurds and Turkmen, and collectively represent considerable ethnoreligious diversity. However, it is important to note that 89 percent of Iran is Shiʿa Muslim. In other words, within this diversity, there is ideological and demographic dominance of the Shiʿa denomination of Islam. This becomes a significant issue, especially from the *realpolitik* disposition of the model for Iran.

From 1982 to 1996, Iran is categorized as a diverse, low-constraint state. Thus it is expected to engage in passive lobbying in support of relevant ethnoreligious minorities. While Iran does not reach a level at which its institutional constraints would be regarded as "high," neither is the post-1996 version a purely "low" constraint state either. Given the shift towards a higher degree of institutional constraint, it would be reasonable to expect post-1996 Iran to feature a combination of passive lobbying and *realpolitik* in its intervention-related behavior. Effects related to affinity and cleavage in the Iranian context with regard to Turkey also are noted below.

Iranian support for Turkish Islamism

Turkey and Iran have been at peace since 1639 – an impressive date that goes back to before the modern era of statehood. During the first half of the twentieth century, Iran and Turkey did not experience significant conflict with each other.[16] Iran under the Shah had a generally favorable relationship with Turkey. Each state featured a commitment to secular government and modernization, along with extensive connections to the US through the Central Treaty Organization (CENTO). A basic change came about with the Iranian Revolution of 1979. This event brought to power an Islamist regime with a very different way of looking at the world.[17] From that point onward, Iran and Turkey represented an "existential threat" to each other.[18] On the one hand, to Iran's mullahs, Turkey's secular constitution in an Islamic country resembles an ongoing call to counter-revolution. On the other hand, to the Turks, Iran's repeated statements about exporting Islamic revolution appear aimed towards any and all who have not already joined in with the cause. Potential for escalation of conflict beyond mere words would seem significant for neighbors with such different worldviews.

During the 1980s, Turkey and Iran remained on relatively positive terms. Iranian support for Turkish Islamists stayed at a rhetorical level.[19] In the 1980s, Turkish fundamentalists advocated an Islamic state but generally eschewed violence. Hizballah, a loose affiliation of Islamist terrorists which hoped for an Iranian-style state to emerge in Turkey, engaged in a few unsuccessful plots, but no direct connection to Iran could be confirmed. Radio Tehran frequently attacked the secular Turkish state, but "the Iranians largely refrained from covert activities to export the revolution to Turkey," and only a few Kurdish Workers' Party (PKK) attacks took place from Iran itself.[20] Tehran even signed a "Security Agreement" on 28 November 1984 that prohibited both sides from engaging in "any activity on its territory aimed against the other's security."[21]

One process that unfolded in the 1980s, with implications for intervention later on, concerned migration from Iran. After the revolution took hold in Iran, many people left in exile and a considerable number ended up in Turkey. It is estimated that the number of Iranian exiles in Turkey peaked at 1.5 million in 1987 and diminished thereafter, although hundreds of thousands still remain. However, in spite of reduced numbers, those who stayed in Turkey constituted "fertile ground for exile politics and infiltration by Iranian agents, providing Iran with a capacity for mischief."[22] In other words, the potential for ethnic affinity and cleavage increased as a result of this migration.

Dramatic change came in the 1990s following the Kuwait crisis. During that time Iran did not actively support terrorist activities in Turkey. The major reason for such restraint was that Iran was "waiting to see the results of a campaign that would greatly influence Iraq's strategic standing."[23] In 1990, Turks found themselves taken aback at statements and actions of the Iranian ambassador to Ankara. Specifically, he weighed in on the Turkish ban on wearing a headscarf. The ambassador's participation in street demonstrations against the policy had an even more unfavorable impact on Turkish opinion. This went a step beyond the usual non-visits by Iranian officials in the 1980s to Ataturk's mausoleum in order to convey disapproval of secularism.[24] In that same year, the journalist Çetin Emeç, along with two other prominent pro-secular and modernist figures, had been assassinated by members of Hizballah, an organization with suspected connections to Iran.

As the 1990s moved forward, Iranian complicity with fundamentalist Islam in Turkey became more consistent and assertive in nature. Ely Karmon describes the year 1990 as "the starting point for the offensive against the Turkish secular establishment."[25] Radical terrorist organizations became highly active in Turkey during that decade, seeking to establish "an Islamic, Shari'a-based state on the Iranian example" and enjoying "wide Iranian support."[26] It is important to note that changes in the early 1990s deviate somewhat from passive lobbying and at times resemble *realpolitik*. A plausible explanation for that development is the onset of change in the Iranian system. In the early 1990s, Iran was in transition from autocracy to an institutionally mixed system. A transition period such as this one can be expected to produce hybrid policies that fall between passive lobbying and *realpolitik*.

Support for the Islamic Movement of Kurdistan (IMK) from the early 1990s onward revealed a pragmatic side to Iranian foreign policy.[27] While not Shi'a in belief, Iran supported the IMK because of its perceived ability to weaken the Turkish government. The IMK provided a "useful link" between the Iranian government and Kurdish Islamist terrorists, such as the notorious Veliğlu.[28]

Perhaps more central to the Islamist factor in Turkey are the actions of Hizballah, noted already for its presumed connection to Iran. The killings attributed to Hizballah in the 1990s include targets ranging from prominent secularists to members of the left-wing PKK. Those who carried out the executions and their accomplices are said to have visited Iran and received training while there. A report issued by the Turkish Parliament in 1995 claimed that "the Iranian consul general in Istanbul and members of his staff had helped set up the Turkish Hizballah, which then enjoyed the support of Iran in all respects."[29] Accusations of Iranian support for Hizballah, at certain times backed by evidence and at others stated as self-evident, would become common for Turkish political leaders and media as the 1990s progressed.

Events in 1993 put the role of Iran, with respect to Islamist terrorism, in bold relief for the Turks. On 24 January 1993, the renowned academic and journalist Uğur Mumcu was killed when a bomb exploded under his car. As with those accused and later convicted of similar crimes, the Islamic militants indicted for the murder of Mumcu had connections with Iranian agents – including diplomats stationed in Turkey.[30] Mumcu's funeral turned into a display of public support of secularism.[31] In February, a Turkish cabinet minister announced at a press conference the government's awareness, for the first time, that members of Islamist organizations "underwent months of military and theoretical training in Iranian security installations, traveled with Iranian real and forged documents, had weapons and explosives of Iranian origin and participated in attacks on Turkish citizens and also Iranian opposition militants."[32]

Other than the assassinations, protest demonstration and accusations noted above, 1993 featured unfortunate events in the city of Sivas on 2 July. Islamic fundamentalists disrupted a cultural festival attended by prominent intellectuals, most notably the secularist author Aziz Nesin, who had angered Islamists with his translation of material from Salman Rushdie's *Satanic Verses*. The fire set by the Islamists killed over 30 people.[33]

Incidents continued in 1994. The Great Eastern Islamic Fighters Front (IBDA-C) engaged in 90 terrorist attacks that year, including the assassination of a prominent movie critic and author, Onat Kutlular, on 30 December 1994.[34] Kutlular died a few days later as a result of his injuries.[35] The killings of Mumcu and Kutlular, identified in the Turkish mind with Iranian sponsorship, indicated a pattern for the rest of the decade.

The overall number of attacks by radical Islamist organization in 1994, 464, represented a high watermark. Thereafter, Turkish security forces began to respond with successful operations.[36] Attacks continued in 1995 but at a lower level, with 86 acts of violence reported and traced mostly to Hizballah and IBDA-C.[37] However, the main point of contention between Turkey and Iran at mid-decade became Iran's support of the PKK. The PKK stepped up its terrorist activity in 1994 and Iran offered a safe haven to PKK fighters.[38] While not Islamist itself, the success of the PKK had the effect of damaging the secularist regime in Ankara, and therefore indirectly furthered the cause of fundamentalist opposition.

By 1996, Iranian involvement in support of Turkish Islamist radicalism appeared more directly after the arrest of Irfan Cagarici, a leader of Islamic Action. Cagarici confessed about his organization's terrorist activities since the early 1990s. This included "assassination of secular politicians and intellectuals, with direct support and supervision of Iranian intelligence."[39] The revelations reinforced Turkish suspicions about Iran and its intentions towards their country. Karmon describes this incident as the cause of a new low in relations between Turkey and Iran.[40]

Tensions continued into the late 1990s between Turkey and Iran. While Iran had agreed in security protocols not to "interfere in Turkey's domestic politics," that did not put an end to the process. For example, in March 1997, Ambassador Mohammed Reza Bagheri publicly called for the institution of Shari'a law in Turkey. This led to his expulsion shortly thereafter.[41]

Ongoing Turkish concerns about Iranian support for the PKK and other entities hostile to the government in Ankara exploded into prominence with the "Kavakçi Affair" in 1999. Merve Kavakçi, a young Islamist recently elected to Parliament, stated that she would wear a headscarf at the May swearing-in ceremony. When she tried to do so, extensive verbal abuse compelled her to withdraw. Although Iran played no direct role in the Kavakçi Affair, Turkish public opinion took out its frustrations about fundamentalist activism on the state known to support Islamism with the greatest enthusiasm. The incident, and its aftermath, increased the level of angry rhetoric exchanged between Iran and Turkey. Most notably, the new Turkish Prime Minister, Bülent Ecevit, attacked

Iran for its support of the PKK. He observed, in particular, that Iran had hosted the Sixth Annual Congress of the PKK.[42] In sum, the way in which the headscarf incident so easily produced intense accusations between Iran and Turkey demonstrated the destabilization of their relationship over time.[43]

Matters intensified in the aftermath of the assassination of Ahmet Taner Kişlali, a prominent professor and journalist who favored Kemalism and secularism, on 21 October 1999. This incident occurred one day after the arrest of 92 members of Hizballah who had been trained in Iran. Accusations of Iranian involvement with Hizballah and the PKK pervaded the Turkish media with high intensity. Iran denied involvement in the murder and a respected academic source speculated that Tehran in all likelihood did not orchestrate the event.[44] Turkish anger over Iranian support of Hizballah, however, did not dissipate in the face of denials about involvement across the board. Accusations about Iranian support for Hizballah proliferated, with many taking a highly specific form, and backed by confessions from members of the organization itself.[45]

Matters became worse in January 2000 following Hizbullah's assassination of Konca Kuriş, a young activist, due to Iran's strong implication in other such events.[46] A few months later, in May 2000, Turkish media "announced that the killers of some 17 well known Turkish journalists, politicians, professors and other public figures had been apprehended."[47] Confessions revealed support from agents of Iranian intelligence. This caused a major crisis in Turkey's relations with Iran. Several of the assassinations stood out in Turkish memory and elicited an especially bad reaction to the possibility of Iranian involvement.[48] At the same time, Turkish media continued to accuse Iran of harboring PKK guerrillas and members of Hizballah. For example, in May 2000, Turkish media claimed that Iran had given safe haven to 1500 PKK guerrillas and 53 Hizballah members.[49] The level of anger among Turks towards Iran reached a magnitude higher than the previous decade, which also included numerous incidents that significantly increased tensions.

Events came to a head with the August 2000 visit of Iranian Deputy Foreign Minister Muhsin Aminzade to Turkey. During that visit, it became clear that a fundamental change had occurred in Iran's position regarding support for Islamic radicalism in Turkey. Olson summarizes the transformation by observing:

> Not only that the Islamic Republic of Iran was no longer able or willing to export its revolution, but also that it would no longer be able to export its discourse among the populace of neighboring countries, if the governments of those countries responded vigorously. Aminzade was forced to accept and made no statements regarding the "decree" (*kararname*), i.e., the Turkish government's attempt to implement measures to root out any civil servants whom government officials felt showed sympathy with the Kurdish nationalist or Islamist movements – the very movements in Turkey that had been most receptive to the Islamic Republic's Islamic discourse. By August 2000, both the Kurdish nationalist and Islamists forces in Turkey no longer looked to Iran for even moral support, let alone military or political support.[50]

While eager to promote Islam abroad, Iran also had to pursue that policy within realistic limitations. After the highly destructive war with Iraq, Tehran could not begin to contemplate serious escalation of its conflict with Turkey. As a result, Iran used Aminzade's visit to signal a cooling off with regard to promotion of Islamism in Turkey – a pragmatic turn that implicitly recognized building public pressure on the Turkish leadership to take firm action against Iran.

Turkey remained suspicious of Iran vis-à-vis the PKK, but even if true, accusations after the millennium point towards much more limited support for Islamists of all varieties. None of the allegations, for example, concerned assassinations or complicity with other acts of violence.[51] In addition, Turkish security forces are credited with taking effective action against groups believed or confirmed to be sponsored by Iran.[52]

Applying the framework to the Iranian case

Events from 1982 to 2003 generally confirm the expectations from the framework developed by Carment *et al.* The preceding case history will be discussed in terms of the breaking-points relevant to the model vis-à-vis institutional constraints: 1982 to 1996, diverse with low constraint; and 1997 to 2003, diverse with a mixed level constraint (i.e., higher constraint). Figure 7.1 displays

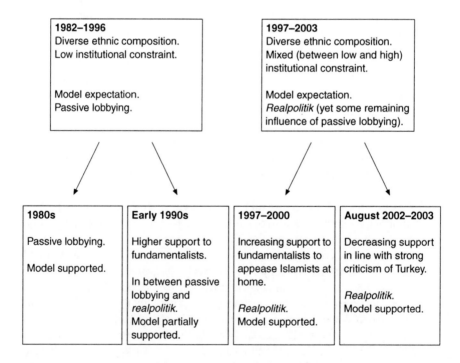

Figure 7.1 The evolution of Iranian interventionism from 1982 to 2003.

expectations from the Carment *et al.* model, in addition to how well Iran fits that model. In the figure, two basic periods are identified: 1982 to 1996 and 1997 to 2003. Each of these periods is divided into two sub-periods in line with changing policies in Iran.

1982 to 1996: diverse with low constraint

1980s: passive lobbying

During the 1980s, Iran clearly engaged in passive lobbying. As expected from the framework, there is not much activity to report. Iran either helped to establish Hizballah or gave the impression that it would offer support through a steady diet of Islamist propaganda. The government in Tehran also allowed the PKK to find refuge on its territory, but there is no evidence of sponsorship beyond this permissive behavior. Over and above the contributions of the framework in explaining Iranian behavior, it is worth bearing in mind the burdens posed by the war with Iraq from 1980 to 1988. This reality undoubtedly reinforced the risks of more active intervention of Iran in Turkey because Iran was already worn out by a brutal war. In addition, the Turks might stir up ethnoreligious cleavages in Iran as a way of retaliating if Iranian support for Islamists, at least from Ankara's point of view, got carried away.

Early 1990s: passive lobbying and realpolitik

Within the period of low constraint, an interesting shift occurs in Iranian behavior around 1990. This change towards more active support for Islamists in Turkey does not contradict the prediction of passive lobbying because other factors from the Carment *et al.* model come into play. First, and as noted previously, the potential for ethnoreligious affinity and cleavage had increased significantly due to the migration from Iran into Turkey. Second, while the Polity project still classifies Iran as an autocracy during the 1990s, its designation changed in 1996 to a hybrid system with democratic tendencies. Thus it would not be unreasonable to see Iran in the 1990s as a state in transition from autocracy to an institutionally mixed system leaning towards democracy, which in turn would predict the presence of passive lobbying with a trend towards *realpolitik*.

Iran's support for the PKK, Hizballah and involvement with high-profile assassinations during the 1990s fits the bill as described. Iran tried to publicly play down its support for Islamism in Turkey, but also clearly hoped to obtain some political pay-offs at home. Faced with a "recent emergence of ethnic nationalism among [its] own minorities,"[53] Iran had the potential to reap political benefits at home through the unifying theme of support for Islam, most notably in a secular state such as Turkey. Iran's increasingly active media, moreover, had criticized the government because it appeared lax in standing up to Turkey, which had an ongoing strategic partnership with Israel.[54] Thus the government in

Tehran engaged in a balancing act: support for Islamism in Turkey should be played up at home and played down elsewhere. Such an approach might reasonably be characterized as pragmatic and realist in nature.

1997 to 2003: diverse with a mixed level of constraint

1997 to 2000: realpolitik *with increasing activism*

From 1997 to 2000, in the initial years of increased institutional constraint, Iranian policy shifted to a higher level of support for Islamism in Turkey, with a concomitant lower level of deniability. The upward change corresponded almost exactly with democratization. Elements of *realpolitik* were reflected in both the escalation and de-escalation, after 2000, of Iran's backing for Islamists in Turkey. From 1997 to 2000, Iran pragmatically supported both the PKK as an instrument to weaken Ankara while also backing various Islamist organizations not identified with the Shi'a tradition. In terms of affinity, Iran is seen as an enthusiastic supporter of Hizballah, which used violence in an attempt to overthrow Turkey's secular regime in favor of one modeled after Tehran.

Initial analysis might give the impression that this contradicts the Carment *et al.* model because a *realpolitik* disposition limits willingness to intervene. However, in this case, more active support was in line with the pragmatic concerns of Iran. The decision makers knew they had to appease Islamists at home, who demanded more effort to export the country's ideology. Iran's shift towards higher institutional constraint created the conditions to promote activism. Unlike before, the Iranian government from 1997 onward dealt with either potential or real outbidding from Islamists who wanted less talk and more action to promote the revolution abroad. Therefore, increasing intervention by Iran in the late 1990s actually reflected a pragmatic approach that combined domestic and international components. Foreign policy cannot be seen as straying too far from this basic goal. Critics are waiting to decry the failures of any regime. In this context, with democratization there comes the potential for religious and other forms of outbidding. The majority in Iran (i.e., 89 percent Shi'a Muslim) demanded more activism in foreign policy. Consider Olson's observations about challenges mounting within Iran during the mid-1990s:

> The internal threats consisted not just of a different "brand" of Islam as represented by the struggle between the reformist and conservatives, but as the July 1999 "student" demonstrations against the conservative clergy suggested, the possible alignment of secular and non-clerical forces within the demonstrators, including Kurdish nationalists.[55]

Thus, the turn to democracy, interestingly enough, had the perverse effect of making the Iranian government more responsive to extremists eager to undermine the Turkish secular state. The government's natural priority became shoring up its position against various threats and solidifying its Islamic "base" at home. Increased activity in Turkey was potentially a "low-cost" option and therefore an attractive alternative.

At the same time, Iran showed pragmatism in how it pursued that goal. Tehran continued to deny, wherever possible, its involvement with radical Islamist actions against the Turkish government. Even when attacks escalated, they still targeted secular intellectual and media professionals rather than military or security personnel.[56] This undoubtedly reflected concerns about provoking an extreme reaction from Turkey, within which, more than virtually any other state, the military is by far the most respected institution.

2000 to 2003: realpolitik *with decreasing activism*

Iran's actions after 2000 supported the idea that it had shifted in the direction of *realpolitik* rather than simply unbridled activism. In other words, Iran decreased its support and activism due to pragmatic concerns. After a series of assassinations attributed to Islamists with Iranian ties, matters came to a head with the Three Ks – Kavakçi, Kyşlali and Kuriş. The headscarf incident and dual assassinations in 1999 to 2000 caused an escalation in Turkish anger towards Iran. The latter, as would be anticipated by *realpolitik* and a lingering disposition towards passive rather than active lobbying, simply backed away from its active support of Turkish Islamists. Put simply, the costs imposed by the increased risk of military confrontation with Turkey outweighed benefits at home from staving off religious outbidding, which is completely in line with realist expectations. Therefore, the foreign policy of the state changes, but the motivation stays the same. Since Iran was an ethnically diverse state with high institutional constraints at the time, it had a minimal win-set in the terms conveyed by Carment *et al.*[57] Due to that minimal win-set, we see a shift in policy from Iran with changing conditions. If the win-set was broader, it might have been possible to continue activist policies in spite of Turkish anger towards Iran.

Iran, in sum, behaves as expected by the framework over the test period of 1982 to 2003. It acted initially like a state that is diverse and low in constraint; where passive lobbying is the norm, with ethnoreligious affinity and cleavage, along with a shift towards a new institutional setting, explained its movement from 1990 onward towards a higher level of sponsorship for radical Islam in Turkey. After Iran was reclassified as a diverse but hybrid state leaning towards high constraint, it became a more active supporter of Islamism in Turkey. This process reversed itself when, as expected, a *realpolitik* mind-set saw the danger of continued provocation of Turkey as too great to accept. Iran reaped the domestic benefits that it could afford and reduced its sponsorship of radical Islam to a level that would not cause it to become the focal point of Turkish wrath.

Alternative frames of reference

This study adopts the Carment *et al.* model and analyzes the relations between Iran and Turkey between 1982 and 2003 according to that view. Yet the

Carment *et al.* model is only one possible way to analyze the evolution of Iranian intervention in Turkey. For instance, an assessment based on relative distribution of power, which would reflect a realist point of view, represents another alternative. In addition, one might pursue an economic approach that focuses on changes in intervention as a function of the oil industry as a central component of Iran's foreign policy. It is feasible to analyze changes in behavior as displayed in Figure 7.1 from the standpoint of both of these alternative theoretical frameworks. This section provides a very basic sense of how the evolution of Iranian intervention in Turkey might be explained by employing these two different but overlapping perspectives.

The relationship between power distribution and conflict is a major theme in International Relations. Many theoretical frameworks such as power transition, long cycles and balance of power emphasize the importance of how power is distributed.[58] Daniel Geller, for instance, observes that "[w]hether conceptualized as military capabilities alone, or as a broader set of military, economic and demographic capabilities, the power base of a state has long been considered to be an important factor shaping foreign behavior."[59]

Empirical patterns show that higher power status for a state is associated with bolder policies. Melvin Small and David Singer reported that major powers have a higher likelihood of becoming involved in a conflict than have minor powers.[60] Similarly, results from Stuart Bremer support the idea that states with a higher composite index of national capability (CINC) are more likely to engage in wars.[61] Wolf-Dieter Eberwein confirms Bremer's study.[62] Similarly, Charles Gochman and Zeev Maoz find a connection between being major powers and the likelihood of being involved in militarized interstate disputes.[63] It is possible to unpack Iran–Turkey relations in relation to the power distribution based on these findings. From this point of view, power distribution between Iran and Turkey might influence Iran's decisions on support for fundamentalists in Turkey. The influence would be that, when Iran is more powerful than Turkey, the likelihood of intervention will be higher.

Although there are multiple ways of measuring state capability, this study employs the Correlates of War (COW) National Capability dataset, version 3.02.[64] The CINC score is used to determine the power distribution between Iran and Turkey.[65] Figure 7.2 displays the CINC annual values of Iran and Turkey for 1980 to 2001.

The CINC scores for Iran and Turkey zigzag from 1980 to 1989. Throughout most of the 1990s, Turkey had a higher CINC score than Iran and the gap enlarged significantly in 1998 and 1999. From 1999 to 2001, Iran moved closer to Turkey.

Passive lobbying in the 1980s does not match up with change in CINC scores of Iran and Turkey for the same time. Throughout the 1980s, the power position of Iran to Turkey oscillates and does not follow a certain trend. However, throughout the 1990s, there is a clear trend of higher CINC scores for Turkey compared with those of Iran. The empirical pattern might still explain increasing support from Iran to fundamentalists in Turkey, in a roundabout way. Iran,

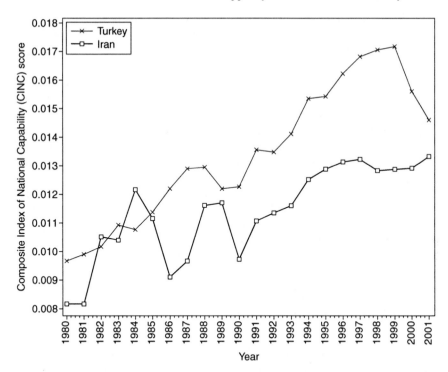

Figure 7.2 Composite Index of National Capability (CINC) scores of Iran and Turkey from 1980 to 2001.

perhaps deterred from directly confrontational behavior by Turkey's superior capabilities, might have shifted from passive lobbying to active intervention. The trend for the 2000 to 2003 period is not clear, since the data go only up to 2001. However, 2000 and 2001 show that Iran is starting to catch up, and there is less support in this period from Iran of fundamentalists in Turkey. In sum, relative capability does not explain the Iran–Turkey dyad in the 1980s, but it does shed partial light on the 1990s. The increasing gap between capabilities between Iran and Turkey, to the advantage of Turkey, may have encouraged Iran to pursue a more activist policy but not in a way that would have much risk of producing open warfare.

Examining the relationship between change in oil prices and evolution of Iranian intervention in Turkey is another way of looking at the same overarching issue (i.e., the role of capability in affecting foreign policy). From the early 1980s until Iraq's invasion of Kuwait, we observe a general decline in oil prices.[66] In the early 1990s there was a sharp increase and then a decrease due to the Gulf War. Throughout the 1990s, if we leave annual shifts aside, oil prices were stable. However, the period starting from 9/11 exhibits a clear upward trend in oil prices.

Recall that the evidence marshaled above profiles Iran's actions from 1982 to

1996 as passive lobbying. From 1997 to 2000, Iran clearly followed a more activist policy – also well confirmed – and that level declined after 2000. Given the preceding set of breaking-points, we do not see parallels between oil prices and level of activism in supporting extremists in Turkey. When oil prices are declining, intervention takes the form of passive lobbying. After the Gulf War, oil prices remained stable, but Iran's level of activism changed from passive lobbying to more activist policies of intervention. After 11 September 2001, oil prices increased, while Iranian support for fundamentalists in Turkey did not. The lack of correlation between oil prices and Iranian intervention in Turkey is therefore surprising, especially because oil revenues are considered to be a significant source of power for Iran.

Taken together, the preceding analyses of relative overall capability and evolving oil prices produced mixed results. At the very least it could be said that while some policy shifts might appear responsive to either changing oil prices or CINC scores, the degree of correspondence is far from perfect. By contrast, the typology from Carment *et al.* seems more in line with the timing of policy change from 1982 to 2003.

Conclusions and future directions

This study confirms the expectations derived from the framework of Carment *et al.* with regard to Iranian interventionism as related to Turkey for the period from 1982 to 2003. One interesting by-product of the results is the emergence of Iran as a state with an open foreign policy, even in areas related to religion. While Iran is *sui generis* in terms of its status as a theocracy, the model from Carment *et al.* does seem to account for variation in its support for Islamists abroad, with the example at hand being those in Turkey.

Iranian conduct in relation to Islamism in Turkey also triangulates with expectations derived from three other frames of reference.

First, Carsten Laustsen and Ole Wæver observe that religious conflicts are usually asymmetric; secular states "are attacked by religious groups."[67] This is certainly true of the struggle between the avowedly secular Turkish state and Islamists within its borders. Despite occasional accusations from Iran that Turkey has meddled in its internal affairs, evidence is lacking. Instead, the story is one of a state-center against ethnoreligious societal groupings that receive varying levels of support from an external state patron.

Second, the results of the present case study also resonate with the aggregate findings of Deepa Khosla on intervention in conflicts within the developing world. From a study of 975 interventions in ethnic conflicts in the broadly defined South during the 1990s, Khosla finds that "militant sects," defined as active in politics and different in beliefs from society in general, are most likely to experience intervention. Although Iran did not engage in full-scale military intervention against Turkey, it clearly supported militant sects of Islam within the country's borders.[68]

Third, Iran's foreign policy in the present context also resonates with "omnibalancing."[69] Iran is seen as balancing both external and internal threats. This situation becomes more challenging with the shift towards a higher degree of institutional constraint.

One possibility for future research concerns the comparison of Iran with other sponsors of radical Islam. A notable priority here is Saudi Arabia.[70] Specifically, do the activities of this state as an intervener on behalf of radical Islam follow the patterns suggested by the model from Carment *et al.*? While Saudi activities abroad on behalf of fundamentalist Islam have been studied, this work is not as yet connected to a cross-nationally relevant model of intervention, which in turn would be a step forward in explanation of such activities on behalf of religious groups.

Notes

1 J. Fox and S. Sandler, *Bringing Religion Into International Relations*, New York: Palgrave Macmillan, 2004.
2 A. Hasenclever and V. Rittberger, "Does Religion Make a Difference? Theoretical Approaches to the Impact of Faith on Political Conflict," in P. Hatzopoulos and F. Petito (eds) *Religion in International Relation: The Return from Exile*, New York: Palgrave Macmillan, 2003, p. 115.
3 P. Hatzopoulos and F. Petito, op. cit., p. 1.
4 Ibid.
5 Recent examples of valuable essays on religion and IR include R. Scott Appleby, *The Ambivalence of the Sacred: Religion, Violence and Reconciliation*, Lanham, MD: Rowman & Littlefield, 2000; and those in the collection from Hatzopoulos and Petito, op. cit. Individual and comparative case studies include C. C. James and Ö. Özdamar, "Religion as a Factor in Ethnic Conflict: Kashmir and Indian Foreign Policy," *Terrorism and Political Violence*, 2005, vol. 17, no. 3, pp. 447–467; and J. Fox, "Variations on a Theme: State Policy Toward Radical Islam in Four Post-Soviet Sunni Muslim States," Unpublished Manuscript, 2006a. Fox and Sandler, op. cit.; J. Fox, "State Religion and Discrimination Against Ethnic Minorities," Unpublished Manuscript, 2006b; and B. Lai, "An Empirical Examination of Religion and Conflict in the Middle East, 1950–1992," *Foreign Policy Analysis*, 2006, vol. 2, pp. 21–36, among others, have carried out quantitative analyses.
6 T. Nardin, "Epilogue," in Hatzopoulos and Petito, op. cit., p. 272; V. Kubálková, "Toward an International Political Theology," in Hatzopoulos and Petito, op. cit., p. 79.
7 H. J. Barkley, "Iran and Turkey: Confrontation Across an Ideological Divide," in A. Z. Rubinstein and O. M. Smolansky (eds) *Regional Power Rivalries in the New Eurasia*, Armonk, NY: M.E. Sharpe, Inc., pp. 147–168.
8 D. Carment, P. James and Z. Taydas, *Who Intervenes? Ethnic Conflict and Interstate Crisis*, Columbus, OH: Ohio State University Press, 2006.
9 The logic of the model that follows is based primarily on Carment *et al.*, op. cit., pp. 17–42. While their framework focuses directly on ethnic intervention, there is nothing that prevents it from being extended in the current study to an *ethnoreligious* context.
10 The category of diverse ethnic composition with low constraint is relevant to Iran, as described momentarily, for the period from 1982 to 1996. From 1997 to 2003, Iran is somewhere in between the pure types of low and high constraint theorized about by Carment *et al.* vis-à-vis intervention. Given that only the two ethnically diverse cells in the matrix of national types from Carment *et al.* (op. cit., p. 25) are relevant,

expectations for ethnically dominant states (whether institutionally constrained or not) are not detailed below.

11 R. D. Putnam, "Diplomacy and Domestic Politics: The Logic of Two-level Games," *International Organization*, 1988, vol. 42, pp. 426–460.

12 Carment *et al.*, op. cit., pp. 34–36.

13 Polity IV codes Iran as "−88," which designates regime transition, from 1979 to 1981. Over the years from 1982 to 1996, Iran's polity score is "0" for democracy and "6" for autocracy, giving it a net value of "−6," which is in the autocratic range. Finally, from 1997 to 2003, Iran's democracy and autocracy scores are "4" and "1," for a score of "3," which indicates a mixed system leaning towards democracy. The conventional Polity thresholds for high and low constraints are scores of "6" and "−6," that is, democracy and autocracy, respectively.

14 The remaining categories are Gilak and Mazaderani (8 percent), Kurd (7 percent), Arab (3 percent), Lur (2 percent), Baloch (2 percent), Turkmen (2 percent) and Others (1 percent). Available online at www.cia.gov/cia/publications/factbook/geos/ir.html (accessed 12 September 2006).

15 These groups include those who are politically active, with a population of at least 500,000, and are taken to experience some kind of risk from the state apparatus, with the possibilities ranging from various forms of discrimination all the way up to genocide in some host countries. Available online at www.cidcm.umd.edu/inscr/mar/ (accessed 12 September 2006).

16 J. Calabrese, "Turkey and Iran: Limits of a Stable Relationship," *British Journal of Middle Eastern Studies*, 1998, vol. 25, no. 2, pp. 75–94.

17 "Islamism" and "Islamic fundamentalism" are defined by Mahmud A. Faksh in "The Prospects of Islamic Fundamentalism in the Post-Gulf War Period," *International Journal*, 1994, vol. 109, no. 2, pp. 183–218, as referring to "Islamic movements or groups that want to use Islam as a political force to mobilize the public, gain control, and reform society and state in accordance with their doctrinal religious agenda." The government of Iran is seen as the epitome of such goals. It is virtually unique among regimes around the world as a theocracy.

An interesting and dissenting view of the Iranian Revolution appears in M. E. Hegland, "Islamic Revival or Political and Cultural Revolution? An Iranian Case Study," in R. T. Antoun and M. E. Hegland (eds) *Religious Resurgence: Contemporary Cases in Islam, Christianity and Judaism*, Syracuse, NY: Syracuse University Press, 1987, pp. 194–219. Based on field research, she makes the case that the events of 1979 had more of a political than religious origin. For example, complaints about socioeconomic inequality played a central role in mobilization against the Shah of Iran. While the evidence offered by Hegland about events in Iran at or around 1979 is compelling, the fact remains that the Iranian Revolution crystallized into a regime identified principally with the promotion of Shi'a Islam.

18 Barkley, op. cit., p. 147.

19 S. Bolukbasi, "Turkey Copes with Revolutionary Iran," *Journal of South Asian and Middle Eastern Studies*, fall/winter 1989, vol. 13, nos 1 and 2, pp. 94–107; see also Calabrese, op. cit., p. 78.

20 Bolukbasi, op. cit., pp. 101–104.

21 Ibid., p. 103.

22 Barkley, op. cit., p. 157.

23 E. Karmon (December 1998), "Counterterrorism Policy: Why Tehran Starts and Stops Terrorism," *Middle East Quarterly*, vol. 5, no. 4. Available online at www.meforum.org/article/427 (accessed 12 March 2007).

24 Barkley, op. cit., p. 157.

25 E. Karmon, "Radical Islamist Movements in Turkey," in B. Rubin (ed.) *Revolutionaries and Reformers: Contemporary Islamic Movements in the Middle East*, Albany, NY: State University of New York Press, 2003, pp. 41–67.

26 E. Karmon, "Radical Islamic Political Groups in Turkey," *Middle East Review of International Affairs*, 1997, vol. 1, no. 1, pp. 1–15.
27 Karmon (op. cit., 1997, p. 2) mentions a report by the Turkish National Intelligence Organization and the Security General Directorate of the Police which, in October 1991, noted ten other Islamic organizations "active in Turkey: Turkish Islamic Liberation Army (IKO), Turkish Islamic Liberation Front (TIK-C), Fighters of the Islamic Revolution (IDAM), Turkish Islamic Liberation Union (TIKB), World Shariʿa Liberation Army (DSKO), Universal Brotherhood Front-Shariʿa Revenge Squad (EKC-SIM), Islamic Liberation Party Front (IKP-C), Turkish Fighters of the Universal Islamic War of Liberation (EIK-TM), Turkish Islamic Fighters Army (IMO) and Turkish Shariʿa Revenge Commandos (TSIK)." Additional organizations, such as Great East Islamic Raiders Front (IBDA-C), are named as active by other sources.
28 A. Mango, *Turkey and the War on Terror: For Forty Years We Fought Alone*, New York: Routledge, 2005, p. 63. In this book, the author provides detailed information about Iranian involvement in Turkey, but the material requires verification because the source is written from a very explicitly pro-Turkish point of view. Mango's assertions, and those of others cited here, frequently rest on fragmentary evidence. This point might be made more generally about all sources in the general area of external state support for terrorism because of the obvious motive, all other things being equal, to conceal involvement to the extent that it has occurred. The point concerning scarcity of source material is made about the activities of Turkish Islamic organizations, in particular by Karmon, op. cit., 1997, p. 3.
29 Mango, op. cit., p. 62.
30 Karmon, op. cit., 1997, p. 7.
31 Ibid., op. cit.
32 Ibid., op. cit.
33 Karmon, op. cit., 1997, p. 5; Mango, op. cit., p. 63. There is a discrepancy in the exact number of fatalities reported, with 36 and 37 as the figures from Karmon and Mango, respectively.
34 Karmon, op. cit., 1997.
35 Mango, op. cit., p. 63.
36 Karmon, op. cit., 1997, pp. 5–8.
37 Ibid.
38 Ibid.
39 Ibid., p. 6. These assertions seem generally accepted in the literature, but not without controversy. Calabrese (op. cit., p. 85), for example, is more cautious about Iranian involvement, asserting that evidence regarding assassinations is "far from conclusive."
40 Karmon, op. cit., 2003, p. 46.
41 Calabrese, op. cit., p. 85; R. Olson, *Turkey–Iran Relations 1979–2004: Revolution, Ideology, War, Coups and Geopolitics*, Costa Mesa, CA: Mazda Publishers, 2004, p. 46.
42 Olson, op. cit., pp. 48–49.
43 In July 1999, Iran alleged that Turkish fighter aircraft bombed sites within Iranian territory. Turkey later acknowledged that it may have bombed Iranian soldiers who had entered Iraqi territory or even that a few bombs had inadvertently struck Iranian soil (Olson, op. cit., pp. 53–55).
44 Ibid., pp. 56–57.
45 Ibid., p. 59.
46 Ibid.
47 Ibid., p. 61.
48 The most egregious examples, from the Turkish point of view, are the assassinations of Professor Bahriye Üçok (6 October 1990), Muammer Aksoy (31 January 1991), Uğur Mumcu (24 January 1993) and Professor Ahmet Taner Kyşlali (21 October 1999) (Olson, op. cit., p. 61).

49 Ibid., pp. 62–63.
50 Ibid.
51 Ibid., p. 69.
52 Mango, op. cit., p. 66.
53 Barkley, op. cit., pp. 147–148.
54 Calabrese, op. cit., p. 87.
55 Olson, op. cit., p. 42.
56 Karmon, op. cit., 1997, pp. 9–10.
57 See also Putnam, op. cit.
58 D. S. Geller and J. D. Singer, *Nations at War: A Scientific Study of International Conflict*, Cambridge: Cambridge University Press, 1998.
59 D. S. Geller, "Explaining War: Empirical Patterns and Theoretical Mechanisms," in M. I. Midlarsky (ed.) *Handbook of War Studies II*, Ann Arbor: The University of Michigan Press, 2000, p. 409.
60 M. Small and J. D. Singer, "Patterns in International Warfare, 1816–1965," *Annals*, 1970, vol. 391, pp. 145–155.
61 S. A. Bremer, "National Capabilities and War Proneness," in D. Singer (ed.) *The Correlates of War II: Testing Some Realpolitik Models*, New York: The Free Press, 1980, cited in Geller, op. cit.
62 W-D. Eberwein, "The Seduction of Power: Serious International Disputes and the Power Status of Nations, 1900–1976," *International Interactions*, 1982, vol. 9, pp. 57–74.
63 C. S. Gochman and Z. Maoz, "Militarized Interstate Disputes, 1816–1976: Procedures, Patterns and Insights," *Journal of Conflict Resolution*, 1984, vol. 28, pp. 585–615, cited in P. James, *International Relations and Scientific Progress: Structural Realism Reconsidered*, Columbus, OH: Ohio State University Press, 2002.
64 Further information on the dataset may be found available online at www.correlatesofwar.org/ (accessed 11 September 2006).
65 The CINC score is calculated in the following way. First, iron and steel production, military expenditures, military personnel, energy consumption, total population and urban population – six components – are summed up for a given year, converting each state's absolute component to a share of the international system. Second, CINC value is calculated by averaging across the six components. Further information is available online at www.correlatesofwar.org/ (accessed 11 September 2006).
66 Many online resources provide facts on oil price change. Available online at www.wtrg.com/prices.htm (accessed 12 September 2006) and www.mises.org/story/1892 (accessed 12 September 2006).
67 C. B. Laustsen and O. Wæver, "In Defense of Religion: Sacred Referent Objects for Securitization," in Hatzopoulos and Petito, op. cit., pp. 147–180.
68 D. Khosla, "Third World States as Interveners in Ethnic Conflicts: Implications for Regional and International Security," *Third World Quarterly*, 1999, vol. 20, no. 6, 1143–1156.
69 Olson, op. cit., p. 42; M. J. O'Reilly, "Omnibalancing: Oman Confronts an Uncertain Future," *The Middle East Journal*, 1998, vol. 1, pp. 70–84.
70 A. B. Prados and C. M. Blanchard, "Saudi Arabia: Terrorist Financing Issues," in N. P. Tollitz (ed.) *Saudi Arabia: Terrorism, US Relations and Oil*, New York: Nova Science Publishers, 2005, pp. 27–60.

8 The Islamic dimension of Pakistan's foreign policy

Rushda Siddiqui

The existence of Pakistan is the realization of a fundamentalist imagination. "Rogue," "problem" and "failed" are some of the prefixes that are given to the state of Pakistan.[1] This chapter explores the mechanisms of defense employed by Pakistan to preserve its unique identity and existence, and discusses how religion influences its foreign policies towards its neighbors.

To understand Pakistan's foreign policy and to explain why Pakistan is seen simultaneously as an ally and as a source of international terrorism, one must analyze the country's creation and the ideology behind the founding of the state. In its 60 years of existence, Pakistan has become a conduit for arms, drugs and money by forces expressing ideological dissent and exhibiting political violence.

Pakistan has been one of the first states in contemporary history to employ non-state proxies to safeguard its interests in the region and in the international arena. Initially, Pakistan benefited from its non-state actors and the mechanisms they employed. For example, the government used its foreign office to support terrorist activities in Kashmir. In the long run, however, the use of non-state actors backfired, increasing the state's vulnerability to a backlash not only by the states affected by Pakistan's terrorist proxies, but also by the non-state actors within Pakistan. Today, Pakistan is considered as a "state sponsor of terrorism" or a "passive sponsor of terrorism."[2] Solutions ranging from imposing economic and political sanctions to direct military action against the state have been debated in the international community.

Background

Pakistan's creation came in the wake of a bevy of political aspirations and forces in India. A diversity of religious practices initially characterized the partition of India into a homeland for Muslims. Today, various intellectual, spiritual, political and academic approaches to Islam are coupled with more institutionalized forms. The existence of varied sects within Islam and the attempt of each to make its variant a "state religion" made the exercise a complex issue.

The concept of religion giving an identity to a society to form a cohesive bond for its adherents is the very idea responsible for the creation of Pakistan.[3]

Religion helped characterize Pakistani identity just as partition defined the state's territorial contours. However, the quest for state identity became mired in sectarian debate as various ideological and religious trends contested the true meaning of Islam. Religious pluralism weakened the concept of a nation-state, and, since 1947, Pakistan still grapples with issues of identity.

This very complex mixture of social aspirations and political ideologies has left the country in a state of flux. Due to the difficulty in characterizing itself, Pakistan has created a set of contradictions that make its domestic and foreign policies complex and paradoxical phenomena. The state defined its strategic interests, threats and alliances based on its ideological affinities. As a result, the economically, politically and militarily weak state of Pakistan tried unsuccessfully to be an ideological leader of the radical Islamic world.

Islam and the creation of Pakistan

Pakistan was established as an Islamic state for Muslims of all ethnic and linguistic backgrounds on the Indian subcontinent. Contrary to other ideological states, Pakistan had little opportunity to develop as a nation-state based on territory, institutions and citizenship: it always adhered to its ideological and transnational goal of gathering together all Muslims in the region. Following the loss of East Pakistan, the Islamic character of Pakistan's foreign policy became more relevant during the Soviet invasion of Afghanistan.[4]

However, Muslims are not a monolithic community, nor is there a single interpretation of Islam. At the country's birth, various schools of Islamic thought, each with their own interpretations and worldviews, complicated the vision of Pakistan's future. It was a weak and floundering state, without a defined goal, and with most of the rights denied to it by the British Raj. Political maneuvering and Gandhi's hunger strike ensured that Pakistan did not starve of funds at birth; cash transfers saved the country from political death. However, the lack of political cohesiveness of the new state and the subsequent takeover of power by the military was not envisaged after the founding.

The role of Islam was not at the center of Muslim politics during the struggle for Pakistan, but emerged after the state was created. Maulana Mawdudi revised the concept that the sole object of the Pakistan movement was the establishment of an Islamic state. His party, the Jamat-i-Islami, soon evolved into a political party that demanded the establishment of an Islamic state in Pakistan.

Jamat-i-Islami's viewpoint contrasted sharply with the views of the leaders of the Muslim League, from Qaid-i-Azam Jinnah onward. In a speech before Pakistan's new Constituent Assembly, Jinnah stressed that the goal of partition was not the establishment of an Islamic state but the creation of a safe haven for Muslims throughout the world. He spelled out a secular future for the new country:

> You may belong to any religion or caste or creed. That has nothing to do with the business of the state. We are starting with this fundamental

principle that we are all citizens and equal citizens of the state. We should keep that in front of us as our ideal and you will find that in the course of time Hindus will cease to be Hindus and Muslims will cease to be Muslims, not in the religious sense because that is the personal faith of each individual, but in the political sense, as citizens of the State.[5]

Jinnah died appalled by the hatred and bloodshed generated by partition and desperately concerned about the difficulty Pakistan faced in establishing a modern state.[6]

Over time, it was apparent that Jinnah failed in his ambitious project. As Stephen Cohen notes, Pakistan's uniqueness centers around the intricate interaction between the physical/political/legal entity of the state and the notion of the Pakistani nation. From its very inception, the state of Pakistan was thought to be more than a physical or legal entity that provided welfare, order and justice to its citizens. Pakistan was to be an extraordinary state – a homeland for Indian Muslims and an ideological and political leader of the Islamic world. Providing a homeland to protect Muslims – a minority community in British India – from the bigotry and intolerance of India's Hindu majority was important.[7] On the one hand, there was Pakistan the state – a physically bounded territory with a legal and international personality. On the other hand, there was Pakistan the nation – mission-bound to serve as a beacon for oppressed Muslim communities elsewhere in the world.

Pakistan has become a classic case for the many forms which fundamentalist politics take; from schools of theology on the government payroll (the Barelvi and the Deobandi) that perform the same role as al-Azhar University in Egypt and yet at the same time also serve as spokesmen for the anti-government Islamists; to running civil service organizations that fill the economic and political vacuum left by the state machinery; from organizing moderate proselytizing movements like the Tabligh-Jammat, to organizing militant camps. The government machinery of Pakistan is a classic example of the conflict over power between state and society. Studies have focused on the manner in which the religious forces have either influenced the state apparatus or have infiltrated it.

The crisis over identity and the propensity towards fundamentalism have also impacted upon Pakistan's relationship with India. Religious extremists on both sides, encouraged by the memory of the violence accompanying the partition, dictated the nature of relations between the two states. The ongoing dispute over Kashmir and the bitter distrust on both sides had a considerable impact on shaping the foreign and domestic policies of both countries. As one military leader succeeded another, the army's vision of Pakistan began to define the state.[8]

Pakistani elites, both civilian and military, felt that their country's security was under threat from their bigger neighbor, India, and that national defense had to take precedence over all other priorities. The twin imperatives of defending Pakistan from India and reclaiming Kashmir provided a powerful backdrop and rationalization for the development of a praetorian state.[9]

Once Pakistan realized that independence from India was inevitable and that partition was irreversible, it tried to formulate a secular and democratic state based on Jinnah's vision. This gave an advantage to the coercive apparatus, and brought the armed forces to the helm of affairs. The social aim had been to constantly rein in the politicians who represented various strands of religious fundamentalisms, parochial and regional pulls within the society.

Sociologists have demonstrated that it was the capacity of religion to lend legitimacy to organized and increasingly centralized use of coercive power (through the appeal to divine authority) that made the consolidation of state power possible where otherwise it might not have been. This, in turn, further facilitated the development of the institutional capacity to govern a geographical territory and the capacity to mobilize militarily. The association between the state and the military persists to the present day. Conquest rapidly became the primary mechanism through which the institutional form of the state became diffused, because the state's organizational capacity conferred upon it a competitive advantage when confronting pre-state-like societies.[10]

The rise of non-state actors

Ideally, the state of Pakistan should not have faced opposition from within its borders and should have served as the ideal Muslim state. However, attempts by the state to create a national identity have been marked by unprecedented violence, corrosion of legitimacy, the spawning of secessionist movements and large-scale external intervention. State-sponsored religious groups created militias. Originally these militias fought in Afghanistan and in Kashmir, but eventually turned against Pakistan and opposed the state as well.

This has not prevented other clerical orders with "street" power to become the mainstay of the state. The use of civil society institutions by political forces represented the paradox of parallel religion-based welfare being run in the Muslim state. The line between public and private spheres was extremely thin. Although it has not been developed to the extent of the Muslim Brotherhood networks, the welfare activity of Pakistani religious groups has acquired and gained strength in its own right. Education is by far their most important means of influencing politics. The *madrasas* started as religious training schools that groomed students into clergy but acquired a new significance post-1970s, filling a void left by the lack of a formal state education system. Many *madrasa* graduates trained to become religio-political mercenaries. Over time these mercenaries have become one of the biggest problems for the state. They represent a parallel apparatus capable of sustaining an armed force that can challenge state authority. The mercenaries represent the power to shape new ideologies and challenge the state's legitimacy.

Society and government represent the contradictions of Pakistan's global policy of fraternization and exclusion. Both work on the principle of exporting the ideology, forming a brotherhood with adherents of the faith across the globe, luring them to support the cause of the nation and seeking strength in the shared faith. At the same time, their exclusiveness does not allow them to work towards a homogenization of religion or of the adherents. The clash of the principles of secularism and egalitarianism are dilemmas faced by the state and society. Both pursue the principles of exclusion and repression of non-religionists to safeguard the identity of the religion. Both have a long history of opposition to each other and a history of cooperation with each other.

According to Joel Migdal, the patterns of domination between a state and society are undermined by key struggles that are spread out in society's multiple arenas of domination and opposition. Officials at different levels of the state are central figures in these struggles, interacting and at times conflicting with an entire constellation of social forces. Any individual part of the state may respond as much to the distinctive pressures it faces in particular arenas as it does to the rest of the state organization.[11]

It is the control at these various levels that gives a state its strength and leverage to be the largest social actor. Moreover, it is at the various levels of interaction that the state should impact most upon the society it purportedly represents. In the case of Pakistan, however, the levels of interaction are minimal. The outreach of the mosques and the social service networks they run far exceeds the outreach of the state, which is limited. Because of this, it is not surprising that after 50 years as a state, Pakistan's leadership has little control over its population or over the non-state actors in its territory. The dilemma between using Islamic militancy as a tool and the danger it represents to the very state that supports it is placing the continued existence of Pakistan in jeopardy.

The political agendas of the non-state actors in Pakistan have been varied, as have been their mechanism of working. The most important of the non-state actors are the trained terrorists who have been most visible in Afghanistan and Kashmir. Their origins are not particularly important; what is important is the manner in which the state has used them to further its own agenda. As a weak state without a clearly defined foreign policy, Pakistan has actively used terrorists to further its interests in South Asia and in other parts of the world.

The functioning of non-state actors can be understood on two levels. The first is at the level of the social welfare system. Over a period of time, the state transformed the social welfare system into a propaganda system harnessing social support for the activities and ideologies of non-state actors. The second level is the active use and creation of non-state actors by the state. The first level can be explained by the use of *madrasas* in garnering support for the activities of organizations like al Qaeda, and in creating the alternative to state Islam. The second level can be understood by the mechanism of creation and use of groomed mercenaries in the form of the Taliban in Afghanistan and the terrorists in Indian Kashmir. These are groups which were created by the Inter Services Intelligence (ISI) units of the Pakistani Army.

Relations between state and non-state actors

The symbiotic relationship between the state and its socio-political forces came into play soon after the creation of Pakistan. The two players conflicted over the nature of the state and the drafting of the constitution. At the same time, they supported each other in achieving the common objectives of the state, i.e., propagating ideology, exporting ideology, and confronting the challenge of being a strategically vulnerable state.

There are two institutions that play the main role in the manner in which non-state actors are used in Pakistan's foreign policy. The first is the agency of social welfare that comes in the form of educational institutions like the *madrasas*; the second is the institution of the ISI. A coordinated effort between the two has been responsible for the implementation of using terrorism as a tool of foreign policy. The ISI has also created organizations that play a role in domestic politics of the countries.

The Taliban in Afghanistan and the Lashkar in India are two examples of the way Pakistan has used militancy to further its foreign policy objectives. The Taliban is an indigenous movement that was overtaken and engineered. Over time, it became an institutionalized movement that was controlled and directed by the ISI. The aim of having a controlled home-grown movement in Afghanistan ensured that Pakistan would not face hostility or opposition on its western border. In addition, a friendly polity in Afghanistan would be an effective counter to the Shi'a government in Iran. Afghanistan could also provide Pakistan with strategic depth in its conflict with India.

In Indian Kashmir, however, the story was different. As Pakistan realized that it could not tap into a local movement or impact upon the Muslim population elsewhere in India, it was instrumental in creating a range of terrorist organizations. Youths and potential mercenaries were picked up from various parts of Pakistan, Afghanistan, and Kashmir, and trained in special *madrasas* so that they could function as non-state actors in India, and in Kashmir in particular. The involvement of the ISI in fomenting violence in Kashmir caused bitter hostilities not only between India and Pakistan, but between Pakistan and the rest of the world.

Pakistan's policy of using non-state actors, particularly in Kashmir, has come under criticism from multilateral civil society organizations like Amnesty International and the International Crisis Group. This has been mostly due to the fact that the ISI used coercive and forcible techniques to recruit terrorists. Their studies, among many, document the manner in which boys were trained in camps in Pakistan and forced to become terrorists, or the way in which mercenary soldiers were used to wage low-intensity conflicts with India. Ahmed Rashid, in his book on the Taliban, discusses how the recruits are caught in a quagmire: they cannot return to their middle-class working populations because they lack the educational or vocational qualifications, and they remain social and political misfits due to their indoctrination of radical ideology.[12]

The political forces of Pakistan have been more aware of the role they play in the global scenario. Their agendas range from saving the Muslims of India to providing leadership to the Islamists across the globe, from Europe to Southeast Asia. For them it has been important to run a parallel state apparatus in Pakistan and in other countries. The roots for the ideological expansion of ideas and the mechanism for propagation came in the form of *madrasas*, while the various sources of funding came from drugs, charities, the arms trade and money laundering.

The State of Pakistan has been aware of its shortcomings as a strong and resilient economy and as a competent military force in the region. Three wars with India in 1948, 1962 and 1971, and the separation of East Pakistan into the independent country of Bangladesh, made Pakistan acutely aware of the need to integrate and strengthen the socio-political forces within the mainstream. Mohammed Waseem explains the relationship between the state and the Islamist forces by pointing out that for nearly a quarter of a century after independence, the modernist Muslim elite firmly maintained control of government. Governments used Islamic ideology to counter the demand for provincial autonomy in pursuit of their agenda for national unity. *'Ulama'*, and Islamists in general, occupied a secondary role in public life. While operating from the *madrasas* and pulpits of the mosque, they demanded Shari'a rule in Pakistan. Under successive parliamentary governments (1947–1958) followed by General Ayub's military and later presidential rule (1958–1969), the ruling elite adopted various strategies to control, cajole and co-opt Islamist elements. The latter condemned the former for being lackeys of the secular West.[13]

Pakistan's foreign policy had as much of an impact on the radicalization of fundamentalism in the country as did internal variables. It is not possible to detach the external variables of change from the developments of the Pakistani polity. Similarly, it would not be possible to detach the role of non-state actors in Pakistan from its foreign and external policy. The Indo–Pak wars had as much of an impact on development as the Islamization processes, started by Zia-ul Haq in the 1970s and 1980s.

What is important in the case of Pakistan is understanding the relationship between the state and the Islamists. Islamists were encouraged to develop into self-sufficient entities to help the state achieve its strategic and long-term goals. The process began with the flow of funds from Saudi Arabia to build *madrasas* and mosques in the country. In the 1970s, the Saudis were in a mode to disburse their charities from the first flush of petro-dollars. With a weak economy and almost non-existent infrastructure, Pakistan depended on these charities to provide social welfare and succor to the economy. The charities were responsible for providing a network of small and medium-sized welfare networks across the country. Since the state was unable to establish an education system, the network of mosques and related institutions took over. The original intentions and ideas of the Saudis were sidelined in the process, as was the process of government control over the organizations.

Mohammed Ayoob explains that although in the 1980s and 1990s the Saudis did finance many *madrasas* in Pakistan, especially on the Afghanistan border, it was the local context – the lack of educational and economic opportunities and the absence of social services – that led to the demand for *madrasa* education and Islamist charitable networks. It was this lack of opportunity, combined with the impact of the Afghan War, that created the *jihadis* now so reviled in the

Western media. Nor would neo-Wahhabi teachings have had much impact in Pakistan had it not been for local circumstances that made them attractive to certain constituencies opposed to the patrimonial and clientist Pakistani state and its great-power patrons. The neo-Wahhabism of the Pakistani *madrasas* went far beyond the original thrust of Wahhabi teachings. The Saudi rulers had envisioned Wahhabism as a socially conservative and politically quiet form of Islam. The idea was that the Wahhabis would help the House of Saud as the "Keeper of the Two Holy Places" to retain power, while turning a blind eye to Saudi Arabia's economic and security relationship with the "infidel" United States.[14]

As the state encouraged the non-state actors to grow in physical and political power and to further their own domestic and international agendas, slowly these very forces became difficult to control. Initially, these forces, combined with religious fervor, provided legitimacy to a failing and weak Pakistani government. As the state was unable to effectively form an alternative to the existing capitalist and socialist forms of government, it fell back on religious forces to provide it with legitimacy.

The role of the madrasas

Understanding the role *madrasas* play in support of Islamist activities across the globe can be explained in terms of the role they play in society. They fill the vacuum that exists between the function of the state and the practice of the state. *Madrasas* cater to the lower middle class, mostly in rural and semi-urban areas of the country. Recently, a politicization of the *madrasas* has been one of the most important political developments in Pakistan, with ramifications in the international arena.

Madrasas played a prominent role in the politics of Pakistan at the end of the 1970s, when democratic and political rule was replaced by military rule. The government of Zulfikar Ali Bhutto (1971–1977) channeled Pakistan's Islamic aspirations towards foreign policy. Pakistan played a key role in developing the Organization of Islamic Conference and opened up special relations with Islamic groups and countries. Through his Islamization efforts, General Zia made Pakistan an important ideological and organizational center of the global Islamist movement.

General Zia-ul Haq (1977–1988) was the first leader who changed the mission of the state. While the concept of religion had been the founding principle of Pakistan, Zia used Islam as a tool for political legitimization of his politics. Zia's claim that Bhutto's government was deviating from the norm helped him garner support from the Islamist political forces. As the Pakistan People's Party (PPP) leader, Bhutto displayed his potential to challenge Zia from jail, thereby successfully manipulating Islamic ideology to stabilize his regime. Zia issued the controversial Hudud Ordinances shortly before hanging Bhutto ostensibly to pre-empt the much feared agitation from his party. Zia castigated democracy as an importation from the West and instead upheld Islam as a source of legitimacy. The Islamic parties JI, JUI and JUP joined Zia's military government in an all-out effort to prevent Bhutto's party from returning to power in the event of elections. Cooperation between army and Islamic parties that started under Yahya Khan came to fruition under Zia. The JI earned the dubious title of Martial Law's B team.[15]

In 1979, the Iranian Revolution and the Soviet occupation of Afghanistan inspired a profound shift in the Muslim world and in the *madrasas*. Shiʿa–Sunni differences in ideology were exacerbated, coupled with clashes between Middle Eastern governments and the ideology of the Iranian Revolution. In the midst of this conflict, and the *madrasa* boom it spawned, the United States helped create an Islamic resistance to communism in Afghanistan. The US encouraged Saudi Arabia and other oil-rich states to fund the Afghan resistance and its supporters throughout the Muslim world. Pakistan's military ruler at the time, General Mohammed Zia ul-Haq, decided to establish *madrasas* instead of modern schools in Afghan refugee camps, where five million displaced Afghans provided a natural supply of recruits for the resistance. The refugees needed schools; the resistance needed *mujahideen* (holy warriors). *Madrasas* would provide an education of sorts, but they would also serve as a center of indoctrination and motivation.[16]

The schools' influence and staying power derived from deep-rooted socio-economic conditions. In some ways, *madrasas* were at the center of a civil war of ideas in the Islamic world. Westernized and usually affluent Muslims lack an interest in religious matters, but religious scholars, marginalized by modernization, seek to assert their own relevance by insisting on orthodoxy. A secular education is expensive and therefore inaccessible to the poor, but *madrasas* are typically free. Poor students attending *madrasas* believe that the West, loyal to uncaring and aloof leaders, is responsible for their misery and that Islam as practiced in its earliest form can deliver them.[17]

During the presidency of General Zia, Islamist groups and parties gained immensely in terms of building an image of street power. Over a period of time, from the presidency of Zulfiqar Bhutto to the government of Pervez Musharaff, the *madrasas* have grown into institutions in their own right. Even if their international support system is cut off, the *madrasas* have developed a system of self-sustenance. They have the support of the local populations and the political opposition to the existing government. Their power to lobby and garner popular support has made them into a force that cannot be suppressed. Successive governments have failed to curb the outreach of the *madrasas*, or to even check the syllabi of their education. Whether it has been a process of providing registration to the *madrasas* or providing an alternative infrastructure for education, governments have been unable to address the issues effectively.[18]

In the post-9/11 scenario, there is immense international pressure on the Pakistani government to crack down on the *madrasas* and the Islamists. The government, therefore, has been seeking an alternative way to incorporate the *madrasas* into the mainstream. Pakistan has sought assistance to strengthen and increase the number of secular and Western education systems in the country in order to counter the radical and fundamentalist rhetoric coming out of these schools.

Second, an increase in the number of Western-style institutions would strengthen the state system and help the government bridge the gap between its functional and societal demands. Educational institutions and welfare organizations that propagate the idea of loyalty to the state help generate avenues for the local population to integrate into the state system. If Pakistan is successful with this, hopefully it will be able to wean away the resource base for terrorists and non-state actors.

Creation of jihadis

Hamza Alavi explains that in the 1980s, Islamic fundamentalism was propagated in Pakistan by General Zia. Zia was recruited by US President Ronald Regan and assisted by the Central Intelligence Agency (CIA) to mobilize Afghan warlords to fight the Soviets in the name of Islamic *jihad*. A *jihadi* culture was propagated within the army, as well as in Afghanistan, with the help of US and Saudi money.[19]

As this involvement became deeper, the ISI took over full control of implementing the state policy. Initially the ISI operatives acquired the services of JI to funnel CIA-procured arms and money to Afghan warlords masquerading as *mujahideen*.[20] The CIA trained *jihadis* in both countries and armed them with sophisticated missiles. After driving the Soviets out of Afghanistan, rival warlords, all invoking Islam, armed by the US and Pakistan, and funded by Saudi Arabia, began tearing their country apart.[21]

After the Soviet withdrawal from Afghanistan and the degeneration of Afghan *jihad* into a prolonged civil war, the ISI shifted its support to Jamiat-e-Ulema-e-Islam (JUI), the more fundamentalist and sectarian of Pakistan's Islamist parties subscribing to the Deobandi–Wahhabi doctrine. In Afghanistan, the Taliban militia that overran the strongholds of earlier *mujahideen* warlords in the mid-1990s and established the Islamic Emirate of Afghanistan under Mulla Omar was mobilized from the *madrasas* of the JUI. The JUI also had doctrinal affinity with the fundamentalist Wahhabi Islam of Osama bin Laden and his Arab followers planted by the CIA in Afghanistan to wage anti-communist *jihad*. The co-optation of Islamist parties as *jihadi* arms of the Pakistan army in Afghanistan sent out a clear signal that waging *jihad* was a legitimate political activity. All types of *jihadi* formations sprouted from existing Islamist parties, as well as independently, to wage their holy wars against unbelievers. Their arena then expanded to free Kashmir from Indian control, as well as to free Pakistan from the rule of secular politicians.[22]

The chaos that ensued following the Soviet withdrawal precipitated Pakistan's decision to take the militant Islamic student movement – which became the Taliban – under its wing. Under the guidance and tutelage of the ISI, Pakistan armed the Taliban, helped them recruit new members, and provided them with the training and battle plans that they used to take over most of Afghanistan in the mid-1990s. Once in power the Taliban did not simply carry out Pakistan's bidding, although a number of Pakistani militant groups were integrated into the

Taliban's command structure. Overall, Pakistan did get most of what it wanted from the installation of a friendly regime in Afghanistan, namely strategic depth and an incubator for fighters to be used against India in the contested Kashmir region. Nevertheless, with these benefits came costs. Because of the ISI's policy, many of its own (and other state organizations') members grew close to anti-Western Islamists, including bin Laden.[23]

According to Frédéric Grare, the military sees ideology as a tool to strengthen its power and rationalize its expansionism, while the Islamists see power as a means to expand ideology. Thus, neither the existence of occasional meeting points nor the prevalence of pre-existing tensions should come as a surprise.[24] Grare goes on to use Waseem's explanation about how the ruling elite opted for Islam as an instrument of policy. The elite conceived religion as a counterweight to demands of the leftist groups and ethnic parties to open up the state system to a wider section of society. Under a bureaucracy, the army and a democratic framework based on mass mandate was considered dysfunctional. Therefore the elites used Islamic ideology and shaped its idiom. The group sought to control the theory and practice of Islamic ideology by passing legislation in the name of the Shari'a, assuming control over the *madrasas* and influencing the growth patterns of Islamic groups and networks.[25]

The ISI established the Markaz al-Dawa, a center for worldwide Islamist activities. Maulvi Zaki, the center's spiritual leader, taught the trainees that their destiny was to fight and liberate "the land of Allah from infidels." The commanders and instructors at Markaz-al-Dawa were primarily from Algeria, Sudan and Egypt, and most of them had more than a decade of combat experience in Afghanistan. In early 1992, some of these Afghans were transferred to Azad Kashmir where new camps were being built for them by the Pakistani Army. By early 1993, there were over 1,000 Afghan *mujahideen* in the Markaz al-Dawa alone. Following the completion of their advanced training, the Afghans were sent to Kashmir, Algeria and Egypt. Furthermore, Islamabad's claims to the contrary notwithstanding, the main offices of the Islamist terrorist organizations have remained functioning in Peshawar.[26]

Pakistan has been facing the problem of terrorism on both the domestic and international front as a result of these non-state actors and the radical world they created. Pakistan's policy severely backfired, mostly due to the weakness of the state and the inability to sustain such a program. To create non-state actors on foreign soil, and then to ideologically and physically sustain their existence, required a vision, and an economic, political and military strength that Pakistan lacked.

The ouster of the Soviet forces from Afghanistan, the failure to produce adequate secessionists in Jammu and Kashmir and the end of the Cold War and the War on Terror post-9/11 led to a total breakdown of the strategy of using non-state actors as instruments of foreign policy execution. The US and allied forces' military intervention in Afghanistan further led to a major influx of refugees into Pakistan, particularly in the Northwest frontier province. The ideology of religious radicalism and political secessionism with which the Taliban was created spilled back into Pakistan. Today, Pakistan is forced to use the armed forces and wage a war on its own population to reintegrate them into the mainstream.

The ideological spill-over of fundamentalism has led to a radicalization of the polity within Pakistan. The earlier political phenomenon within Pakistan of having opposition parties that supported fundamentalism now has an armed base. The political leadership of Islamist parties in Pakistan is also acquiring further leadership and support from cross-border leaders.

Variables impacting upon Pakistan's foreign policy

Pakistan's security environment derives its origins from the circumstances in which the state was created and is complicated by its location in a "dangerous" neighborhood. With borders of India to the east, China to the north, and Iran and Afghanistan to the west, security remains at the center of Pakistan's foreign policy. Relations with its neighbors have been the chief basis for alliances and partnerships between Pakistan and countries around the world. To counter the potential threats, Pakistan has repeatedly been involved in Afghan internal politics in the hopes of influencing the nature of its regime. For instance, following the 1979 Soviet invasion of Afghanistan, Pakistan joined with the US in supporting opposition to the Soviet occupation force. This support included backing extremist *mujahideen* guerrilla groups, which in turn created its own set of problems for Pakistan upon Soviet withdrawal a decade later.

The violence accompanying the period prior to partition of Pakistan and India generated hostility. This hostility continues to affect relations between the two countries due mainly to the unresolved issue of Jammu and Kashmir. This region is the source of continuing tensions and conflict, has shaped the unstable and tense security environment in the region[27] and has played a major role in the development of Pakistan's foreign policy after 1947. From the UN enforced cease-fire of 1949 to the 1965 war over Kashmir, Pakistan allied itself with the West by joining the Baghdad Pact and its successors, CENTO and SEATO. The motivation underlying the membership of the alliances had been the need to redress defense vulnerability and to achieve a reasonable military equilibrium with India.

The second variable was the Indian intervention in the creation of Bangladesh as a separate country. From 1965 to the 1971 crisis in East Pakistan, the two countries were in a constant state of hostility. The 1965 war, sparked by the Jammu and Kashmir issue, led to a drastic reduction in economic and military assistance to Pakistan. The increase in defense expenditure together with the decline in foreign assistance created economic difficulties and aggravated political problems, producing a sense of alienation in East Pakistan. In 1971, India intervened militarily to assist East Pakistan in ceding and forming Bangladesh.

The threat of increasing Soviet presence in Afghanistan had a major impact on Pakistan's foreign policy. Similar to the border dispute with India, Pakistan also encountered a disputed border on its western front. The recognition of the Durand line between Pakistan and Afghanistan has been as much an issue as the

Radcliffe boundary. Following the separation of Bangladesh, Pakistan was too busy to allow for instability in Afghanistan. As a result, from 1971 to 1989, Pakistan was actively involved in rebuilding itself and facing the challenge of the Soviet military intervention in neighboring Afghanistan.

Nuclear tests may be identified as the fourth variable that has impacted upon Pakistan's strategic threat perception from the 1990s to May 1998. Pakistan began working intensively to become a nuclear state in order to deter the perceived threat of war from India. Both countries had sanctions imposed on them.

The next and most important variable in shaping Pakistani foreign policy has been US policy towards Pakistan. During the Cold War era, Pakistan was an ally and a buffer in containing the spread of communism in south Asia. With increased Soviet military presence in Afghanistan, the US government became actively involved in arming, training and supporting the Pakistani policy of using non-state actors as weapons.

However, with the withdrawal of Soviet troops from Afghanistan and the end of the Cold War, two important events in 1990 influenced Pakistani security. The 1985 Pressler Amendment had authorized the banning of most military and economic assistance to Pakistan if an annual presidential determining that Pakistan did not possess a nuclear device was not given. In 1990, US President George H.W. Bush was the first to withhold such a determination. Pakistan, on the other hand, saw the ban as US partiality towards India.[28]

The US should not be understood as the only external variable that influenced the foreign policy of Pakistan. Apart from individual countries, international forums and multilateral institutions, such as the United Nations and the Organization of Islamic Countries, played a role in shaping foreign policy.

9/11 and the War on Terror shifted paradigms and set in motion the fifth phase of Pakistan's foreign policy. Pakistan was forced to decide between allying with the US and becoming part of the war, or not joining America and positioning itself at the receiving end of the war. To become a front-line ally in the War on Terror, Pakistan has had to modify its previous stands on its policies towards Afghanistan and towards curbing non-state actors. Pakistan is now working actively with the US and Western forces in Afghanistan to curb the economic lifeline of the *jihadis* and the terrorist training camps.

Conclusion

Pakistan provides an interesting case study of how domestic politics influence International Relations and how international politics impact upon domestic politics.

The creation of Pakistan was an attempt to form a religion-based state, unique from Muslim majority states elsewhere in the world. The ambition of the state was to serve as the guiding force in shaping state–society relations throughout the Muslim world. By intervening actively in international politics, Pakistan aims to be the leader of all Muslim communities. Pakistan attempts to set the agenda of what Islamic or international organizations should be doing, by actively propagating causes and raising issues in international forums.

However, since the time of its inception, Pakistan has been unable to clearly define or understand the nature of its relations with India. Pakistan views its neighbor as both a threat and a potential ally. On the one hand, a conventional military confrontation with India may not just result in another military defeat for Pakistan but may also cause a nuclear conflict in the region. On the other hand, Pakistan is aware of the need for increased economic cooperation with India to improve its own economy.

The biggest problem for Pakistan is the lack of a formal and organized state apparatus. The outreach of the state machinery is very limited. An example illuminating this fact is the 2005 earthquake in Kashmir that demonstrated the state's limited administrative abilities. The Islamist aid workers and parties were able to network and provide relief much faster than the government. The inadequacy of the aid and support reaching the earthquake refugees rendered them vulnerable not only to poverty, death and disease, but also to radicalization and anti-government political leanings. Many fear that the radicalization of Pakistan's deprived regions – characterized by low-intensity conflict, refugees, poverty, lack of democracy, corruption and mismanagement – will become too virulently anti-government and anti-Western for the armed forces to handle.

Olivier Roy points out that while Islamists adapt to the nation-state, neo-fundamentalists embody the crisis of the nation-state, squeezed between intrastate solidarities and globalization. The state level is bypassed and ignored.[29] Pakistan's foreign policy is characterized by a radicalization of society and a growth of armed and unarmed non-state actors. Over time, these actors will be able to overrun the state apparatus and potentially ignite a civil war, reminiscent of the current situation in Iraq. Therefore, the solution in Pakistan lies not in coercive actions that would damage the infrastructure of the state but in strengthening the institution of the state. Coercive alternatives, like sanctions or direct military intervention, will only lead to a more chaotic Asia. The increased outreach of the state, along with an increase in the infrastructure of social welfare, would be the most effective weapon in countering fundamentalists. Basic social welfare services like the educational institutions and the healthcare system are examples of institutions to be strengthened. In addition, an economic system that addresses the issues of population, poverty, unemployment and human security would need to be established to set Pakistan on a course for improvement.

Notes

1 For how the fundamentalist imagination of the state works, see M. Juergensmeyer, *The New Cold War? Religious Nationalism Confronts the Secular State*, Berkley and Los Angeles: University of California Press, 1993; and R. Scott Appleby, "History in the Fundamentalist Imagination," *Journal of American History*, September 2002, vol. 89, no. 2, pp. 498–511.

2 See D. Byman, "Passive Sponsors of Terrorism," *Survival*, winter 2005–2006, vol. 47, no. 4, pp. 117–144. Byman has categorized Pakistan as one of the states that are passive sponsors of terrorism. This means essentially that though the state may not be

directly involved with international terrorism, it allows the terrorists to operate at its expense. The state allows the terrorists to operate from its soil, and, by turning a blind eye to the terrorists, has become a passive sponsor of terrorism.

3 See Samuel Huntington's argument on the clash of civilizations based on the identity of religion in his famous article "Clash of Civilizations," *Foreign Affairs* summer 1993, vol. 72, no. 3, pp. 22–49.

4 See O. Roy. "Pakistan and the Taliban." Available online at www.ceri-sciencespo.com/archive/octo00/artor.pdf (accessed 26 August 2006).

5 Available online at http://pakistanspace.tripod.com/archives/47jin11.htm (accessed 2 October 2006).

6 Ibid., p. 111.

7 S. Cohen, "The Nation and State of Pakistan," *Washington Quarterly*, summer 2002, vol. 25, no. 3, p. 109.

8 Ibid., p. 112.

9 S. Bose, "Decolonization and State Building in South Asia," *Journal of International Affairs*, fall 2004, vol. 58, no. 1, pp. 95–114.

10 C. Hay *et al.* (eds) *The State: Theories and Issues*, New York: Palgrave Macmillan, 2006, pp. 4–5.

11 See J. S. Migdal, "The State in Society: An Approach to Struggles for Domination in State Power and Social Forces: Domination and Transformation in the Third World," in J. S. Midgal, A. Kohli and V. Shue (eds) *State Power and Social Forces: Domination and Transformation in the Third World*, New York: Cambridge University Press, 1994, p. 9.

12 See A. Rashid, *Taliban: Militant Islam, Oil and Fundamentalism in Central Asia*, New Haven, CT: Yale University Press, 2000.

13 See M. Waseem, "Origins and Growth Patterns of Islamic Organizations in Pakistan," in *Religious Radicalism and Security in South Asia.* Available online at www.apcss.org/Publications/Edited%20Volumes/ReligiousRadicalism/Religious Radicalism.htm (accessed 18 April 2006).

14 See Mohammed Ayoob, "Political Islam: Image and Reality," *World Policy Journal*, fall 2004, vol. 21, no. 3, pp. 3–4.

15 Ibid., p. 22.

16 See H. Haqqani, "On Madrasas." Available online at http://ics.leeds.ac.uk/papers/vp01.cfm?outfit=pmt&folder=10&paper=992 (accessed 2 June 2006).

17 Ibid.

18 See Waseem, op. cit.

19 H. Alavi, "Pakistan between Afghanistan and India," *Pakistan Perspectives*, January–June 2002, vol. 7, no. 1, pp. 5–16.

20 See Hassan N. Gardezi. "The Politics of Religion in Pakistan: Islamic State or Shari'a Rule." Available online at www.sacw.net/new/Gardezi140403.html (accessed 24 October 2006).

21 Hamza, op. cit.

22 Ibid.

23 See J. Cole, "Pakistan's Foreign and Domestic Policy Since September 11th," Massachusetts Institute of Technology. Available online at http://web.mit.edu/SSP/seminars/wed_archives_02spring/cole.htm (accessed 21 November 2006).

24 F. Grare, "Islam, Militarism, and the 2007–2008 Elections in Pakistan," Carnegie Paper No. 70, July 2006, p. 6.

25 Ibid., pp. 6–7.

26 For Further details about how the Markaz Dawar operates and how it is connected to global networks of terror like those of Osama bin Laden, see Yossef Bodansky (22 June 1994), "Pakistan Supports Terrorists Rebels in Pakistan," *Globalsecurity.org*. Available online at www.globalsecurity.org/security/library/congress/1994_cr/h940622-terror-pak.htm (accessed 27 March 2007); see also M. Chossudovsky, *War*

and Globalization: The Truth Behind September, Quebec, Canada: Global Outlook Press, 2004.
27 Available online at www.pakistan.gov.pk (accessed 26 October 2006).
28 For a list of sanctions against Pakistan, see www.pbs.org/wgbh/pages/frontline/taliban/pakistan/uspolicychart.html.
29 O. Roy, "Neo-fundamentalism," Social Science Research Council. Available online at www.ssrc.org/sept11/essays/roy.htm (accessed 1 November 2006).

Part III
Responding to the Islamist challenge

9 The potential dangers of a "real" *jihad*

Max Singer

Introduction

The key proposition of this chapter is that a much more dangerous and destructive *jihad* than has been seen so far is possible, and I predict that the danger will either be averted or come to pass within the next few years.

A number of implications follow from this hypothesis. First, it follows that one of the primary policy goals must be to prevent a more destructive *jihad* from occurring. Second, in order to prevent a worse *jihad*, it is necessary to use strategies designed to work in the short term. Third, limiting *jihad* to current levels has been an important partial success, especially if it stays so limited.

A fourth key proposition is that it is important to distinguish between Muslims who are engaged in or promoting "*jihad*-now" and those who are either against or not willing to support *jihad*-now, even though they favor *jihad* in principle, or at some other time. By "*jihad*-now" I mean violent actions against the West or against Muslims who oppose *jihad*-now.

This proposed distinction – between supporters and opponents of *jihad*-now – is one that is rarely made.[1] There are many other sensible ways to divide or analyze Muslim organizations, schools of thought and policies. The policy approach suggested here is that the US perspective should focus on what is directly relevant to the US's main short-term concern: preventing a greater *jihad*. In a practical sense, our enemies are those who are promoting *jihad*-now, and anyone who opposes *jihad*-now, for whatever reason, and however hostile to us and to other non-Muslims, is serving our purposes.

The present situation

There is now an attempted *jihad*. Al Qaeda and other groups have said, "It's time for *jihad*, follow us."[2] They succeeded in producing 9/11 and many terrorist attacks around the world, but most of the Muslim world has not joined the fight. Although probably tens of millions of individual Muslims support *jihad*-now in varying degrees, currently there is not a Muslim population that as a society is clearly committed to *jihad*-now.

Nor have Muslim governments rushed to join the *jihad*. Iran is the Muslim government that is most committed to *jihad*-now, although it preserves some ambiguity.[3] Syria, for political reasons, tacitly supports *jihad* but actively denies involvement.[4] However, Syria is too small to matter if events turn serious. The Saudi government allows perhaps $4 billion per year of Saudi money to be the key force in spreading *jihadi* ideology through the world,[5] although officially the government opposes anti-Western terrorism. In addition, a strong part of the Saudi leadership is against *jihad*-now, even though for various reasons they feel it prudent to give some aid to advocates of *jihad*-now. In addition, there are probably elements of Pakistan's government that, despite President Parvez Musharref, also support *jihad*-now.[6] Despite this, there are dozens of other Muslim governments that have not been conspicuously moved by the call for *jihad*-now.

There would be a much larger *jihad* – I would call it a "real *jihad*" – if several large Muslim governments, such as Pakistan[7] and Bangladesh,[8] and several large Muslim populations, such as the Baluchis or the Bengalis, decided to support *jihad*-now. If there were large regions or countries where terrorist organizations could organize, recruit, train, and openly plan, free from pressure or fear of attack, homeland defense would have a difficult time protecting the US.

Before continuing, clarification of some key terms is necessary. "*Jihad*" means making war against the infidels, or those who resist the extension of Muslim rule and law.[9] One person can make a *jihad*, although it would not be very significant. The whole Muslim world could, theoretically, make *jihad*, but that is not very likely. There is a point in the spectrum between one and everyone where *jihad* is large enough to be called a "real *jihad*," or "big *jihad*." A "real *jihad*" is one that has the support of a substantially larger share of the Muslim world than is supporting *jihad*-now today, but much less than the whole Muslim world.

The US can probably defeat the current level of *jihad* without great disruption to civilian life if it seriously pursues a sound policy. However, there is a plausible level of increased *jihad* which would entirely change the intensity and scope of the conflict and its harm to the world. If the US continues to respond only weakly to the current *jihad*, the danger of a much greater *jihad* will increase. The current *jihad* will be a footnote in history; a real *jihad* will create a new historical era. The level of *jihad* that changes the world as much as it was changed by 9/11 is what I refer to as a "real *jihad*." In other words, if enough people and governments support "*jihad*-now," a "real *jihad*" would exist. For this discussion, however, it is not necessary to calculate precisely the increase in *jihad* before a "real *jihad*" exists. It is sufficient to say that some increase in support for *jihad*, involving much less than the whole Muslim world, would be enough to radically change the conflict.

Governments and populations

While governments are the key actors for and against *jihad*, it is also important to consider Muslim populations or communities, despite difficulties in defining such groups or in understanding their "position" or "decision." Despite ambiguities, it often becomes clear when a population has made the decision to support *jihad*-now. "Support" means not only sympathizing with the idea of *jihad*, but also includes a willingness to face the consequences. For example, it is clear that the Palestinian population supports a terror war against Israel, although undoubtedly many Palestinians disagree with this approach; the support is not great enough to prevent the Israeli security service from acquiring sufficient information to prevent terror attacks.[10]

Why would it matter if a major Muslim population decided to support *jihad*-now today, since there are already millions of Muslim individuals who already do so? The first reason is that when a "population" supports *jihad*-now it is more difficult for the government to act against *jihadi* terrorists, putting pressure on the government to also support *jihad*-now. Second, when one Muslim population makes *jihad* it encourages other populations to also make *jihad*, which may in turn cause an avalanche effect. Third, if there is a Muslim government supporting *jihad*-now, and it is supported by its population, the US cannot solve the problem by simply removing the government.

Fourth, one reasonable explanation for the absence of successful *jihadi* attacks on the US since 9/11 may be that no major Muslim community has decided to make *jihad*-now. Al Qaeda and other terrorist organizations primarily comprise not only numerous citizens who feel themselves to be acting with the support of their communities, but also more typically young men and fanatics (of whom there are millions in a total population of over a billion). Most of the more ideologically centerist parts of Muslim populations are still waiting to see whether *jihad*-now is Allah's will and the right course for Muslims to take. It seems plausible that if the mainstream of some large Muslim communities decided to join *jihad*-now, they would eventually create organizations capable of presenting a much greater problem for US internal security forces than these forces have had to face thus far.

The stereotypical fear of *jihad* is of a billion Muslims swept up in emotional fervor attacking those standing in their way.[11] This fear is baseless. While it is easy to exaggerate the importance of the Arab or Muslim "street," it is also necessary to recognize the emotional potential in the Muslim world. It is essentially impossible that "*jihad* fever" will sweep over the world of Islam. The Muslim world is too diverse and divided for that reality. It is not impossible that such a *jihad*-now favoring a wave of emotion or ideas could catch hold in one or a few large Muslim populations, or that waves of public feeling might arise in élites rather than among the masses. Muslim élites, comprising 1 to 10 percent of their populations, are subject to sudden turns and probably wield more influence over Muslim governments than do the opinion and emotions of the majority of the population.

Real *jihad*

It is plausible that a realistically imaginable increase in support for *jihad*-now by Muslim governments and populations ("real *jihad*") would lead to a more effective effort to overcome US Homeland Security. "Real *jihad*" has the potential to kill tens of thousands of American civilians either by dramatic 9/11-type attacks or by a profusion of smaller attacks. Imagine how Americans would react to large-scale deadly explosions over a month or two in Syracuse, NY, Sarasota, FL, and Sacramento, CA. Lurking beneath the fear of unexpected attacks is the realization of what could happen if the increased support for *jihadi* terrorists enabled them to acquire a nuclear or biological weapon capable of killing hundreds of thousands of people.

Paradoxically a real *jihad* cannot be started without additional successful terror attacks in the US, because not enough Muslims are likely to believe that *jihad*-now can succeed if enough Americans are not killed. Nor are they likely to believe that a *jihad* that cannot kill Americans has divine support. Muslim belief dictates that faith brings success, and conversely, lack of success shows lack of the necessary faith to garner Allah's support.[12]

Increased attacks in the US would quickly produce multiplied defensive measures in addition to actions overseas. It is impossible to predict the balance that would eventually be reached between a serious program of attack and multiplied defensive measures, but the process required to reach that balance would not be pretty. What are considered inconveniences today, such as long queues at airports and international phone call monitoring, would seem quaint in retrospect to the necessary response of large-scale attacks.

The largest indirect effect of an increase in 9/11-type attacks would be on the Muslim population in the US and other countries targeted by *jihadis*. Perhaps a million or more Muslims would move from the West back to Muslim countries. For the Muslims remaining in the West, the problems they face and the necessary and unnecessary injustices would be much worse because there is still no widely accepted Muslim organization in the US that speaks against *jihadi* terror and exposes Muslims in the US who support terror. Therefore, if multiplied Islamist terror leads to a popular backlash, there will not be a Muslim group that has earned the credibility needed to represent and defend the Muslims who choose loyalty to American law over allegiance to fellow Muslims. I believe this to be true in Europe as well.

It seems clear that a *jihad* with increased Muslim support would be able to produce at least a moderate amount of terrorism in the US and would change the world more dramatically than the events of 9/11. Today the world is still essentially "normal"; a real *jihad* would produce a perceptibly different and dangerous global situation. While the suffering and costs of that reality would be widely felt, Muslims are likely to suffer more from separation; they need the West much more than the West needs them. While the West needs Muslim oil (although less than most people think)[13] it is quite possible for a great deal of oil to flow even if there is a high degree of separation between Muslim countries and the rest of the world.

Is the danger of such a horribly conflicted world just hypothetical? Is there a substantial chance that there could be a larger *jihad*? No one can assess the odds precisely, but there seems to be enough evidence to support the real danger of a larger *jihad* for prudent measures to be taken in government policy to make the prevention of a real *jihad* a major goal.

Preventing real *jihad*

What must be done in order to prevent a real *jihad*?

Since preventing a real *jihad* is something that must be done in the next few years, little effort should be put into convincing Muslims that they should not believe in *jihad*. Most Muslims understand the Qur'ān and Islamic tradition to say that Islam is the one true religion and that Allah intends that it should rule the world. Muslims also believe that any government or society that refuses to accept Islamic rule and Shari'a law is not legitimate for Muslims. Therefore, there is automatically a theoretical state of war between the world of Islam and the rest of the world, which is referred to as *Dar al Harb* ("the world of war"),[14] although the war does not have to be prosecuted every day.

The majority of Muslims believe in either *jihad*-now, *jihad*-as-soon-as-possible, or, most commonly, *jihad*-someday. These *jihad*-favoring views are so deeply held, and have such strong support in Islamic writings and traditions, that there is no hope of significantly reducing this majority in the next decade or two. However, there is the possibility of influencing Muslims to move from one of these *jihad*-favoring views to another, particularly to prevent those who favor *jihad*-as-soon-as-possible from deciding that now is the time.

If *jihad* were conducted solely by words, economic boycotts, or by military invasions, it would not be as big a problem for the US. However, today, the principal weapon of *jihad* is terror – that is, deliberately killing large numbers of civilians chosen for their convenience as targets and not because of their actions or views. Supporting *jihad*-now means promoting, organizing, and conducting terrorist attacks. Therefore, although the US can live with a Muslim commitment to *jihad* as a principle, it cannot live with a Muslim commitment to *jihad*-now.

In 1966 or 1976, there was no substantial movement for *jihad*-now, although all the fundamental reasons for *jihad* were just as great then as they are today.[15] This shows that the question of *jihad*-now is separate from the question of *jihad*. The most that the US can do in the short term is to bring Islam's relationship to the West back to where it was 30 years ago. Recent experience shows that neither Muslim beliefs, nor the long history of Muslim grievances and humiliation, necessarily create an immediate danger of *jihad*-now.

Muslim decisions about whether this is the time for *jihad*-now depend primarily on their perceptions of the chance that *jihad* will succeed and of the degree of danger to the Muslim community from making *jihad*. Muslims will wage *jihad* if it looks as if they can succeed and as if they face little danger from trying. They will postpone the struggle if the West appears indomitable and dangerous. They will not stop because we are nice or reasonable or fair. They will not go ahead because they hate us, so long as they fear us. We have no possibility in the time available to make all Muslims like us or to convince them that we are legitimate. All we can do, and need to do, is to convince them to respect our power and determination – or even ruthlessness.[16]

Which battle of ideas?

There has been much talk about the battle of ideas. The most urgent battle of ideas in which the US must be engaged is the battle to convince Muslim governments and populations to reject the call for *jihad*-now. While this is a struggle of *ideas* it must be conducted primarily by *actions* rather than by words. The only "argument" that is effective against *jihad*-now in the short term is the argument that it is too dangerous for Islam. This is an argument that can best be made by actions that demonstrate US power over Muslim countries and the lack of power of *jihadi* organizations.

To prevent a real *jihad*, the US must make two demands on the Arab and Muslim countries: don't harbor terrorists and don't acquire nuclear or biological weapons. There are two separate reasons for these demands. The first reason is that the US and world order will benefit if terrorists are not harbored and WMDs are not spread in the Middle East. The second reason is that by compelling these countries to comply with US demands, the US demonstrates to the Muslim world that the US is too powerful to attack.

The Bible tells the story of how God taught Pharaoh and the Jews a lesson about His power. He demanded, "Let my people go!" and when Pharaoh rejected the demand He inflicted ten plagues on the Egyptians, one at a time, until Pharaoh was forced to comply. Note that if Pharaoh had replied to Moses' first request by saying, "Good idea, I was thinking about something like that myself; when do you want to leave?" God's plan would have been foiled. God's intention in the story was to harden Pharaoh's heart.

If the US tries to "buy" compliance with its demands by appeasing Arab governments, it subverts its second major purpose. Trying to buy compliance from Arab countries for essential US security needs demonstrates American weakness. It shows that the US understands neither its own power nor Arab weakness and that the US will never be able to buy the necessary compliance. In other words, Arab governments may promise but they will not deliver unless they are afraid for their own survival (afraid in most cases of political measures, not military attack). Of course, as a practical matter we need to follow a mixed strategy, with carrots as well as sticks. However, we need to be clear about the basic message we are delivering because there is a fundamental conflict between appeasement and compulsion.

The critical issue in Washington

This analysis has an important implication for the fundamental unarticulated dispute in Washington over the Middle East. That central question, which the US Administration has not yet faced, is whether the US should get the help it needs to fight terrorism from Arab governments by appeasing them or by frightening them – by buying or compelling their decision. The actual practical policy, of course, must be mixed and varied from country to country. Since the two basic approaches are contradictory, the US must decide which is primary. In the long run, there are arguments supporting an approach that primarily buys, not compels, support. In the short run – when the decisions about *jihad*-now are being made – it is very hard to make a case for appeasement, even if it is the main direction of US policy today.

The following is the model I believe should guide US policy. There is a major effort by al Qaeda and some Muslim leaders to call for *jihad*-now. The Muslim world is currently "thinking" about whether to accept the call for *jihad*-now – that is whether to commit to violent attacks against the West and especially the US. (This is why a US defeat in Iraq would be dangerous.) In the next few years there will either be an implicit rejection of the call or some major populations and governments will unite and make a real *jihad*. If the current call for *jihad*-now is rejected, *jihad*-now will become a dead letter for some years, although individuals will continue to try to make attacks. A decision will have to be made that will end the matter for a decade or even a generation. After *jihad*-now has been clearly rejected there will be a different dynamic within Muslim communities. Perhaps a more open discussion will become possible, and the realities and temptations of the modern world will have time to work on the Muslim public and thinkers.

The alternative view of how Muslim behavior will be determined is that the possibility of real *jihad* is essentially constant. This view suggests that there never will be a decision against *jihad*-now, just a lack of decision to make *jihad* today, which does not reduce the possibility of a decision to make *jihad* tomorrow.

The best evidence that this model is correct are the signs from some of the most pro-*jihad* Muslims, including various off-shoots of the Muslim Brotherhood, and even some of al Qaeda, that they may want to pull back the call for *jihad*-now.[17] They are afraid that too few Muslims will join *jihad*-now and that if the call for *jihad*-now is rejected it will be a long time before they can try again.

Today many believers in *jihad*-as-soon-as-possible, the West's most fervent long-term enemies, are serving our interests by opposing *jihad*-now out of fear that *jihad*-now will fail and damage the possibility of trying again soon.

The US has been too concentrated on the importance of a fundamentally *jihadi* view of the world within Islam, as well as on the very long-term process that will eventually enable Islam to be a part of the modern world. In addition, the US has been too focused on the pattern of today's conflict with *jihadi* terrorists and has not appreciated the perspective of the possible range of conflicts.

The focus must be to ensure Muslim decisions against *jihad*-now. The US will be dealing with *jihadism* for a long time, but it is primarily an issue that Muslims will have to deal with. The immediate danger to the US comes not from support for *jihad* but from *jihad*-now. The choice between these two depends on decisions over which we can have a decisive influence by demonstrating how much harm will come to Muslims from this decision.

We can hope that if the current call for *jihad*-now is defeated in the next few years, which seems reasonably likely, it will give the world a respite before the challenge is brought again – similar to the situation 30 years ago. But even if short-term victory does not provide a respite, and the fight continues to discourage *jihad*-now, that struggle will remain the most urgent task. Muslim reformers who are engaged in the long-term effort of trying to move Islam away from the *jihadi* view of their religion are unlikely to be heard and unlikely to make headway as long as the possibility of *jihad*-now is on everyone's mind.

Notes

1 Arab-American psychiatrist Wafa Sultan, in an interview with the Arabic news channel *Al-Jazeera* on 21 February 2006, condemned acts of terrorism carried out under the banner of Islam, stating, "We have not seen a single Jew blow himself up in a German restaurant" in response to a negative comment about Judaism.

2 *The World Islamic Front for Jihad against Jews and Crusaders*, al Qaeda, February 1998.

3 Paula A. DeSutter, Assistant Secretary for Verification and Compliance, testified that "Iran is the most active state sponsor of terrorism." Testimony to the Joint US–Israeli Parliamentary Committee, Washington, DC, 23 September 2003.

4 See Ambassador Cofer Black, Coordinator for Counterterrorism, Testimony to the Senate Foreign Relations Committee, Washington, DC, 30 October 2003.

5 The Kingdom of Saudi Arabia reports that it has spent $70 billion on charitable and Islamic foundations to promote the radical Wahhabist ideology throughout the world. D. E. Kaplan, "The Saudi Connection: How Billions in Oil Money Spawned a Global Terror Network," *US News*, 15 December 2003.

6 See E. Kaplan (10 October 2006), "The ISI and Terrorism: Behind the Accusations," Council on Foreign Relations. Available online at www.cfr.org/publication/11644/isi_and_terrorism.html?breadcrumb=%2Fregion%2F283%2Fpakistan (accessed 11 January 2007).

7 See S. P. Cohen (Summer 2003), "The Jihadist Threat to Pakistan," *The Washington Quarterly*. Available online at www.brook.edu/views/articles/cohens/20030601.htm (accessed 23 January 2007).

8 See I.P. Khosla's concluding remarks in "Recent Developments in Bangladesh and Elections 2007," Institute of Peace and Conflict Studies, Article No. 2178, 5 January 2007. Available online at www.ipcs.org/newIpcsSeminars2.jsp?action=showView&kValue=2193 (accessed 23 January 2007).

9 G. Kepel, *The Trail of Political Islam*, trans. A. F. Roberts, London: I.B. Tauris, 2004.

10 Evidence of this has been gathered through polls conducted among the Palestinian people in the West Bank and Gaza by Dr. Khalil Shakaki of the Palestinian Center for Policy and Survey Research in Ramallah. In December 1996, 39 percent of Palestinians polled supported armed attacks against Israel. Available online at http://pcpsr.org/survey/cprspolls/96/poll25a.html (accessed 27 January 2007). However, ten years later, after the failed peace process and the Second Intifada, 56 percent supported armed attacks within Israel against Israeli citizens (27 June 2006). Available online at http://pcpsr.org/survey/polls/2006/p20e1.html (accessed 27 January 2007). Sixty-three percent agree that Palestinians should emulate Hizbollah's tactics used against Israel in the last war (26 September, 2006). Available online at www.pcpsr.org/survey/polls/2006/p21ejoint.html (accessed 27 January 2007). Seventy-seven percent support the Beer Sheva bombing attack (23–26 September 2004). Available online at http://pcpsr.org/survey/polls/2004/p13a.html (accessed 27 January 2007).

11 For example, "A poll carried out by the Council on American–Islamic Relations (CAIR), an advocacy group, found that for one in three Americans, the word Islam triggers negative connotations such as 'war,' 'hatred' and 'terrorist.'" B. Debusmann, "In US, Fear and Distrust of Muslims Runs Deep," *Reuters*, 1 December 2006.

12 *Tawhid* is one of the pillars of Islam. It asserts the oneness of Allah and His power to create and destroy as He wills. Those who truly believe in Allah and take Him into their hearts will be looked upon by Him with love and success; but without it, a person is not considered a real Muslim and therefore does not deserve the blessings of Allah. "The acceptance or denial of this phrase produces a world of difference between man and man. The believers in it become one single community and those who do not believe in it form an opposing group. For the believers there is unhampered progress and success in this world and in the hereafter, while failure and ignominy are the ultimate lot of those who refuse to believe in it." S. Abul A'la Maududi (11 January 2007), "Tawhid: Faith in the Unity of Allah," *Toward Understanding Islam*. USC Compendium of Muslim Texts. Available online at www.usc.edu/dept/MSA/ fundamentals/tawheed/mautaw1.html (accessed 27 January 2007).

13 I address this topic in "Saudi Arabia's Overrated Oil Weapon," *The Weekly Standard*, 18 August 2003, vol. 8, no. 46.

14 See A. G. Bostom (21 April 2001), "The Global Jihad," *FrontPageMagazine.com*. Available online at www.frontpagemag.com/Articles/ReadArticle.asp?ID=22141 (accessed 11 January 2007).

15 The assassination of Anwar Sadat in 1981 by Egyptian Islamists "added the idea of *jihad* as the path to world domination." Pipes, "*Jihad* Through History," *New York Sun*, 31 May 2005.

16 Support for this understanding of Muslim behavior comes from virtually all descriptions of Muslim history and sociology. The leading scholar is Prof. Bernard Lewis, but many others present essentially the same understanding. While there are Professors of Middle East Studies who recommend different policies, they do not describe a different paradigm for Muslim patterns of behavior. They have a different view of politics but not a different description of Muslim ethos.

17 D. Pipes (23 September 2003), "The Islamic State of America?" *FrontPage Magazine.Com*. Available online at www.danielpipes.org/article/2100 (accessed 11 January 2007).

10 Deterring those who are already dead?[1]

Laurent Murawiec

Introduction

Whether in a bar brawl or in nuclear escalation, deterrence works when one is able credibly to threaten or upset the enemy's center of gravity and inflict unacceptable losses upon him. Deterrence relies upon the question: *Is it worth it?* Is the price-earning ratio of the contemplated action so negative that it would wipe out the capital? Deterrence works if the price to be paid by the party to be deterred largely exceeds his expected earnings. But deterrence only works if the enemy is able and willing to enter the same calculus. If the enemy plays by other rules and calculates by other means, he will not be dissuaded. If the enemy's calculus is that he wishes to exchange his own life on earth for eternal bliss and to extol Allah's triumph, and if to him the Apocalypse is more desirable, he will not be deterred.

This chapter explores the possibility of deterring fanatics and reaches the conclusion that it is not possible to deter the modern Gnostics, the *jihadis*. Despite this conclusion, there are effective means of response, which may lessen, hinder or hamper their *jihadi* aims.

Ideological religion: the politics of Mahmoud Ahmadinejad

When Mahmoud Ahmadinejad was the mayor of Tehran, he insistently proposed that the main thoroughfares of Tehran should be widened so that on the day of his reappearance, the Hidden Imam, Mohamed ibn Hassan, who went into the Great Occultation in 941 AD, could tread spacious avenues. More recently, he told the Indian Foreign Minister that "in two years, everything will be settled," which the visiting dignitary mistook to mean that Iran expected to possess nuclear weapons in two years. He was later bemused to learn that Ahmadinejad had meant that the Mahdi would appear in two years, at which point all worldly problems would disappear.

This attitude is not new, nor should it surprise us. Religious notions and their estranged cousins, ideological representations, determine not only their believers' beliefs but also their actions. The difference between the religious and the ideologically religious is this: the religious believer accepts reality and works at improving it, while the fanatic rejects reality, refuses to pass any compromise with it and gambles everything in his effort to destroy it and replace it with his fantasy.

Ahmadinejad inhabits his beliefs rather than common reality. His politics cannot be labeled "radical," as opposed to "moderate." Rather, his politics are apocalyptic and eschatological. Ahmadinejad wants to hasten the reappearance of the Hidden Imam, whose coming will be the Sign of the Hour that the End of Days is nigh, according to traditional Muslim and especially Shi'a apocalyptics.[2] Its vanishing point is not earthly but otherworldly. Ayatollah Khomeini famously stated, "We have not made a revolution to lower the price of melon."[3] The task of the Mahdi, when he reappears, will be to lead the great and final war which will bring about the extermination of the Unbelievers, the end of Unbelief and the complete dominion of God's writ upon the whole of mankind. The *umma* will then inflate to absorb the rest of the world. That Ahmadinejad believes this will happen in two years exemplifies his utopian visions.

The politics practiced by those who wield power in Tehran such as Ahmadinejad, the Pasdaran, the Basiji, the Ministry of Intelligence and Supreme Guide Khomeini are not only apocalyptic and millenarian, but also autistic. They believe that everything in the world contradicting their perverted sense of what is and what ought to be must be eradicated. In their revolt against the world's reality, they are determined to impose an order that is incompatible with most institutions and people, and they are prepared to destroy a world that refuses their *dawa*, or their Islamic message.

Contemporary *jihad* as a form of modern Gnosticism

On 28 September 1971, the Prime Minister of Jordan, Wasfi al-Tell, walked into the lobby of the Sheraton Hotel in Cairo. Al-Tell had previously been threatened by the Palestinians in retaliation for Black September of 1970.

> Five shots, fired at point-blank range, hit [him] … He staggered … he fell dying among the shards of glass on the marble floor. As he lay dying, one of his killers bent over and lapped the blood that poured from his wounds.[4]

The multiplicity of similar incidents indicates that they are neither "collateral damage" nor incidental occurrences. These incidents do not belong in the sphere of traditional politics; they are instead located in an alternate sphere of geopolitics.

Soldiers kill. Terrorists kill. Modern *jihadis* lap their victims' blood. Inseparable from contemporary Arab-Muslim *jihad* are the idealization of blood, the veneration of savagery, the cult of killing and the worship of death. Gruesome murder, gory and gleeful infliction of pain are lionized and proffered as models and exemplary actions pleasing to Allah. These are not merely reflections of a pre-modern attitude towards death which shares none of our sensitivities regarding human life. I have collected dozens of examples of human sacrifices inflicted by all types of Islamic *jihadis*. This pornography of crime is endless; from the gratuitous killing of Leon Klinghoffer in 1985 to Mohammad Atta's instructions, "You must make your knife sharp and you must not discomfort your animal during the slaughter."[5] From the *Behesht Zahra*, the "Paradise of Flowers" graveyard near Tehran with its Fountain of Blood, to this report on the killing of an Algerian intellectual:

> Dr. Hammed Boukhobza who was killed by a group of Islamist terrorists in the city of Telemly.... He was not just killed in his apartment, but his wife and children who wanted to escape were forced to watch how he was literally cut to pieces, his entrails slowly drawn out while he was just barely alive. The terrorists obviously liked to watch the suffering, and they wanted his family to share their enjoyment.[6]

The accumulation of such deeds shows that they are not an epiphenomenon but are central to the purpose of the *jihadi*. They are aired 24 hours a day on TV channels such as *al Jazeera*. They are avidly watched and celebrated. Images and videos of assassinations such as that of Daniel Pearl and Paul Johnson are shown as "live" killings for the viewing public. Perhaps the worst symbol was the picture taken on 12 October 2000 in Ramallah: a young man raises his red hands dipped in the blood of two murdered Israeli soldiers in front of an exultant Palestinian crowd. There is a public demand to meet the supply: snuff movies are served as identity markers. They bespeak the triumph of a theology of death, a "manufacture of death" according to Baathist ideologues (the purported division between supposedly "secular" Arab or pan-Arab nationalists and religious types is meaningless when the matter is life and death), and an "industry of death," as leading Saudi *'ulama'* proudly say. Listen to the hypnotic threnody of the Muslim Brotherhood's chanted motto: *Allah ghayatuna/Al Rasul zaimuna/Al Quran dusturuna/Al Jihad sabiluna/Al mawt fi sabil Allah asma amanina/Allah akbar* ("God is our goal, The Prophet is our leader, The Quran is our constitution, *Jihad* is our way, *Death in the service of God is the loftiest of our wishes*, God is great, God is great").[7] These are words to be taken seriously, even literally, as events have shown. Hassan al-Banna repeatedly praised his Brotherhood's "art of death" (*fann al-mawt*). This is *thanatolatry, martyropathology* or *nihilism*. When an entire society orients itself towards killing and actively seeking death, that society becomes suicidal.

If you deprecate life and conversely focus all your desires upon death, trading your earthly life for the afterlife, or *shahada*, becomes easier. Taking the life of others is a mandate, an obligation, an offering. Suicide-killing as practiced so often against Israel, India and more recently the United States, is caused by this collective pathology of the mind, the Gnostic religious ideology. There are secondary, contributing causes, but they are just that: auxiliaries to the ideology.

The believers – here, the *jihadis* – are the Elect and only they know God's plan for the world. They have been chosen by Him to fight and win the final, cosmic battle between God and Satan and bring about perfection on earth, in this case the extension of God's writ and dominion, *dar al-Islam*, to mankind as a whole. The nonbelievers are wrong and evil, *jahili*, an enemy liable to be killed at will. According to this view, reality and creation are irretrievably perverted. The Perfect are "an elite of amoral supermen,"[8] who know what reality "really" ought to be. They are engaged in transforming the world so that it conforms to the "second reality" that they alone know, thanks to their special knowledge, *gnôsis*. In order to travel from the evil today to the perfect tomorrow, torrents of blood must be shed, the blood of all those whose actions, or whose very being, hinder the accomplishment of the Mahdi's mission. Owing to their extraordinary status, the Perfects are above all laws and norms. Everything they do is willed and sanctioned by God. Their intent (*niyyah*) vouches for their acts. They alone are able to determine life and death. The power this ideology confers upon its believers is intoxicating. They love death more than we love life.

Contemporary *jihad* is not a matter of politics (of occupation, grievances, colonialism, neocolonialism, imperialism or Zionism), but a matter of Gnostic faith. Consequently, attempts at dealing with the problem politically will not have any effect. Just as aspirin and penicillin, while beneficial drugs, will not counter maladies of the mind, political solutions will not touch the problem of *jihad*. Modern *jihadis* are not crazy, but they are possessed by a disease of the mind. That disease is the political religion of modern Gnosticism in its Islamic version, as shown in the examples above.

Gnosticism in Europe: 1100 to 1600

Gnosticism, or the belief in a fantasy that is taken to be more real than the common reality, is not a new concept. For 500 years, from 1100 to 1600, Europe was wracked by Gnostic insurrections, from Flanders to Northern Italy, from Bohemia to France. The adherents mobilized hundreds of thousands of people, threatened kingdoms and overthrew dukedoms, slaughtered Jews, priests and people of wealth, and created their own, grotesque, bloody, totalitarian "republics."

"Soon we shall drink blood for wine," stated one of the leading insurgent writers, "those who do not accept baptism ... are to be killed, then they will be baptized in their blood."[9] "Accursed be the man who withholds his sword from shedding the blood of the enemies of Christ. Every believer must wash his hands in that blood," wrote another.[10] While Thomas Müntzer preached:

> Curse the unbelievers ... don't let them live any longer, the evil-doers who turn away from God. For a godless man has no right to live if he hinders the godly. The sword is necessary to exterminate them ... if they resist let them be slaughtered without mercy ... the ungodly have no right to live, save what the Elect choose to allow them.... Now, go at them ... it is time.... The scoundrels are as dispirited as dogs ... Take no notice of the lamentations of the godless! They will beg you ... don't be moved by pity... At them! At them! While the fire is hot! Don't let your sword get cold! Don't let it go lame![11]

Gnostics killed indiscriminately to try to create their own vision of the world.

Gnosticism in the modern era

Similarly, in the modern era, a variety of Islamic radicals echo these same words. "Die before you die!" Ali Shariati tells the Shi'a believer. "He who takes up a gun, a kitchen knife or even a pebble with which to arm and kill the enemies of the faith has his place assured in Heaven," said Ayatollah Fazlallah Mahalati, organizer of Iranian assassination squads.[12] According to Ruhollah Khomeini,

> To allow the infidels to stay alive means to let them do more corrupting. To kill them is a surgical operation commanded by Allah ... we have to kill ... war is a blessing for the world and for every nation. It is Allah himself who commands men to wage war and kill.... It is war that purifies the earth.[13]

Article 15 of the Hamas charter states: "I indeed wish to go to war for the sake of Allah! I will assault and kill, assault and kill, assault and kill!"[14]

In modern times in the West, as Eric Voegelin[15] and Norman Cohn[16] have shown, Gnostic ideology morphed and took on secular forms – Nazism and Bolshevism in particular. Islam was heavily burdened by Gnostic contents and historically shaped by a tribal matrix that inherently fostered Manichean tendencies ("them" vs. "us"). The jump from mere religion to religious ideology was easy. It was achieved in the nineteenth century by Jamal al-Din al-Afghani and was followed by Abu Ala Mawdoodi, Hassan al-Banna, Sayyid Qutb, Ali Shariati, Ruhollah Khomeini and Osama bin Laden. In addition, groups such as Hamas, Hizballah, the Deobandi of South Asia, the Indonesian Jemaah Islamiyya, the Talibans and the Wahhabis all share this outlook.

Strategies for dealing with the *jihadi*

Looking at past and present examples, how do we deter the modern Gnostic warriors, the *jihadi*? Mainly, we do not. Those who wish to die generally cannot be deterred. Imagine facing Osama bin Laden: How do you deter him? Or Zawahiri, or Zarqawi? Faith has been described as a belief in things invisible. Gnostics do not believe what they see, they see what they believe.

Deterrence might have worked long before contemporary *jihad* was able to reach critical mass, some time in the early to mid-1990s. Had we powerfully counter-punched earlier, deterrence might have been effective. Events such as the Suez crisis of 1956, the great oil robbery in 1973, the Tehran hostage crisis in 1979, the slaughter of US Marines and French *legionnaires* in Beirut in 1982, and the countless other unpunished outrages that emboldened perpetrators and strategists beyond any reasonable limit, have rendered deterrence ineffective.

If our enemy was merely "terrorism" we could defang it, admittedly at great cost, by destroying the Saudi–Wahhabi nexus and their grip on power. This could be done by wiping out the Iranian Ayatollahs' strength and by coming down hard on the noxious Pakistani military intelligence establishment, the linchpins of Muslim terrorism. Not a modest program. The collapse of the terrorist infrastructure would render the terrorist groups largely ineffective. But terror itself is nothing but the principal paramilitary instrument of *jihad*. The operative concept is *jihad*, not terror. The *jihadis'* purpose (in Clausewitzian terms, *zweck*) in the very words of the Qur'ān is to strike terror in the hearts of nonbelievers. This purpose has a quasi-military objective: once terrorized, the nonbelievers, the schismatics and the polytheists will convert, submit or die. The strategic aim (*ziel*) of *jihad* is the Gnostic takeover of the world. To some extent, we may be able to lessen, hinder or hamper the *zweck*. But the *ziel* is unconditional and cannot be altered. Can we defang *jihad* by pulling its terrorist teeth?

Some work-arounds are effective. The way in which Israeli military and security forces have ruthlessly sapped the strength of Islamic terror, notably by a high-tempo attrition of its leadership cadre, is exemplary and should be studied and emulated elsewhere. When efficiently hunted down and terminated, *jihadi* terror leaders must spend more time protecting themselves instead of plotting attacks. Their age and level of experience decreases, making them less adept at their trade. Successful closing in on their operations boxes them in. Leadership must be learned and practiced: eliminating leaders thwarts the emergence of new leadership. The certainty of dying without being able to forestall it, or hurting your enemy, is demoralizing. Targeted assassination is an efficient response.

Contemporary *jihad*, like its emanation, terrorism, is an integral chain: as long as it is islamico-glamorous to be a cleric who issues *fatwas* calling for the murder of Israeli civilians or American GIs, the cleric will go on. Once dead, he will stop. So will the chairman of a charity that funnels money to *jihad*. So will the senior intelligence officer who trains or smuggles terrorists, the predicator who incites, the *madrasa* or university professor who brainwashes, the prince who lies for the sake of terror, the ayatollah who sends out teams of killers, and so on. This is deterrence after the French expression, *"il est bon de tuer de temps en temps un amiral pour encourager les autres"* ("it is good from time to time to kill an admiral to encourage the others.") *Jihad* is the operative ideology of a number of states. States can be pinned down and hit. This approach is a variant of the notion of decapitation, or of the formulation of nodal targeting given by air power theorist Col John Warden.[17] Less than the *jihadi* hardware, it is the *jihadi* software that has to be hit. However, soft power will only play a role, not lead the way.

What did Europe do to crush the insurrectionary Gnostics in the Medieval and late-Medieval era? Churchill once said: "If Hitler invaded Hell I would make at least a favorable reference to the Devil in the House of Commons." Likewise, I will put in a kind word for the Inquisition (not the Spanish Inquisition), which did quite a job of rounding up and killing the Gnostics. Thomas Müntzer was defeated, captured and beheaded in 1525. The "King" of the Anabaptists of Münster, John von Leyden, and his aides were executed in 1535. As a terrible warning, their bodies were suspended in iron cages from the tower of St. Lambert's church in the town. Those who survived hid to wait for better days. They found that their insurgency was hopeless and they learned that sticking out one's neck was a sure way to lose it. Their will had been broken.

One martyr will have followers; ten martyrs will be admired and emulated. One thousand dead martyrs who die unheralded die in vain. If Ahmadinejad and others die in vain they will not be extolled. Death is the only thing that matters to the Gnostic, to the *jihadi*: take away his death and he is left with nothing. This does not mean, as the jurors of the Zacarias Moussaoui trial were led to believe, that "you cannot make a martyr out of him, since this is what he wants," as various ill-informed journalists commented at the time. Make his death a lonely, useless, ignored death. Unextraordinary, unromantic, trivial deaths shatter the glory of the *jihadi's* purpose. It was George Patton who said: "No bastard ever won a war by dying for his country. He won it by making the other poor dumb bastard die for his country." The recipe is not pretty, nor is it easy.

This puts to the test our own, cherished values: the rule of law, the worth of human life, the importance of sovereignty and international law. Some say, "If we behave in such a way, we become like the enemy." I believe this to be a foolish view. After all, not even Dresden made the Allies into Nazis, nor did Hiroshima turn America into its enemy. Instead, after using the worst instruments of war, the US turned enemies into friends, ruins into blooming cities. Contrary to the *jihadis*, we believe in this anguished remark by Robert E. Lee: "It is well that war is so terrible. We would grow too fond of it." We as a democratic society are not fond of war, but war we wage if we must, albeit often too late.[18]

I am often asked about "Muslim moderates" by those in search of alternative strategies. I invariably answer that anti-Nazi Germans existed but were inaudible, and therefore played no role. Muslim moderates will only be a factor if they are heard, at whatever the cost to them.

Conclusions

The defeated European Gnostics went underground. Their sole hope resided in the clandestine transmission of their beliefs, especially to their children. Society cannot eliminate the Gnostic beliefs, but can make the strain dormant instead of virulent. *Jihad* is integral to Islam and derives from its most fundamental tenets. The severing of that link will not happen in the near future. Throughout history, when Islamic conquerors met their match, they stopped. When they met crushing defeat, they retreated, and found the *'ulama'* and the *faqih* to justify that, like prophets who, having announced the Rapture for 8:09 a.m. yesterday, rescheduled it for next year.

Once their leaders had been exterminated, the Medieval insurgents of Europe disbanded and scattered. Applying high-tempo attrition and nodal targeting to the *jihadi* apparatus worldwide (by which I emphatically do not mean "terrorists" alone or even in the first place) seems to be a modern equivalent. In homage to the chain of command that orchestrated his elimination, Sheikh Yasin was not in the habit of wielding pistols – he wielded death. It is those who deploy the undead who must be the priority targets.

Notes

1 This chapter is a report on the essential conclusions of the author's *The Mind of Jihad*, Washington, DC: Hudson Institute Press, 2005.
2 See, e.g., D. Cook, *Studies in Muslim Apocalyptic*, Princeton, NJ: The Darwin Press, 2002.
3 Quoted by D. Pipes, "It's Not the Economy, Stupid: What the West Needs to Know about the Rise of Radical Islam," *Washington Post*, 2 July 1995.
4 J. Becker, *The PLO: The Rise and Fall of the Palestine Liberation Organization*, New York: St. Martin's Press, 1984, p. 77.
5 Translation of the hijacker letter by Hatem Bazian. Available online at www.mindfully.org/Reform/Photos-Hijackers-DOJ27sep01.htm (accessed 15 March 2007).
6 W. Laqueur, *No End to War: Terrorism in the 21st Century*, New York and London: Continuum, 2004, pp. 43–44.
7 R. P. Mitchell, *The Society of the Muslim Brothers*, Oxford and New York: Oxford University Press, 1969, p. 194.
8 N. Cohn, *The Pursuit of the Millennium: Revolutionary Millenarians and Mystical Anarchists of the Middle Ages*, revised and enlarged edn, Oxford and New York: Oxford University Press, 1961–1970, p. 148.
9 Ibid., p. 122.
10 Ibid., p. 212.
11 Ibid., pp. 235–250, *passim.*
12 A. Taheri, *Holy Terror: The Inside Story of Islamic Terrorism*, London: Sphere Books, 1987, p. 8.
13 Ibid., p. 113.
14 R. Israeli, "The Charter of Allah: The Platform of the Islamic Resistance Movement (Hamas)," in Y. Alexander and A. H. Foxman (eds) *The 1988–1989 Annual on Terrorism*, Dordrecht, The Netherlands: Kluwer Academic, 1990, pp. 99–134.
15 E. Voegelin, *Autobiographical Reflections*, Columbia, MO: University of Missouri Press, 2005; and *Science, Politics and Gnosticism*, Washington, DC: Regnery, 1968–1977.
16 Cohn, op. cit.
17 J. Warden III, *The Air Campaign: Planning For Combat*, New York: National Defense University Press Publication, 1988.
18 Victor Davis Hanson has developed the point in several of his books, notably V. D. Hanson, *Carnage and Culture: Landmark Battles in the Rise to Western Power*, New York: Anchor Books, 2001.

11 Fighting terrorism with democracy?

Daniel Byman

At his second inauguration, President Bush issued an eloquent call for America to spread the blessing of liberty: "For as long as whole regions of the world simmer in resentment and tyranny – prone to ideologies that feed hatred and excuse murder – violence will gather, and multiply in destructive power, and cross the most defended borders, and raise a mortal threat." That "the force of human freedom" can defeat such a threat is a theme that senior Bush Administration officials have echoed ever since.

This argument for freedom is not partisan politics as usual. The President's lofty rhetoric is shared by political pundits and many in the Democratic Party. Even anti-Bush voices, such as Senator John Kerry and *New York Times* columnist Thomas Friedman, share the President's view that autocratic countries that lack liberty produce terrorists who pose an immediate threat to the United States.[1] If Bush, Kerry, and Friedman are correct, then the solution to the problem is the spread of freedom and democracy throughout the world.

Skeptics who view US foreign policy through the lens of power and wealth may be surprised to learn that the Bush Administration has put democracy in the Middle East higher on its agenda than any other administration in US history. Given the absence of weapons of mass destruction or links between Saddam Hussein's regime and terrorists, spreading democracy to Iraq has become the major justification for America's war and continued occupation of Iraq. The attempt to broaden democracy worldwide, however, includes more than just Iraq. The United States spends at least $1 billion a year on promoting democracy throughout the Middle East, excluding Iraq.[2] The Bush Administration has tried to foster democratic opposition to authoritarian enemies such as Iran and Syria. Pressure is even put on Saudi Arabia, Yemen, and Egypt, countries that cooperate closely with Washington on counter-terrorism.[3]

However laudable the goal, many Middle East and terrorism specialists are skeptical of the President's use of democracy as a tool for fighting terrorism. Richard Clarke, President Bush's former top counter-terrorism official, scoffed, "It is not the lack of democracy that produced *jihadist* movements, nor will the creation of democracies quell them."[4] Middle East specialist F. Gregory Gause III argues forcefully that there is no security rationale for promoting democracy: the presence of democracy does not reduce terrorism nor decrease popular support for extremism, but it would increase the number of anti-US regimes in the Middle East.

Efforts to promote democracy in Iraq, Palestine, Lebanon, and even Saudi Arabia make this debate more than a rhetorical issue. Democratization is occurring: at times promoted by the United States, at times without any significant outside intervention. Unfortunately, neither side in this debate appears to understand the nuanced and conflicted relationship between democracy and terrorism. The President is correct: the absence of freedom does indeed lead many individuals to take up arms. But democracy is not a panacea. Indeed, it can weaken governments, foster strife, and increase the strength of anti-Western organizations, thus making the job of counter-terrorism officials far more difficult.

The answer is neither to embrace democracy uncritically nor to reject it completely. Rather, policy-makers should recognize when the promotion of democracy should be pursued and when it should be rejected.

Are the fruits of freedom poisonous?

Let us consider first the advantages of democracy. A free form of government offers many advantages in countering terrorism (though not all of them apply to the struggle against al Qaeda). To understand these advantages, it is vital to understand the adversary. On the one hand, democratization would further enrage core activists; on the other hand, it would offset some of the grievances espoused by local insurgents upon whom al Qaeda draws. Although democratization would have little direct impact on the inner circles of the *jihadist* movement, it could theoretically reduce the base on which it draws, and individuals disaffected with their governments would be drawn instead to peaceful politics. Having chosen their own government, the radicals would receive far less popular support, particularly from other Islamists. Thus, they would be isolated from mainstream politics and placed where they belong – on the fringe.

We must also distinguish support for terrorism in general versus support for anti-US terrorism. There are studies and historical examples that illustrate how democratization affects the attitudes of local terrorist groups towards their governments. But these examples do not necessarily apply to al Qaeda because of its global ambitions. Thus, history offers little guidance in regard to al Qaeda. While increased involvement in politics helped move the Provisional IRA away from anti-British violence, that experience does not tell us how democratic participation affects groups with far greater ambitions. In theory, a group in Egypt might turn away from violence and cease attacks on an Egyptian regime that espouses more popular input into decision-making, but that does not mean that members of the group would not then instead devote themselves to attacking the United States.

The case for democratization

At a most basic level, some terrorists take up arms because they cannot shape government policy to address their grievances. Give them a voice, and they have no need for violence. Many Americans can sympathize with this position: if denied the right to vote, the right to speak freely, and the right to practice our religions, we too would rise up. Presumably most citizens would draw the line at killing innocents, but violence itself would become far more justifiable.

Democratic governments are also more likely to have open economic systems and the rule of law, both of which spur economic growth. In a democracy, over time, high-quality jobs are likely to be more plentiful. Ideally, corruption will diminish, and a meritocracy will arise.[5]

Together, these political and economic opportunities offer two related advantages. First, the level of grievance is lower. If there are fewer contentious issues, there will be fewer angry people. Second, even if individuals are angry, they can turn to the ballot-box rather than the rifle to express their grievances. People in democracies as varied as the United States, Finland, Japan, and Costa Rica all have grievances that they resolve by electing new leaders.

A genuine offer to allow terrorist leaders to participate in politics might not convince them to change course by itself, but their constituents, hopeful that talks might lead to peace, may become less supportive of violence. This increases pressure on the group to hold off on violence for fear of losing recruits, money, and overall sympathy.[6] Just as engagement in politics can change the opinions of constituents, they can also strengthen more moderate elements of a terrorist group, which in turn increases the chances of successful negotiation. For example, the US dialogue with PIRA leader Gerry Adams that began in 1994 contributed to the PIRA cease-fire decision later that year. As a result of the dialogue, Adams' stature was strengthened at the expense of those in the PIRA's senior ranks who favored continued violence.[7]

Although political participation does not always soften the group's violent stance, it may create divisions among its members. When peace talks lead to an offer of concessions, fractures arise within a movement, especially if some members oppose compromise. When members' goals are not uniform, terrorist groups that once enjoyed widespread support become vulnerable to fissures. The British hoped that if talks failed to produce a settlement with the PIRA, they would at least create divisions within its ranks and weaken the group as a whole.[8]

There are risks in excluding groups from the political process. Terrorism is not static: a refusal to include a particular group in the political process may strengthen rather than weaken extremists by showing that non-violent means offer no hope. In addition, some terrorist organizations spring from moderate movements that encountered only government repression. A refusal to talk may thus discourage new leaders who might otherwise have preferred peaceful means of change. Hamas, for example, historically gained more support when peace talks were foundering.[9]

Even if autocratic regimes adopt pro-Western policies, it does not necessarily help the United States to gain the goodwill of their citizens. Many Arab governments have used state-run media to spread anti-Western and anti-US messages to divert anger from the regimes' shortcomings, but in so doing, they bolster the *jihadist* message. A freer press, David Hoffman argues, would reduce the anti-American vitriol.[10] More broadly, the fall of such regimes might reduce anti-US propaganda.

Critics of democratization rightly point out that the bin Ladens of the world are hostile to democracy despite the greater economic opportunities a free government would offer. Bin Laden himself is a scion of a staggeringly wealthy Saudi family, and his deputy 'Ayman Zawahiri comes from an extremely distinguished Egyptian family: neither experienced poverty or political isolation. Al Qaeda attacks the United States primarily for policy reasons such as the US military presence in the Middle East and its support for Israel rather than the presence or absence of democracy. Many if not all of the international terrorist attacks on the United States involve operatives who lived in democratic Western European countries like Germany and Britain. Indeed, *jihadists* have repeatedly denounced the idea of democracy, claiming that it replaces the law of God with the law of man. After all, lawgivers could legalize homosexuality, give women equal status under the law, forge a lasting peace with Israel, or otherwise violate what the *jihadists* see as God's guidance. US support for democracy would be simply one more strike against the United States.

But this criticism of democracy is too narrow. Even if democracy would not influence bin Laden and his followers, it can isolate them by changing their popular image from Robin Hoods to that of thugs. As befits a people who know the true face of tyranny, the Arab world is highly supportive of the idea of democracy. A survey in the UN-backed *Arab Human Development Report* reports that over 60 percent declare that "democracy is the best form of government," a result higher than in Western Europe or North America.[11] Democratization would thus place the *jihadists* on the defensive. Their opposition to a truly democratic system would expose one of the least popular points in their agenda. Some families that now offer the *jihadists* their sons or their money would instead help the police and security services. Terrorists would have to expend much of their time and effort ensuring the silence of the people around them.

Surprisingly, the experience of Western Europe offers some support for the pro-democracy camp. Although France and the United Kingdom are clearly democracies and thus appear to be glaring counter-examples to the argument that freedom reduces terrorism, the Western European political systems have not satisfied young Muslims. They feel angry and alienated from the traditional European political process and culture. They believe that the Europeans do not respect their values or their aspirations. If, however, they felt truly included in European society, their anger might diminish. Perhaps, more importantly, the scope of violence in Europe will always be limited. That is not to minimize terrorism as a serious and sustained problem in Europe. But terrorism has not led, nor will it lead to broader insurgencies as it has in parts of the Muslim world. The European terrorists are isolated, and while they can wreak death and horror as they bomb trains and buses, they cannot rouse thousands of their fellows and convince them to take up arms as they can in non-democratic countries like Algeria.

Another important consideration is the popularity of Islamist political parties. Because they would undoubtedly do well in elections, the divide between peaceful and violent Islamists would in theory widen. Thus, the success of moderates at the polls would undermine the *jihadists'* claim that violence is necessary to bring about a just society. *Jihadists*, therefore, would turn their vitriol on their peaceful counterparts, further isolating themselves. Moderate Islamists, understanding that they are likely to be the target of violence, would have a strong incentive to marginalize their violent counterparts. They would know full well that these attacks could provide a pretext for regimes to abort democratization. For the United States, the intelligence advantage of acquiring Islamists as allies could be immense. Because the Islamists would know who are violent within their tight-knit communities, they could identify them to the authorities.

Elections would also separate more moderate Islamists from the extreme *salafis* (literally "predecessors" but used to refer to Muslims who embrace a puritanical version of Islam). Many *salafis* are extremely suspicious of politics, viewing the process as inherently corrupting. As the inevitable exigencies of power weigh down Islamist politicians, this critique would become even more widespread: some supposed Islamists would prove to be corrupt, while others would get sidetracked by the goal of preserving power. In Iran today, traditional religious scholars are often scathing about what they see as the corruption and compromises of clerics who have joined the political process. In their eyes, politics and religion must be separated in order to preserve the sanctity of the faith.

Social scientists maintain that groups do a better job policing themselves than do outsiders.[12] When groups identify, ostracize, and suppress radicals on their own, the job of the police and intelligence services is relatively easy. Jewish terrorism against the British government before Israel's independence illustrates this principle. In 1944 and 1945, the Irgun, the Stern Gang, and other radicals attacked a range of British targets while the more mainstream Haganah sought to cooperate with the British authorities. The Haganah handed over perhaps 1,000 activists and effectively destroyed the radicals' operational capability. Itzhak Shamir, a Stern Gang member who later became Israel's Prime Minister, related, "We were really a hunted group.... The prisons were the only place where we were a majority."[13] Several years later, when the Haganah resolved to push the British out, they ceased cooperation and the authorities lost their ability to repress the radical groups – a loss that over time led to attacks that eventually drove the British out of Palestine.[14]

Once the democratic system is in place, the process can over time reinforce moderation over radicalism. In part this moderation occurs because the political system pays off: the groups obtain positions of power, and can enact real changes without violence. In addition, if radical Islamists participate in the governing process, they will be forced to moderate their stance due to the mundane realities of governing. Political Islam expert Ray Takeyh contends, "Many radical groups find that once they are part of the governing order, the imperative of getting re-elected leads many to actually abandon their disruptive and costly utopian schemes in search of more practical solutions."[15] Movements such as Morocco's Justice and Development Party and Jordan's Islamic Action Front are increasingly characterized by pragmatism. In power, Turkey's Justice and Development Party has proved quite pragmatic. The commonplace realities of governance became its focus, not backing radicalism. Analyst Amr Hamzawy asserts, "Instead of clinging to fantasies of theocratic states, Islamist movements in these countries now see the wisdom of competing peacefully for shares of political power and working within existing institutions to promote gradual democratic openings."[16]

Like pragmatic politicians, radicals are judged not only by their ultimate aspirations but also by the quality of trash removal and the level of corruption. Indeed, power may result in discrediting mainstream Islamists in favor of more secular alternatives. As Islam specialist Graham Fuller notes, Islamists have powerful critiques of their countries' problems but have few practical solutions to offer.[17]

Regardless of whether and how much these benefits would materialize in countries like Egypt and Pakistan, an argument can be made that the United States would win simply by changing public perceptions of its views towards democracy. The United States can rightly be accused of supporting despots of different stripes from Uzbekistan to Saudi Arabia to Morocco. Not surprisingly, when the President of the United States is photographed shaking hands with Egyptian President Mubarak, who despite his title is a classic strongman, the world assumes that the United States is the foe of democracy. In justifying anti-US violence, bin Laden himself regularly cites such support in his decrees. By changing the US approach, the United States will be less vulnerable to the charge of hypocrisy, even if the reality on the ground remains the same.

Again, this approach is likely to have a stronger impact among the outer circle of the radical movement and ordinary Muslims than on the *jihadists* themselves. The *jihadist* list of grievances is long, and US support for brutal regimes is only one small part of their complaints. But US support for better governance may offset the *jihadists'* remaining charges and diminish the level of anger among potential sympathizers.

Hard realities

Yet the case against democracy as a counter-terrorism instrument is strong. One of the most powerful criticisms is that there is no inherent link between the presence of democracy and the absence of terrorism: indeed, several studies suggest that democracies are more vulnerable to terrorism than autocratic governments. Two scholars of terrorism, Leonard Weinberg and William Eubank, compare democratic rule with authoritarian regimes and contend that "stable democracy and terrorism go together."[18] Since their founding, India and Israel are two democratic countries that have suffered from terrorism by an array of enemies.

The danger is even more considerable for countries that are transitioning to democracy. Mature democracies like Sweden and Germany may be peaceful and have established means for airing and redressing citizens' grievances, but terrorists can find opportunities in countries where the institutions of democracy have not yet coalesced. James Fearon and David Laitin, two leading political scientists, find evidence that insurgencies are more likely to break out among countries with weak governments.[19] Because new democracies are fragile, they become more vulnerable to insurgency and unrest. Turmoil often ensues early on when the senior political leadership attempts to purge the police and security services, while old rivals watch eagerly for opportunities to re-establish themselves. The pillar of the ancient regime, fear, may have been toppled but the ideas of equal citizenship and the rule of law still have shallow roots. In such circumstances, limited violence can easily bubble over. Violence from the Basque separatist group ETA surged as Spain underwent a transition from fascism to democracy in the late 1970s, in part because the security services were reorganized as a necessary component of democratization.[20]

The problem goes beyond weakness. The democratization process itself is likely to create new grievances. Suddenly, people are free to express their anger over the exclusion of their ethnic or religious group from power, the rampant corruption of many governments, and other problems. Even in the absence of objective grievances, the process of democratization creates political winners and disgruntled losers: for one group to win, another has to be usurped. In Afghanistan, for example, the Pashtun community that once held near-absolute control under the Taliban became less dominant, and now play second fiddle to the Tajiks. In Iraq, the Sunni Arab tribes who enjoyed Saddam's largesse suddenly found themselves purged from the armed forces and senior government ranks, with their former victims now holding power. Not surprisingly, terrorists found these communities to be fertile sources of recruits.

But as Weinberg and Eubank's work suggests, success also has its perils. Democracies can be feeding grounds for terrorists even when the state is functioning well. In free states, targets are widespread, and usually poorly defended. And because democratic legal systems impose restraints on the security services, it is difficult for them to monitor and disrupt terrorist plots. Unlike Egypt, the government of Germany cannot round up thousands of suspects simply to find the few dozen that might be supporting terrorism.

Radicals also exploit democracy's embrace of free speech and free assembly. Until the bombings in London in July 2005, the British capital was home to Islamist militants of all stripes to the point where counter-terrorism officials dubbed it "Londonistan." The governments of Saudi Arabia, Algeria, Egypt, France, and Israel all complained to the British government that firebrand preachers were stirring up hatred against these governments and organizing for their overthrow.[21]

The benefits of a democratic government are even greater for the branches of the organization not directly involved in violence. Extremists can raise money in the guise of charity – for, say, the widows and orphans of the Chechen war. Preachers can lambaste the United States, Russia, India, or other countries fighting insurgencies, so long as they are careful not to directly endorse violence. The initial steps of recruitment are also protected. "Spotters" in mosques or other areas where young Muslim men hang out can identify potential recruits. Free to move about as they wish, the spotters introduce them to members of the movement, turn them against traditional Islamic teachings, and otherwise start to transform them into extremists. Spotters can help launch potential recruits on a journey to Iraq, Pakistan, or other parts of the world where they can become yet more radicalized.

Even the economic advancement that may accompany democracy – so often touted as the main perquisite of democracy – can be risky, especially when the nascent government is shaped. Although becoming a wealthy democracy seems to correlate with a decline in domestic strife, simple economic growth has at best mixed effects. Some young activists find the inevitable disparities that arise disquieting. Though it may seem counter-intuitive, the decline in poverty enables recruits to join terrorist organizations. One of the myths of terrorism is that it is linked to poverty and a lack of learning. Studies of terrorists in the Gaza Strip have found that many are well educated and hold jobs – this in a region where the majority of young men are unemployed. Peter Bergen and Swati Pandey found that the masterminds of most of the worst anti-Western terrorist attacks in the past 15 years all had university degrees, and of the 79 involved in total, over half had attended college: slightly more than the average American.[22]

One only has to look at domestic politics to see the reasons for this phenomenon. People who enter politics typically have some degree of education. The truly poor usually worry more about their next meal than educating their children and engaging in sustained political activity. Political activity is limited if losing a family member to a political organization means that the family is deprived of his vital economic contribution. As development spreads in a new democracy, radical ideas can be easily exchanged among people and, at the same time, they often find their recently fired ambitions frustrated by corruption, cronyism, or a simple lack of jobs.

The dirty little secret of United States counter-terrorism is the benefit it often derives from its partners' lack of democracy. If one is not concerned with civil liberties, there are advantages to arresting thousands of "the usual suspects" in the hopes of ferreting out the dozen or so who may be culpable. The United States can ask Egypt to eavesdrop, detain, or otherwise gain information about a suspect and even take him off the streets. To do the same thing with Germany requires a much higher standard of evidence: commendable from a human rights point of view, but costly for counter-terrorism.

In its use of renditions, the United States has exploited the – how else can one say it? – lower standards of its allies. Renditions are extra-judicial transfers of suspected terrorists from one country to another. Typically, a rendition occurs when the local government, in cooperation with US officials, bundles a suspect on to a plane and sends him to another country where charges stand against him. In contrast to an extradition, the suspect does not go through the legal system of the country where he is arrested. More rarely, US officials or their agents may pull a suspect off the streets without the cooperation of the host government. Several notable terrorists, including Ramzi Yousef who masterminded the 1993 World Trade Center bombing, were rendered to face justice in the United States. Most, however, are sent instead to a country in the Middle East.

Counter-terrorism officials find renditions attractive because they get terrorists off the streets. Although the world is not totally safe now that Ramzi Yousef is in a supermax prison in Colorado, it is indeed somewhat safer. In 1998, the *Wall Street Journal* reported that CIA officers and the Albanian police closed down an Egyptian Islamic *jihad* cell that planned to bomb the US Embassy in Tirana. The suspects were sent to Egypt, where two were executed, and others jailed. Their interrogations also led to the arrests of numerous affiliates, dealing a crushing blow to the organization.[23] Renditions are also a source of information even when they do not lead to a lengthy imprisonment. Security forces can ask suspects questions, examine their documents, and otherwise gather information that may be relevant to past or future attacks. In keeping with democratic traditions, free societies wrestle with the murky ethical problems surrounding terrorism. Renditions are one such problem. When a suspect undergoes rendition, he is often transferred to a country such as Egypt where human rights abuses are common. Counter-terrorism officials find renditions attractive because of the high bar US law sets for convicting suspected terrorists. Intelligence agencies often cannot meet the legal standard that requires proof "beyond a reasonable doubt." Often, the only available intelligence is hearsay, rumor, and circumstantial evidence, information that can be maddeningly imprecise, incomplete, and at times contradictory. Because they are not democratic, many US allies in the Middle East have a far lower standard of evidence and are willing to bend their rules in response to a US request.

Invariably, the debate about renditions leads to questions regarding interrogation, which in turn leads to the greatest drawback of renditions – torture. A number of countries used for renditions, such as Egypt, Jordan, Morocco, and particularly Syria are often brutal to prisoners. Although the US government demands that foreign governments promise not to use torture, officials have little control over suspects once they leave US custody – one US government official called these promises a "farce."[24]

The pragmatic use of authoritarian regimes creates a fundamental tension in US policy, particularly as the United States tries to sell itself as a benevolent friend of the Arab and Muslim worlds. The United States needs a stable Middle East to ensure its interests. As Abdelwahab El-Affendi notes,

> The United States is presently trying to walk a tight-rope between engaging the populace in public diplomacy dialogue while still doing business with the regimes it has openly identified as their oppressors; officials want to have their despotic cake and eat it too.[25]

Although the United States might espouse democratic goals in the Middle East, the actual outcome of free and open elections may not be in its favor. Thus, if an Islamist political party is freely elected, the United States may be caught between theory and practicality: that is, the desire for a democratically elected government and a party with goals antithetical to those of the United States, even though the rise of Islamist political parties may in theory lessen the eventual level of violence. Democracy might divide radical and moderate Islamists but the moderate Islamists could easily oppose US foreign policy goals. As Gause contends, "The problem with promoting democracy in the Arab world is not that Arabs do not like democracy; it is that Washington probably would not like the governments Arab democracy would produce."[26] For example, the same Arab Human Development Report that describes the strong support for democracy in the Arab world also notes that less than 20 percent of those polled favor gender equality in the workplace.[27]

Some Islamist groups advocate a very conservative social agenda. In foreign policy they oppose what they see as "imperialism," championing struggles against Russia, China, Israel, India, and other supposed oppressors.[28] The "democratic" result of an Islamist victory in Egypt, for example, might be a decrease in women's rights, a harsher stand against Israel, or more criticism of the US position in Iraq. At the very least, such a government would be less inclined to cooperate with the CIA in hunting suspected terrorists. At most, it might expel the US military from the bases it uses in Egypt and actively support groups like Hamas that use terrorism against Israel.

Many of these Islamist parties may also prove to be fair-weather democrats. Once in office some of these groups have, in the past, rejected democratization or embraced philosophers who, like the *jihadists*, are hostile to the idea of putting man's law above God's. The jury is still out on whether they are embracing the democratic process only if it helps bring them to power or if they recognize its validity, regardless of whether they win or lose. Part of the problem is that the historical experience in the Middle East draws on movements that came to power by violence, whether a bloody revolution in Iran or a coup in Sudan. Their repressive policies may bode ill for Islamists in power elsewhere, but it is not surprising that such movements would not suddenly embrace democracy.[29]

Make no mistake, the Islamists would do well if free elections swept the Middle East. In Palestine, Lebanon, and Iraq, candidates linked to the terrorist group Hamas and pro-Iran militants have emerged victorious from elections. Morocco, Egypt, Yemen, Bahrain, and Saudi Arabia are other countries where Islamists have done well in elections and probably would have won outright were it not for tight regime control over the results. To keep their hold on power, regimes have used many tricks, including limiting access to the media, bribing politicians, gerrymandering districts, passing laws that criminalize those who criticize the government, and imposing outright bans on religious parties to offset their popularity.[30]

Nor does the United States have many alternatives. Years of regime persecution and corruption have made secular and nationalist voices weak, particularly when compared with Islamists. Even if all these problems could be overcome and the price of Islamists in power proves to be worth paying, it is important to note that success, if it came, would be incremental rather than complete. Some groups may engage the political process while continuing their brutal business as usual. When the PIRA accepted a cease-fire in September 1994, it kept its cell structure and logistics network and continued such brutal behavior as beating supposed collaborators and criminals with iron bars. Even after talks had progressed for several years, it made no effort to shut down its infrastructure of cells or decommission any weapons, including its stockpiles of explosives like Semtex and mortars.[31] Government efforts to split a movement and wean away the moderates may succeed, but enough hardcore members remain to guarantee that terrorism continues. Many members of the Basque separatist movement ETA's political wing, Herri Batasuna, responded to the Spanish government's policy of "social reinsertion" (concessions that maximized Basque cultural and political rights), but some radicals maintained control over the movement and continued violence in the name of complete independence.[32] Many members of M-19 in Columbia also turned away from bloodshed, but a violent fringe remained.[33] While far from ideal, even this limited success can reduce the scale of violence and make it easier to gather intelligence on the perpetrators.

An engaged movement itself may reject violence, but new groups may form from rejectionist remnants. The Continuity IRA and the Real IRA both rejected the PIRA's embrace of negotiations over violence and conducted several bloody attacks after the PIRA had signed the Good Friday agreements.[34] In an effort to derail promising peace talks, fringe players may actually escalate their use of violence.

The difficulty of promoting democracy

Despite the high level of funding for democratization programs – including support from the President himself – the United States thus far lacks a coherent strategy for democracy promotion. J. Scott Carpenter, who heads one effort to foster democracy in the Middle East, noted that "We don't know yet how best to promote democracy in the Arab Middle East. I mean we just don't know.... I think there are times when you throw spaghetti against the wall and see if its sticks."[35]

This lack of a strategy is not due to arrogance on the part of policy-makers: the academic and analytic community has at best a limited understanding of how democracy promotion should function in countries that lack such a tradition. There is no formula comparable to economic policies that transform a command economy to one that is free market. Many questions have yet to be resolved. What aspects of democracy are the most important? What is the proper sequence: must there be the rule of law before free elections, or the other way around? Is democracy a path out of civil strife, or must there be domestic harmony first? What means do outsiders have of influencing the spread of democracy? Promoting civil society, everyone's favorite tactic, sounds desirable but it is unclear how a stronger human rights group can lead to the collapse of an authoritarian regime.

A related problem of promoting democracy is that its formal components, elections, for example, are easier to create and monitor than the more amorphous elements of toleration, trust, and social cohesion. Without these components, elections frequently become a means by which a majority dominates a minority. Havoc can result if communities mobilize for fear that the new government in power "democratically" will disenfranchise or impoverish them. The United States has often successfully pushed for elections in divided societies ranging from Kosovo to Iraq but has had much less success in creating the less formal conditions under which elections result in a true liberal democracy.

The formula for spreading democracy throughout totalitarian regimes has yet to be written. Sometimes, even inoffensive attempts to bolster democracy can anger local regimes. The spread of democracy flies in the face of the interests of Arab rulers, most of whom are US allies. The Yemeni government, which cooperates closely with the United States on counter-terrorism, opposed a seemingly innocent US effort to encourage different tribes to work together to stop revenge killings because it feared that if the tribes worked together they would be more effective in uniting and opposing the government: a divided country is more easily controlled.[36]

Unfortunately, today's daunting unpopularity of the United States in the Muslim world risks diminishing the very voices we are trying to support. The United States today has a poison touch. Reformers hoping to capture popular support thus shy away from a US endorsement, fearing that they will lose face with the very people they hope to lead. Authoritarian regimes, including many that are close allies of the United States, cleverly play on this tension and accuse human rights activists of all stripes of being Western puppets.

Thus, even if it is committed to spreading democracy in practice, the United States is caught between a rock and a hard place: US attempts to spread democracy can alienate allies and discredit would-be reformers, and at the same time there is little guarantee that US policies will produce success.

Tread carefully

If a nation can succeed in transforming itself into a democracy, it can reap manifold benefits. Democratic states, when consolidated, do not fight with one another. Democratic states have far better avenues for fighting corruption and ensuring the rule of law than autocracies. If a society is stable and lawful, economic growth follows. And most important, democracy, more than its alternatives, assures the dignity and well-being of its citizens. The rival to democracy is tyranny – a tyranny that is no less miserable because it is inspired by Middle Eastern variants of nationalism, Islam, kleptocracy, and a glorification of the military.

One useful step towards democracy's aim is to bolster alternative voices to anti-US Islamist parties. The United States should work with secular and liberal political organizations to make them effective rivals. The first step might be to sponsor party-building activities, to issue grants for start-up newspapers and websites.[37] But generating rivals to the Islamists will take years if not decades, and even then prospects for success are limited. Liberal democrats are few in the Arab world, and they have little popular support. As Hamzawy notes, "Unfortunately, though, while Arab liberals are celebrities in the West, they are marginal back home."[38] For now, if the United States pursues democratization, there are few alternatives but to seek out allies among moderate Islamists.

When working with both liberals and their Islamist rivals, Washington must recognize that any assistance given with a US label is poisonous to Middle Eastern reformers. Thus assistance must be given indirectly, ideally through international agencies or non-governmental organizations not directly affiliated with the United States. However benevolent the motives of the US may be, its lethal political image will hinder attempts to promote change in the Middle East. Washington must recognize that it can only do so much to transform local political systems and that too much effort may not just fail, but may even backfire.

Because it must tread local politics carefully, the United States may have better luck focusing on two issues central to effective counter-terrorism. The first way is to promote good governance by encouraging an independent judiciary. The second is government penetration of society, which can be accomplished by strengthening the police. These are just some of the means that can pave the way to a successful democracy in the Middle East. For the United States, the stakes are high. When a democracy fails, it becomes a vehicle for cronyism. When it succeeds, it can bolster counter-terrorism efforts and reduce the risk of another attack in this country.

Even as Washington tries not to discredit reformers, it must recognize that being seen as doing good is at times as important as the actual results. When possible, attention should focus on strengthening democracy, whereas any US efforts that could undermine the process, such as bolstering the security services of a regime in order to better monitor terrorists, should be undertaken as quietly as possible.

Not if but where

Choosing our battles is essential. Given the complexity of democracy's impact on terrorism, the real question is not whether the United States should support democracy but when it should do so. Several principles should guide policymakers. First, Western efforts should focus on consolidating democracy in Muslim countries that are already in transition – a daunting task in itself. While success could pay substantial dividends, the ongoing process of democratization means that the West is already running the risk of instability, weakness, and a hostile government, even without coming to the aid of a fledgling democracy. In short, there is less to lose and – because the process has already started due to indigenous efforts – the hope for success is stronger.

Indonesia, the world's most populous Muslim country, is the obvious place to begin. So too is Palestine, where the democratization process has begun, though it is far from complete. Already in these countries, democratization is widening the rift between moderate Islamists and *jihadists*, but it is also fostering new forms of rivalry and strife.

The United States must be particularly careful to avoid repeats of Algeria in 1991 and 1992, where aborted elections that Islamists were poised to win tipped the country over into massive civil war. In the Algerian case, the military *junta* destroyed its own legitimacy while simultaneously "proving" that the radicals were right all along – that the gun, not the ballot-box, was necessary for serious change. As a result, the radicals gained tens of thousands of recruits and perhaps millions of sympathizers at the start of their campaign. It took the carnage of war, and the radicals' extreme brutality, for them to lose this support.

Where democracy is non-existent and democratic groups are weak, Western attention would be better spent building institutions such as the courts and police. These institutions will strengthen government counter-terrorism efforts and, if democratization occurs, make strife and government weakness less likely. US pressure for elections would only destabilize the regime and inhibit vital counter-terrorism cooperation without putting anything positive in its place.

Acknowledgment

An earlier version of this chapter was presented at the conference on "Radical Islam: Challenge and Response" organized by the Begin-Sadat (BESA) Center for Strategic Studies at Bar-Ilan University, 24–25 May 2006. It has been reprinted with permission of John Wiley & Sons, Inc., Chicester, from *The Five Front War: The Better Way to Fight Global Jihad,* © Daniel Byman, October 2007.

Notes

1 W. Oremus (9 February 2005). "Friedman sees pros to Iraq war," *The Stanford Daily Online.* Available online at http://daily.stanford.edu/article/2005/2/9/friedmanSees ProsToIraqWar. Daniel Benjamin and Steven Simon, two leading counter-terrorism analysts who worked in the Clinton Administration, call for "deep engagement" with the Middle East to change regimes' policies on human rights, democracy, and the treatment of minorities. Benjamin and Simon, *The Next Attack,* New York: Henry Holt & Co., 2005, p. 225.
2 D. Finkel, "US Ideals Meet Reality in Yemen," *Washington Post,* 18 December 2005, p. A1.
3 D. Finkel, "In the End, a Painful Choice," *Washington Post,* 20 December 2005, p. A1.
4 R. A. Clarke (6 February 2005), "No Returns," *New York Times Magazine.* Available online at www.nytimes.com/2005/02/06/magazine/06ADVISER.html?ei=5090&en=f4c8c80563cd1fca&ex=1265432400&partner=rssuserland&pagewanted=print&position=.
5 Some may go so far as to say that non-democracies are inherently illegitimate and unstable. By this argument, even apparently stable regimes like Saudi Arabia and Egypt are in reality brittle: their lack of democracy will doom them, if not today then

soon. Supporting democracy, from this point of view, is simply backing the winning horse early on. The non-democratic regimes are likely to collapse into chaos, so they are poor choices as allies. Thus, it does not really matter that authoritarianism has advantages for counter-terrorism as it is doomed to failure.

6 M. Crenshaw, "How Terrorism Declines," *Terrorism and Political Violence*, spring 1991, vol. 3, p. 86.
7 J. Stevenson, "Northern Ireland: Treating Terrorists as Statesmen," *Foreign Policy*, Winter 1997, no. 105, pp. 125–140; L. Richardson, "Britain and the IRA," in R. J. Art and L. Richardson, *Democracy and Counterterrorism: Lessons from the Past*, Washington, DC: USIP Press, 2007.
8 Richardson, op. cit.
9 S. Roy, "Hamas and the Transformation of Political Islam in Palestine," *Current History*, January 2003, p. 17.
10 D. Hoffman, "Beyond Public Diplomacy," *Foreign Affairs*, March/April 2002, vol. 82, no. 2, pp. 1–5.
11 Arab Human Development Report (2003), United Nations Development Program, 19. Available online at www.miftah.org/Doc/Reports/Englishcomplete2003.pdf.
12 See in particular J. D. Fearon and D. D. Laitin, "Explaining Interethnic Cooperation," *American Political Science Review*, December 1996, vol. 90, no. 4, pp. 715–735.
13 N. Bethell, *The Palestinian Triangle*, New York: B.P. Putnam's Sons, 1979, p. 160.
14 J. Bowyer Bell, *Terror Out of Zion: Irgun Zvai Leumi, LEHI, and the Palestine Underground, 1929–1949*, New York: St. Martin's Press, pp. 88, 133–135; S. Zadka, *Blood in Zion: How the Jewish Guerillas Drove the British Out of Palestine*, Washington, DC: Brassey's, 1995, pp. 52–53.
15 R. Takeyh, "Let Democracy Derail Radicalism," *Baltimore Sun*, 21 March 2005.
16 A. Hamzawy, "The Key to Arab Reform: Moderate Islamists," Policy Brief no. 40, Carnegie Endowment for International Peace, August 2005.
17 G. E. Fuller, *The Future of Political Islam*, New York: Palgrave MacMillan, 2003, p. 14.
18 L. B. Weinberg and W. L. Eubank, "Terrorism and Democracy: Perpetrators and Victims," *Terrorism and Political Violence*, spring 2001, vol. 13, no. 1, p. 158. To be fair, many studies are inconclusive. As F. Gregory Gause, an expert on the Middle East, contends rather blandly, "Data available do not show a strong relationship between democracy and an absence of or a reduction in terrorism." Gause, "Can Democracy Stop Terrorism?" *Foreign Affairs*, September/October 2005.
19 J. D. Fearon and D. D. Laitin, "Ethnicity, Insurgency, and Civil War," *American Political Science Review*, February 2003, vol. 97, no. 1, pp. 75–90.
20 F. Reinares, "Democratic Regimes, Internal Security Policy, and the Threat of Terrorism," *Australian Journal of Politics and History*, 1998, vol. 44, no. 3, p. 367.
21 R. Israeli, "Western Democracies and Islamic Fundamentalist Violence," *Journal of Terrorism and Political Violence*, January 2001, pp. 160–173.
22 P. Bergen and S. Pandey, "The Madrassa Scapegoat," *Washington Quarterly*, vol. 29, no. 2, p. 118.
23 R. Chandrasekaran and P. Finn, "US Behind Secret Transfer," *Washington Post*, 11 March 2002, p. A1; A. Higgins and C. Cooper, "Cloak and Dagger: A CIA-backed Team Used Brutal Means to Crack Terror Cell," *Wall Street Journal*, 20 November 2001, p. A1.
24 D. Priest, "CIA's Assurances on Transferred Suspects Doubted," *Washington Post*, 17 March 2005, p. A1.
25 A. El-Affendi, "The Conquest of Muslim Hearts and Minds? Perspectives on US Reform and Public Diplomacy Strategies," Saban Center for Middle East Policy at the Brookings Institution working paper, Washington, DC, September 2005, p. v.
26 Gause, op. cit.
27 Arab Human Development Report, 2003, p. 19.

28 Fuller, op. cit., pp. 38–40.
29 Ibid., p. 29.
30 Ibid., p. 139.
31 Wilkinson, *Terrorism versus Democracy*, Portland, ME: Frank Cass, 2000, p. 86; Stevenson, op. cit.
32 Wilkinson, op. cit., p. 90.
33 Ibid.
34 Ibid., p. 88.
35 D. Finkel, "U.S. Ideals Meet Reality in Yemen," *Washington Post*, 18 December 2005, p. A1.
36 Ibid.; D. Finkel, "A Struggle for Peace in a Place Where Fighting Never Ends," *Washington Post*, 19 December 2005, p. A1; D. Finkel, "In the End, a Painful Choice," *Washington Post*, 20 December 2005, p. A1.
37 Gause, op. cit.
38 A. Hamzawy, "The Key to Arab Reform: Moderate Islamists," Policy Brief no. 40, Carnegie Endowment for International Peace, August 2005.

12 Counter-terrorist strategies

Jonathan Stevenson

The period between the terrorist attacks on 11 September 2001 and the present has been one of reaction. The priority for the United States, Europe and other key "fields of *jihad*" has been, quite understandably, self-protection and, therefore, "hard" security and counter-terrorism. Thus, as the five-year anniversary of the 9/11 attacks draws near, the War on Terror continues to be prosecuted with some vigor and tactical coordination (for example, through counter-terrorism intelligence centers established between the US and other governments) but with a deficit of strategic direction. Hard power – military counter-insurgency in Iraq, Afghanistan and elsewhere; law enforcement and intelligence cooperation; homeland security – still constitute the bulk of the overall effort. Yet, since the US-led takedown of al Qaeda and the Taliban in Afghanistan in late 2001 and early 2002, the indisputable overall tendency of the global Islamist terrorist network has been to disperse and atomize, such that groups in Europe and potentially the US inspired by 9/11 and other spectacular *jihadist* operations will spring up more or less autonomously and spontaneously in largely urban areas, manned more by "local talent" than by imports from Afghanistan, the Gulf, South or Southeast Asia, or other fields of *jihad*. The attacks in Madrid and London are consistent with this observed pattern. The current overall approach to counter-terrorism appears inadequate for redressing this development. There is, in particular, an acute need to tailor global and local policies so that they harmonize with one another – or at least do not work at cross-purposes.

US strategy and the militarization of counter-terrorism

Since the US, however embattled, is still the lone superpower and bears correspondingly heavy security burdens, its counter-terrorist strategy is the most global one. As of early 2006, the US seemed intent on militarizing counter-terrorism. While acknowledging that defeating terrorism requires winning the war of ideas in the long run, the new *National Security Strategy*, released on 16 March 2006, tends to stress military means for preventing attacks; denying terrorists support, sanctuary and access to weapons of mass destruction; and denying them control of any nation or territory that they might use as a base and a platform.[1] The Department of Defense (DoD)'s 2006 Quadrennial Defense

Review (QDR), though acknowledging that transnational terrorists "cannot be defeated solely through military force," broadly embodies the view that the so-called Global War on Terrorism integrally involves the military in that aggressive intervention abroad is necessary to forestall terrorist operations in US territory. The QDR envisages a "long war" not against nation-states but rather against non-state networks, which calls for a US capability to engage enemies in countries with which it is not at war "in many operations characterized by irregular warfare" and an ability "to operate clandestinely and to sustain a persistent but low-visibility presence."[2]

The QDR's principal prescribed counter-terrorist instruments are special operations forces (SOF), which "will possess an expanded organic ability to locate, tag and track dangerous individuals and other high-value targets globally."[3] The fact that after 9/11 US Special Operations Command (SOCOM) became a "supported" as well as a "supporting" combatant command, with substantial budgetary and operational independence from the regional combatant commands, and was assigned the lead military counter-terrorist role under the 2004 Unified Command Plan, reinforces this mission. So does the 9/11 Commission's recommendation that the military take over the Central Intelligence Agency (CIA)'s paramilitary division, as well as Congress's decision in 2005 to provide SOCOM with $25 million annually in discretionary money that can be used to buy foreign allegiances – a function previously the CIA's alone. In turn, the National Military Strategic Plan for the War on Terrorism (NMSP), promulgated in early 2006, tasks SOCOM with preparing a "Global Strategic Plan" for the war on terrorism that will become the centerpiece of the American counter-terrorist enterprise. Consistent with this plan, SOCOM is now the only supported command with a geographically unlimited remit.

By the end of the 2006 fiscal year, US SOF are expected to number 52,846 – the troop strength of three or four infantry divisions.[4] SOCOM's baseline budget has increased by 81 percent since 2001, and for fiscal-year 2006 will reach $6.6 billion.[5] Over the next five years, the DoD plans to increase its personnel by more than 13,000 (15 percent), and to add $9 billion to SOCOM's budget.[6] The DoD will also increase the number of active duty US Army Special Forces battalions by one-third; expand psychological operations (PSYOPs) and civil affairs units by 3,700 personnel, or 33 percent; establish a 2,600-strong Marine Corps Special Operations Command; establish an SOF unmanned aerial vehicle (UAV) squadron; and enhance SOF capabilities for insertion into and extraction from denied areas from strategic distances.[7] Underlining SOCOM's institutional significance is Secretary of Defense Donald Rumsfeld's inclusion of the SOCOM deputy commander on the 12-person Deputies Advisory Working Group (DAWG), which was made a permanent part of the DoD's senior management structure in March 2006. No other combatant commander was so privileged.[8]

The Pentagon has allowed SOF to operate as "military liaison elements," with considerable independence, in countries with which the US has a full diplomatic and civilian intelligence presence.[9] Advocates of SOCOM's growing role in the campaign against terrorism believe that SOF should be engaged in all of the 60-odd countries in which *jihadist* cells are believed to operate.[10] In the counter-terrorism arena, then, the Pentagon has continued to win the bureaucratic contest with the State Department and the CIA. While the Bush administration paid lip-service to the importance of public diplomacy in the campaign against terrorism, it has not expedited its pursuit. Karen Hughes, the current undersecretary of state for public diplomacy and public affairs, did not assume her post for six months following her nomination. Her disastrous "listening tour" in fall 2006 merely confirmed to Muslim populations American naïveté and ignorance about Islam and the impact of US policies.[11]

Phenomena such as the ascent of Islamists in Egypt's slowly liberalizing political system have demonstrated that, contrary to what some US officials might wish, democratization is an unreliable counter-terrorism instrument.[12] Yet the United States has not, thus far, formulated a strategic alternative save for the heightened use of SOF for both counter-insurgency and information warfare – a plainly incomplete, and potentially perverse, device. The Istanbul, Madrid and London bombings suggest that the *jihad*'s epicenter is moving to Europe, where mature and broadly US-friendly democracies are the norm. In that theater, even the most covert and discreet military activity would carry prohibitive risk. So, indeed, would a heavy-handed civilian operation, as demonstrated by the criminal investigations that Germany, Italy and Sweden have undertaken of the CIA's alleged abductions of terrorist suspects in the execution of "renditions."[13] These episodes serve only to demonstrate the even greater infeasibility of even low-visibility *military* operations in what is arguably becoming the most critical field of *jihad*. Even in less sensitive places, potential political liabilities attending the covert deployment of SOF abound. In late 2004, one of the inaugural "military liaison elements" had to be withdrawn from Paraguay after killing a street criminal and causing the US – which had not disclosed the deployment of the SOF team to the host government – diplomatic embarrassment. While the teams now operate under more restrictive guidelines established by the national intelligence director, CIA officials view the teams as conditioning unilateral US military activity that could ultimately impair operational as well as diplomatic relationships with other governments.[14] Clandestine US civilian collaboration with authorities in countries harbouring terrorists (e.g., in the arrest of 9/11 mastermind Khalid Shaikh Mohammed in Pakistan, and that of al Qaeda–Jemaah Islamiah liaison Riduan Isamuddin (Hambali) in Thailand) have yielded more frequent and durable and less diplomatically troublesome gains.

Counter-arguments: more soft power

Some governments have acknowledged the need for more focused and inventive applications of soft power, particularly in the form of public diplomacy in the Muslim world and more integrative state outreach to Muslim communities in Europe.[15] But the intensifying *jihadist*-assisted insurgency in Iraq and the July 2005 London bombings (and attempted bombings) indicated that actual efforts in those areas were proving insufficient to stem *jihadist* recruitment and activity. The global *jihad*, as noted, has continued its post-Afghanistan evolution as a horizontal, atomized network in which the core al Qaeda leadership (headed by Osama bin Laden and Ayman al-Zawahiri) had diminished command and control but could inspire and influence regional insurgencies (e.g., al Qaeda in Mesopotamia, Kashmiri separatists, and several Southeast Asian groups) and local upstart groups (e.g., those that staged the Madrid and London bombings). This pattern, driven by Internet-spread propaganda and further accelerated by the ongoing US-led military occupation of Iraq, is likely to continue. While a flat structure makes the network less capable than it was with its base in Afghanistan of pulling off a large-scale coordinated attack in the order of 9/11, it also makes the network less vulnerable to military power and harder to neutralize decisively. After settling for targets of opportunity immediately after the Afghanistan intervention, an ever more dispersed *jihadist* network now appears capable of striking a wider range of targets in addition to Iraq (e.g., Jiddah, Saudi Arabia, December 2004; London, UK, July 2005; Sharm al-Sheikh, Egypt, July 2005; Bali, Indonesia, October 2005; Amman, Jordan, November 2005; and Dahab, Egypt, April 2006) in the course of a little over a year.

While terrorist operations continue and protective measures remain important, it is equally central to countering terrorism to determine what applications of softer forms of power will lead to the diminution of transnational political violence. And although Americans and others tend to view counter-terrorism as an endeavor closely akin to a war, Europeans and others are still inclined to see it as a law enforcement and public policy challenge. (Israel, arguably in a unique position, appears to regard terrorism as an ongoing operational challenge – which is perhaps a pedantic way of saying "a fact of life" – that can eventually be marginalized via conflict management.) Yet most parties agree that each approach has its merits, and neither should be discarded. Both foreign policy and domestic policy are therefore critical. Arguably the greatest impediment to prospective gains in the war on terror is the Bush Administration's reluctance to recognize the galvanizing effect that the Iraq occupation and counter-insurgency effort is having on terrorist recruitment, morale and capability. The most salient impact of the Iraq intervention, roundly perceived by European governments, is that it has reinforced bin Laden's narrative depicting the US and its allies as seeking to establish Western hegemony in the Arab and wider Muslim world, to loot Islam's oil, and to support Israel against its largely Muslim neighbors. Furthermore, the US, Canadian and European intelligence communities broadly agree that Iraq has replaced Afghanistan as a training ground for *jihadist* terrorists. The Iraq engagement also allowed a new charismatic *jihadist* leader – Abu Musab al-Zarqawi – to emerge; though he was killed by a US airstrike in June 2006, he built a formidable network and recruiting base that is proving difficult to dislodge. And it has arguably led the US to neglect other areas ripe for growth in terrorism recruitment or activity such as sub-Saharan Africa.

An especially salient and sobering development has been Islamist terrorists' consolidation of Europe as a field of *jihad*. The social, economic and political marginalization of Muslims in a number of European countries has made Muslim communities susceptible to radicalization. These countries have tried various mixtures of integration and tolerance, none to adequate effect. There are distinctly different views of the breadth and depth of the Muslim radicalization problem in Europe, with the French considering the problem to be less dire than the British and the Spanish. What is undisputed is the fact that some young Muslim men placed in limbo between home country and European host country were following radical leaders' exhortations to seek an authentic and more satisfying identity in the Islamic *umma*.

Europe's crisis and the need for social reform

The population of the European Union (EU) includes approximately 15 million Muslims (about 4 percent), and the Muslim share is set to double by 2025 – a consequence of both immigration and high fertility rates. It has become less and less likely that the perpetrator of a terrorist attack in Europe will be a member of, or affiliated with, a pre-existing terrorist organization; that is, European Muslim terrorists are increasingly home-grown. Some of the determinants of Muslim radicalization in Europe are motivational and facilitational, but the overriding factors are probably structural. Colonial legacies help determine the geographical distribution of Muslims in Europe, and some of the violently inclined take their cue from various home conflicts (e.g., British Muslims from Pakistan's political and religious strife, French Muslims from Algeria's, Spanish Muslims from Morocco's, and perhaps Dutch Muslims from Indonesia's). But by perpetuating social, economic and political marginalization, most major European nations have also fueled Muslim grievances. Muslims in Europe tend to be segregated in Muslim "ghettos," and are disproportionately unemployed, imprisoned and under-educated. Furthermore, while first-generation refugees tend to stay connected to their home countries, Muslim citizens or permanent residents who have been in Europe for longer generally do not maintain close links. Thus, second- and third-generation Muslims find themselves in an unsettling limbo, whereby they are not fully integrated into Europe but have no affinity with the language, culture or politics of their home countries. For these reasons it is harder for Muslims to assimilate in Europe than in the US, a nation founded on immigration. Older European Muslims simply become insular, but younger ones undertake a more aggressive search for alternative identities that feel more authentic. While such circumstances have not always led to radicalization and political violence – for example, on the part of European Jews – the wider rise of Islamist radicalism and the salience of transnational terrorism present dangerously attractive alternatives that were not available to other marginalized groups.[16]

European intelligence agencies generally agree that most European *jihadists* (about two-thirds) are upwardly mobile. While extremist recruits can be underachievers who may have resorted to criminality, the other likely pool consists of university undergraduates with technical qualifications. Historically, university students have typically been the first to be radicalized – even in groups, such as the Baader–Meinhof Gang or the Red Brigades that style themselves proletarian. In the context of social marginalization, Muslims moving up the social ladder are more likely to run into significant discrimination or racism as they venture outside their own religious and ethnic circles. Clearly government programs maintaining a high level of education will not necessarily diminish terrorism. Finding neither their home countries nor their host countries especially hospitable, many European Muslims seek a home in the *umma* (that is, the notional single nation comprising Muslim believers worldwide), where bin Laden's worldview now flourishes independently of his personal fate or actions. While it is true that the al Qaeda leadership gave the Madrid and London bombings its blessing because of Spain and the UK's participation in the Iraq war, more significant is the likelihood that the bombings would have occurred regardless of that leadership's specific sanction.[17]

On top of adding potent fuel to the *jihadist* argument that Western bellicosity warrants the mobilization of Muslims, the Iraq issue has led many Middle Eastern governments worried about their respective "streets" to distance themselves publicly from the US and its allies and stoked *secular* European anti-American anger and rejection of war. Iraq, then, is a triply potent motivational factor for European Muslims, among whom the war has been broadly and deeply unpopular. The irony is that the European political bond against the war has now crossed ethnic lines. It is true, as French scholar Olivier Roy has noted, that other conflicts (e.g., Israel/Palestine, Kashmir, Chechnya) and more general circumstances (structural marginalization) gave rise to European Muslims' radicalization and violent activity before the Iraq war occurred.[18] Non-Muslim European anti-Americanism also pre-dated Iraq. But Iraq confirms and intensifies the *jihadist* narrative of Muslim humiliation and subjugation by presenting the acute antagonism of Americans killing Arabs, and offering the possibility of a triumphant moment during which a Muslim can kill an American in battle. So far, at most only 200 to 300 European Muslims are believed to have joined the *jihad* in Iraq, and few returnees have surfaced back in Europe. Those who do return, however, are likely to have unique cachet and to increase terrorist recruitment, capability and activity. And they will find at least passive political sympathy in Europe's non-Muslim population. Overall, Europe appears to be approaching a tipping point at which localized Muslim insurgencies – potentially coordinated by knowledgable veterans of the Iraq *jihad* – could become a fact of life.

Central to whether this outcome materializes are the directions of Muslim communities and security apparatuses in three key countries: France, the UK and The Netherlands. These countries putatively cover the spectrum of domestic national counter-terrorism approaches in Europe, from, respectively, enforced assimilation to a balance of encouraged assimilation and hard enforcement to liberal integration. The rise of Islamic radicalism in Europe, however, has challenged the status quo in each country. The Netherlands seems to have responded the most dramatically, with far stricter enforcement and more aggressively assimilative requirements. France, by contrast, has resisted – though not entirely discounted – empirical indications that its Muslim population is becoming more vulnerable to radicalization and defaulted to rigorous intelligence collection and law enforcement as the principal instruments of counter-terrorism. The UK has recognized that even its ramped-up program combining community outreach and infiltration and prevention was insufficient to stop the July 2005 terrorist bombings, but appears to have concluded essentially that the central problem is one of execution rather than design. On balance, then, The Netherlands is moving expeditiously to the UK's middle position while France is moving more slowly towards that position. Given the nature of Europe's current Muslim crisis, this trend is a positive one. Security would likely be improved, however, if France adopted a mixed approach on a more accelerated basis.

There are more than four million Muslims in France, constituting about 6 percent of the population. About three-quarters originate from the Maghreb, over 1.5 million from Algeria. Over half of France's Muslims are French citizens. But Muslim immigrants are twice as likely as non-Muslim ones to be unemployed. France's domestic state policy of resolute secularism – laicité – dictates an immigration policy of strict assimilation: Muslims, like others, are required to pass a French language and culture test in order to be naturalized, and are pushed to embrace French civil ideals and to keep their religion private. In response to the looming problem of radicalization and potential Islamist terrorism, however, the French Council for the Muslim Religion was established in May 2003 as an integrative moderating mechanism for the nation's Muslims and Muslims' official interlocutor with the government. The Council is increasingly pressing the government to respond to Muslims' religious grievances. But its effectiveness is unclear, as many Muslims – radical and moderate alike – view it as potentially reinforcing marginalization. France has not otherwise compromised its official secularity. For example, it has not moved to allow a greater degree of religious expression in schools, and has thus far given little energy to initiatives for improving public religious education or the training of France's broadly unassimilated imams (though this may be changing).

The French government's muscular, centrally controlled and integrated counter-terrorism apparatus has undoubtedly produced positive security results. The French authorities have arrested over 230 terrorist suspects since 2002. They have prevented numerous major terrorist operations, including the bombing of the Eiffel Tower and that of the US embassy in Paris, and dealt highly disruptive blows to Europe-wide al Qaeda facilitation and recruitment networks. Unlike Spain and the UK, France has not suffered a major attack since 9/11.[19] By the same token, however, France's aggressive approach to hard counter-terrorism, combined with an institutionalized intolerance of overt piety that is at odds with the sensibilities of many Muslims and certainly those attracted to Salafism, appears to have rendered significant portions of its Muslim population hostile to the state – or at least reinforced their hostility. Evidence includes the fall 2005 urban riots – which the government tends to think were about Marx and discrimination on the basis of religion and race rather than bin

Ladenism per se – and the Muslim community's anger over France's ban on headscarves in public schools. More pronounced government outreach to the Muslim community, involving greater tolerance and probably a relaxation of France's rigid state secularism, would appear desirable.

There are approximately 700,000 Muslims in The Netherlands, and they constitute almost 5 percent of the population. Dutch Muslims come primarily from Turkey and Morocco, but there are substantial minorities from Suriname, Iraq and Somalia, and are concentrated in large Dutch cities. Muslims are concentrated in urban centers, in particular the four largest cities: Amsterdam, Rotterdam, The Hague and Utrecht. Dutch Muslims' unemployment levels are high, and their educational achievement low. The Netherlands, however, has adopted a broadly liberal policy towards religion. Church and state are separate, freedom of religion legally enshrined, and religious-based discrimination illegal. At the same time, the state does provide certain religious groups – including Muslims – with funding and resources for schools (which must still fulfill a secular national curriculum) and other activities. Dutch liberalism and multiculturalism, however, are under siege. The murder of filmmaker Theo Van Gogh in November 2004 by a Moroccan Muslim, in reaction to what much of the Muslim community considered to be a blasphemous portrayal of Muslim women, precipitated a steep and reactionary increase in anti-Muslim hostility and violence, and rendered intercommunal relations in The Netherlands far more tense than before. Furthermore, the General Intelligence and Security Service (AIVD), which has primary operational responsibility for domestic counter-terrorism, has established that radical Islam has taken root in Dutch society and that extirpating it will be a long and arduous task.

The authorities responded to these realizations in a measured rather than a reactionary way, bolstering security without appearing to become tools of right-wing extremists who had been gaining favor even prior to 9/11. The government's working hypothesis is that such groups are generally not directly operationally linked to any global network, but will often develop transnational relationships with similar groups – or with individual members of al Qaeda – and thus form new, flatter networks.[20] One such local entity in The Netherlands was the so-called "Hofstad group," with which Van Gogh's assassin was associated. The Dutch's threat perception is also marked by an assessment that the Hofstad group is interested in not only mass Western casualties but also in targeting key individuals (politicians or pundits) – a departure for *jihadists*. In addition, the AIVD became worried about sectarian backlash, noting that arson attacks on churches, mosques and schools had been virtually unheard of in The Netherlands until the Van Gogh murder. These realizations – along with the discovery of plans for attacking several targets, among them an AIVD office, during the arrest on suspicion of robbery of a key Hofstad group member – led to expanded and tightened security in public buildings and sites and to a tougher preventive enforcement policy. The AIVD has also become directly involved in monitoring immigrants in cooperation with four other government organizations.

The AIVD has assumed a very proactive role in addressing deeper social problems contributing to radicalization and terrorism. The agency initiated and spearheaded a highly probative investigative study, conducted under the auspices of the EU Counter Terrorism Group, of *jihadist* recruitment in Europe, focusing on methods of recruitment, characteristics of recruits, and recruiting locales. A 2004 AIVD study entitled "From Dawa to Jihad" further chronicled modes (e.g., Saudi Wahhabi missionary organizations, itinerant Salafist preachers, the Internet) of radical indoctrination and recruitment in The Netherlands. This path appears to have had qualifiedly positive effects. Both anti-Muslim sentiment and Islamist radicalization may have now leveled off, and there have been no major terrorist attacks in The Netherlands. The intercommunal divisions and mistrust that have emerged, however, are not likely to be remedied merely by amplified political and social traditions. The government will probably have to intensify affirmative steps to bring Muslims into mainstream social, economic and political life.

The UK has extensive experience in combating the Provisional Irish Republican Army (IRA), and has tough counter-terrorism legislation in place – amplified following 9/11 – that has facilitated its counter-terrorism effort. The vexing operational challenge has been to strike a balance between tough enforcement, which is necessary for the immediate protection of the public, and tolerance for the free expression of often inflammatory ideology or religious beliefs, which is viewed as conducive to longer term conciliation between Muslim and non-Muslim Britons. The ripening *jihadist* threat to the British homeland has rendered the optimal balance even harder to achieve. Thus, although December 2001 legislation substantially increased UK authorities' latitude for detaining terrorist suspects, they have not used their detention power too liberally. France, in particular, criticized the UK for being too lax, which inclined UK authorities to undertake more preventive arrests and detentions starting in late 2002. Shortly after the Madrid bombings in March 2004, British security services seized a 1,600-kilogram cache of fertilizer used to make explosives in a raid on a self-storage facility in West London. This discovery prompted the United Kingdom's Foreign and Commonwealth Office (FCO) and Home Office jointly to undertake a detailed examination – entitled "Young Muslims and Extremism" and leaked to *The Times* of London after the tube bombings of 7 July 2005 – of the security risks posed by the UK's Muslim population.[21]

In addition to setting out the social marginalization of British Muslims, the presence of radical Islamist groups and their recruitment activity, the FCO/Home Office paper cited two primary policy goals: (1) "to isolate extremists within the Muslim community, and to provide support to moderates"; and (2) "to help prevent young Muslims from becoming ensnared or bullied into participation in terrorist or extremist activity."[22] A program emerged, codenamed *Operation Contest*. MI5 would lead an all-out interagency effort to win Muslim hearts and minds while also more directly preventing imminent radicalization. The FCO and the Home Office continued to conduct very public community relations and anti-discrimination efforts, and added focus groups to their repertoire. In addition, however, MI5 and other law enforcement and intelligence agencies dispatched hundreds of undercover officers in regional "intelligence cells" or "Muslim Contact Units" to monitor suspected terrorists and mapped the "terrorist career path" with an eye towards developing a comprehensive "interventions strategy" whereby government agencies would confront Muslims at "key trigger points" before they were drawn into the radical fold.[23]

The bombings in London on 7 July 2005, appeared to skew the balance even more decisively towards enforcement. Nevertheless, the UK's mixture of rigorous intelligence and law enforcement and forward-looking social policies worked well in taming the IRA's insurgency, and British officials tend to perceive Northern Ireland as highly relevant to, even if very different from, the global *jihadist* challenge. For that reason and others, the UK is likely to stick to its mixed approach, resolving simply to apply it more efficiently and comprehensively. This mixed approach, under which soft and hard policies hedge each other, makes the most sense in a dynamic security environment in which both short- and long-term risks must be managed and cannot be completely eliminated. It could be observed that because Britain has suffered a major *jihadist* terrorist attack while the other two countries have not, privileging its counter-terrorism strategy is rash. But the UK's singularly close strategic alignment – especially with regard to the Blair government's unequalled military and political support for the US-led intervention in Iraq – also made it a higher value target. In that light, its strategy may appear more efficacious. While the EU provides some coordinative security mechanisms and baseline standards for social policy, its supranational power – diminished by the recent constitutional crisis – realistically cannot supplant national authority over counter-terrorism matters. And the Muslim situations in separate European countries are, in any case, sufficiently different as to require customized approaches.

Counter-insurgency, the *umma* and America's dilemma

US counter-terrorism strategy ostensibly continues to pivot on the application of military force to engage terrorists outside US borders and thereby deny them access to US territory. Analytically, this makes a certain kind of sense: the American presence in Iraq diverts *jihadist* attention from civilians on US soil to more accessible military targets in Iraq; and the US, unlike Europe, has not been infiltrated. As a group, Muslims in the United States have shown no sign of violent protest, let alone terrorism. The US Muslim population, though multiethnic and variable in terms of income, is generally prosperous and assimilated. Whereas European Muslims' average income is generally below the poverty line, that of American Muslims is slightly above the national average. Their reaction to 9/11 was, on balance, reserved. In short, Muslim violence within the US is indeed more likely to come from foreigners, so the military denial strategy has an appealing logic. In practice, however, the strategy is failing. The essence of that failure consists in the fact that the United States' first iteration of the strategy occurred against a country – Iraq – that turned out not to pose a serious security threat to the US. This single fact allowed radically inclined Muslims to think the worst about America's true intentions, which won al Qaeda recruits and followers. America cannot rewind the tape, and now faces a dilemma. It can either withdraw expeditiously from Iraq or stay there indefinitely to complete the task of state building. Either way, the *jihadists* are handed a propaganda victory: withdrawal reads as a superpower's humiliation, ongoing occupation as its imperialism. The only hope seems to be for the US to stay long enough to prove itself to be a benevolent midwife rather than a malign hegemon.

Staying is not easy. While the Iraq war may have diverted a few *jihadists* from the US in favor of Iraq, the more momentous effect has been to antagonize Muslims worldwide and swell the ranks of the *jihadist* movement, resulting in an overall intensification rather than a diminution of the threat to the United States. The longer the US military stays, the longer this effect lingers. Although Iraq presents a more difficult and lethal operating environment for *jihadists* than did pre-9/11 Afghanistan, the fear is that some foreign fighters will survive US-led counter-insurgency efforts and relocate in Saudi Arabia, Jordan, Europe and possibly the United States better trained and motivated to perpetrate and direct terrorist operations. Although few, if any, have surfaced in Europe and none have turned up in the US, a number have returned to Saudi Arabia and Jordan and staged attacks – notably the suicide bombings in Amman in November 2005. More generally, the advent of Iraq as a field of *jihad* is also prompting *jihadists* to refine and propagate urban warfare techniques, and they may choose to apply them robustly to cities elsewhere.

The received view is that the insurgency in Iraq opposing American, other coalition and new Iraqi government forces is primarily and in substantial major-ity an indigenous movement composed of Sunni Arab Iraqis associated with Saddam Hussein's Baathist regime. This group fears domination and reprisals from a reconstituted Iraqi government controlled mainly by Shi'ite Arab Iraqis, who make up about 65 percent of Iraq's population, and to a lesser degree by Iraqi Kurds, who account for about 23 percent of the population, both of which Saddam's regime brutally oppressed. It is also generally accepted that the *jihadists* have infiltrated the network of Baathist holdouts driving the insurgency and have incrementally gained influence within the movement. This latter view is fairly well substantiated, but largely inferential. It is drawn from the increas-ing incidence of suicide attacks, which are consistent with *jihadist* tactics and psychology, and from the rising proportion of sectarian attacks, which squares with a memorandum, apparently written by Zarqawi, intercepted and leaked by US intelligence in February 2004, indicating that a Sunni/Shi'ite civil war is necessary if the US effort to create a US-friendly state in Iraq is to be thwarted.

An important aspect of the insurgency on which there is less reliable intelli-gence, and no real consensus, is the mindset of the bulk of *jihadist* recruits, a large number of whom are native Iraqis.[24] In addition to al Qaeda in Mesopotamia, two of the best-known and most active insurgent groups are Ansar al-Sunna and the Islamic Army of Iraq, both home-grown.[25] This probably reflects a broader reality: that, like the rest of the Arab world, a substantial portion of the Sunni population of Iraq had been pressured to Islamize since the First Gulf War. Recordings of the sermons of radical preachers widely circulated in the Arab world have also been available in Iraq. Just as other Arab leaders used Islam to enhance their claim to authority or outflank political competitors, Saddam and his Baath party began a "Faith Campaign" in 1993 in the realization that (1) the Baath Party's secular ideology (which turned on pan-Arab nationalism, Iraqi patriotism and Sunni tribal patronage) was losing steam, and (2) political Islam was on the rise in the Arab world. Although most of those who turned to religion did not espouse radical views, a minority did. Despite its secularist roots, the regime tolerated these groups because they were anti-Saudi and thus were politically useful to Saddam.[26] Thus, it is likely that Zarqawi and a small network of foreign *jihadists* gained some influence over Iraqi Sunnis *before* the US and its coalition partners invaded and occupied Iraq. While there is no evidence of a substantial, planning-level connection between Saddam and bin Laden, it is now believed that Zarqawi was present in Iraq well prior to May 2003. US officials considered Iraqi Sunnis to be essentially secular, and therefore did not entertain the possibility of serious *jihadist* penetration. But the subsequent difficulty that US intelligence has experienced in distinguishing with any certainty *jihadist* from Baathist holdout operations suggests a relatively seamless link. That, in turn, could imply a thorough and fairly long-standing infiltration rather than the emergent alliance of convenience that was initially assumed.

On balance, most Iraqi Sunni insurgents are probably now focused on gaining Sunni Arab primacy within Iraq against increasingly active and ruthless Shi'ite militias and wresting Iraq from perceived American control and influence. Because many have been radicalized and indoctrinated with the *jihadist* point of view, though, the majority are likely to be amenable to eventually broadening the geographical scope of their activities. Such a shift would be a reasonable possibility if they achieved their primary Iraq-centric objectives. Yet it could be even more likely if they see themselves as *failing* to achieve them: much as the defeat of political Islam in Egypt, Jordan and elsewhere prompted the transnationalization of the movement, the defeat of both Sunni nationalism and political Islam in Iraq could transnationalize both Iraqi *jihadists* and their foreign abetters. This would inject new militant energy into the *umma*. Whether a dispersed transnational movement is less dangerous than a terrorist-hijacked state is a matter for debate. Here, it suffices to note that neither is good, and the one feeds prospects for the other.

Conflict management and Israel's dilemma

Despite hopeful signs from Northern Ireland and elsewhere that conflict management could be a promising counter-terrorism device, it took a hit when 9/11 drove home the vast differences between "old" and "new" terrorism – in particular, the latter's mass-casualty intent and non-negotiable global demands – that made *jihadists* appear insusceptible to political compromise.[27] As the global *jihadist* movement has dispersed since being denied a physical base in Afghanistan, however, it has become easier to disaggregate it into constituent elements, some of which may be more tractable than al Qaeda's maximalist core.

For example, most Southeast Asian government officials tend to discount the connection between national Islamist resistance groups and the global *jihad*. Southeast Asia has always been considered the Islamic fringe, and there is an active debate as to how closely aligned even Jemaah Islamiah (JI) – before al Qaeda in Mesopotamia coalesced, probably the most operationally effective of the al Qaeda affiliates – remains with the core al Qaeda leadership. The one aims for a regional caliphate, the other for a global one – which suggests that at some point their agendas will diverge. JI now receives less financial and operational support from the al Qaeda nucleus. To be sure, JI is still active – it is suspected of committing the September 2004 bombing of the Australian embassy in Jakarta, and the October 2005 bombings in Bali. But the movement of the global *jihad's* focus away from Southeast Asia, and a domestic mobilization against terrorism by the Indonesian authorities (over 200 arrests and the detention of spiritual leader Abu Bakr Bashir), seem to have produced internal discord about ideology and the use of political violence. Indonesian analysts identify two broad internal groupings: terrorists (bombers) and proselytizers. Abu Sayyaf, the MILF and the southern Thai groups have maintained their distance from the global *jihad*. A loose association may be useful for recruitment and political purposes and to give national authorities some pause, but a closer one unleashes too many counter-terrorism resources (e.g., heavy US assistance and involvement) to be beneficial to the terrorist group in question. The upshot is that the Southeast Asian groups may be more tamable than they once appeared.

Part of the reason, of course, is that both their operational and their political trajectory remain severely limited. That is less true of Hamas, which tends to make Israeli security forces resigned to a counter-terrorism posture without an integral political component, viewing the task as a matter of simply "mowing the grass" when required. Yet even clear-eyed counter-terrorism practitioners recognize the limits of such a program. In September 2003, Ephraim Halevy announced his resignation after four years as head of the Mossad and a year as director of Israel's National Security Council. By his reckoning, the Israeli government must "offer more and demand more" for a stable final settlement to be possible. It had to offer more hope to the Palestinians for a state of their own, and former Prime Minister Ariel Sharon's Gaza withdrawal plan at least tentatively provided such hope.

What it must demand is that the Palestinians recognize the legitimacy of the State of Israel. Hamas has always been the most formidable obstacle to the fulfillment of that imperative, and its political success – culminating in its control of the Palestinian Authority (PA) by virtue of its stunning electoral victory in January 2006 – has made it even more difficult to circumvent. Now, for instance, the prospect that Fatah could dismantle Hamas is even further away. The preferable alternative would be to consolidate Hamas's foray into non-violent politics via conflict management. But while a number of Hamas leaders may be somewhat pragmatic, it seems doubtful that the movement as a whole could make the concession to Israel's legitimacy that any political solution would require.[28] As a matter of doctrine, the group still insists on the extinguishment of the State of Israel and the establishment of an Islamist state in historical Palestine. Yet starving the PA to force Hamas' political ejection – the current dispensation – or, even more improbably, forcibly dismantling Hamas, are problematic precisely because the election gave Hamas legitimacy and indicated the willingness of the Palestinian people to continue to endure considerable pain to resist being politically railroaded by Israel.

The default course, at least in the longer term, still seems to be some form of conflict management. And the Israeli–Palestinian confrontation presents the hard case for political solutions. This is in no small part because Hamas is a kind of hybrid terrorist organization – "old" in the sense that its aims are geographically limited and its violence calibrated to leave room for political dialogue, but "new" in that its stated political objectives are baldly unacceptable to its adversary. The conflict also has a global overlay because it involves Islamists, locally focused though they may be, and is the single most aggravating local conflict to Muslims worldwide. As a result, the al Qaeda leadership politically exploits the conflict to provoke restive Muslims in multiple regions (the Israeli–Palestinian conflict appears to be substantially more resonant than Iraq in Southeast Asia, for example) and spur them to radicalism and ultimately violence.

Arguably, then, the three essential strands of a comprehensive counter-terrorism strategy coalesce in considering the Israeli–Palestinian conflict, such that Israel and the Palestinian territories constitute a rough microcosmic version of the global conflict. Palestinians' social and political marginalization has made Hamas' maximalist (if geographically circumscribed) Islamism attractive. That marginalization must be addressed by Hamas' secular Palestinian rivals in order for them to speak for the Palestinian people and thus provide Israel with a reasonably trustworthy interlocutor. Then the conflict will be remediable through conflict management, and its amelioration will reduce *jihadist* recruiting power and render the "far enemies" – the United States and Israel – less inherently antagonistic to Muslims. Residual terrorism will continue, and will require a hard response, but that response would logically involve less force and therefore be less inflammatory. Co-existence would be possible.

Secular Palestinians stand in relation to Hamas roughly as moderate Muslims generally stand in relation to *jihadists*. The vexing key to the global as well as the local strategy is how to politically empower or re-empower those who are disengaged or discredited. This task, wherever it is undertaken, is fundamentally political. The military slice of the counter-terrorism pie is small and continues to decrease – in part because the conflict within Islam is ideological, in part because the transnational Islamist terrorist network's further dispersal appears more likely than its reconcentration. The capstone task in Iraq is not counter-insurgency – which is a means to a political end – but rather civil state building and the requisite resolution of political differences. Furthermore, the most

alarming sub-trend of the *jihadists'* operational dispersal is the *jihadist* infiltration of Europe. Europe served very effectively as a recruitment, planning and
staging area for al Qaeda's attacks on US interests prior to 9/11. If its infiltration
proceeds further, Europe could once again become a platform for striking the
United States and its assets. This potential outcome clashes with current US
policy, which leverages challenging terrorists abroad militarily as a means of
strengthening the security of the homeland. From a political perspective, the
notion of American SOF operating robustly in, say, Western Europe is little
short of absurd.

The US and its strategic partners, then, need to consider policy adjustments
that account for the likelihood that the global *jihad* will collectively regard itself
as better off as a maximally decentralized and virtual network fully infiltrated
into locales in which the military instrument is subject to severe political and
operational limitations. Those adjustments should include an orderly withdrawal
of US forces from Iraq and a removal of emphasis on direct military action in
general, such that "hard" counter-terrorism becomes primarily a function of
civilian intelligence and law enforcement cooperation. The premium should be
an internationally coordinated blend of regional economic initiatives and proactive conflict management in key areas (especially the Middle East, but also
Kashmir and Chechnya), and on quietly urging and supporting national efforts –
customized according to particular circumstances – to better integrate alienated
segments of society otherwise vulnerable to radicalization.

Notes

1 *National Security Strategy of the United States of America*, March 2006, pp. 11–12.
2 US Department of Defense, *Quadrennial Defense Review Report* (QDR), 6 February
   2006, pp. 9, 11.
3 Ibid., p. 44.
4 Ibid., p. 16.
5 Ibid., p. 44.
6 US SOCOM, News Release No. 6, January 2000, 8 February 2006; QDR, p. 5.
7 QDR, pp. 44–45.
8 (20 March 2006) "Rumsfeld Gives 'Group of 12' Permanent Role, New Name,"
   InsideDefense.com. Available online at http://insidedefense.com/secure/insider_
   display.asp?f=defense_2002.ask&docid=3202006_march20b.
9 B. Gellman, "Secret Unit Expands Rumsfeld's Domain," *Washington Post*, 23
   January 2005, p. A1; S. M. Hersh, "The Coming Wars," *New Yorker*, 24 and 31
   January 2005; T. Shanker and S. Shane, "Elite Troops Get Expanded Role on Intelligence," *New York Times*, 8 March 2006.
10 See, e.g., B. Graham, "Shortfalls of Special Operations Command are Cited," *Washington Post*, 17 November 2005, p. A2.
11 See, e.g., "Diplomatic Toast," *New Republic*, 17 October 2005.
12 See F. G. Gause III, "Can Democracy Stop Terrorism?" *Foreign Affairs*, vol. 84, no.
   5, pp. 62–76.
13 See, e.g., C. Whitlock, "Europeans Investigate CIA Role in Abductions," *Washington
   Post*, 13 March 2005, p. A1.
14 T. Shanker and S. Shane, "Elite Troops Get Expanded Role on Intelligence," *New
   York Times*, 8 March 2006, Available online at www.nytimes.com/2006/03/

08/international/americas/08forces.html?ex=1299474000&en=20fecad5a871e6b2&ei
=5088&partner=rssnyt&emc=rss, (accessed 11 March 2007).

15 The term "soft power," originated by Joseph Nye and Robert Keohane, refers to the
use of attractive and persuasive rather than coercive means – such as technical
support, social legislation, diplomatic dialogue, and economic advantage or assistance, as opposed to military threats or actions – to constrain political actors from
acting in adverse ways or to compel them to act in favorable ways. See, e.g., J. S.
Nye, Jr., *Soft Power: The Means to Success in World Politics*, New York: Public
Affairs, 2005. See also J. S. Nye, Jr., "The Decline of America's Soft Power,"
Foreign Affairs, May/June 2004, vol. 83, no. 3.

16 See generally R. Leiken, "Europe's Angry Muslims," *Foreign Affairs*, vol. 84, no. 4,
July/August 2005.

17 S. Simon and J. Stevenson, "Her Majesty's Secret Service," *The National Interest*,
winter 2005–2006, no. 82, pp. 49–50.

18 See, e.g., O. Roy, "The Ideology of Terror," *New York Times*, 23 July 2005.

19 See generally A. Debat, "Terror and the Fifth Republic," *The National Interest*,
winter 2005–2006, no. 82, pp. 55–61.

20 See Andreas Ulrich (12 July 2005), "Radical Islam's Rising War in Europe," *Salon*.
Available online at http://dir.salon.com/story/news/feature/2005/07/12/terrorism_eu/
index.html, (accessed 11 March 2007).

21 R. Winnett and D. Leppard, "Leaked No. 10 Dossier Reveals Al Qaeda's British
Recruits," *The Times* (London), 10 July 2005. Available online at www.times
online.co.uk/printFriendly/0,,1–523–1688261–523,00.html (includes links to PDF
version of report).

22 "Young Muslims and Extremism," FCO/Home Office paper, pp. 16, 22–24.

23 Summary of "Young Muslims and Extremism," pp. 2–3, attached to letter to Sir
Andrew Turnbull, Cabinet Secretary, Whitehall, from John Gieve, Permanent Secretary, Home Office, dated 10 May 2004.

24 R. Paz, "Arab Volunteers Killed in Iraq: An Analysis," *PRISM Series of Global
Jihad*, March 2005, no. 1/3. See also A. Ghosh, "Inside the Mind of an Iraqi Suicide
Bomber," *Time*, 4 July 2005.

25 M. Abedin, "Post-election Terrorist Trends in Iraq," *Terrorism Monitor*, 11 March
2005, vol. 3, no. 5.

26 "Who are the Insurgents? Sunni Arab Rebels in Iraq," *Special Report 134*, United
States Institute of Peace, April 2005. Similarly, Syrian President Bashar al-Assad has
recently been more tolerant of Islamist groups because they tend to be anti-American.

27 See, e.g., S. Simon and D. Benjamin, "The Terror," *Survival*, Winter 2001, vol. 43,
no. 4, pp. 5–17.

28 See, e.g., S. Simon and J. Stevenson, "Confronting Hamas," *The National Interest*,
Winter 2003/2004, no. 74, pp. 59–68.

Index